IMAGES
of America

WINCHESTER

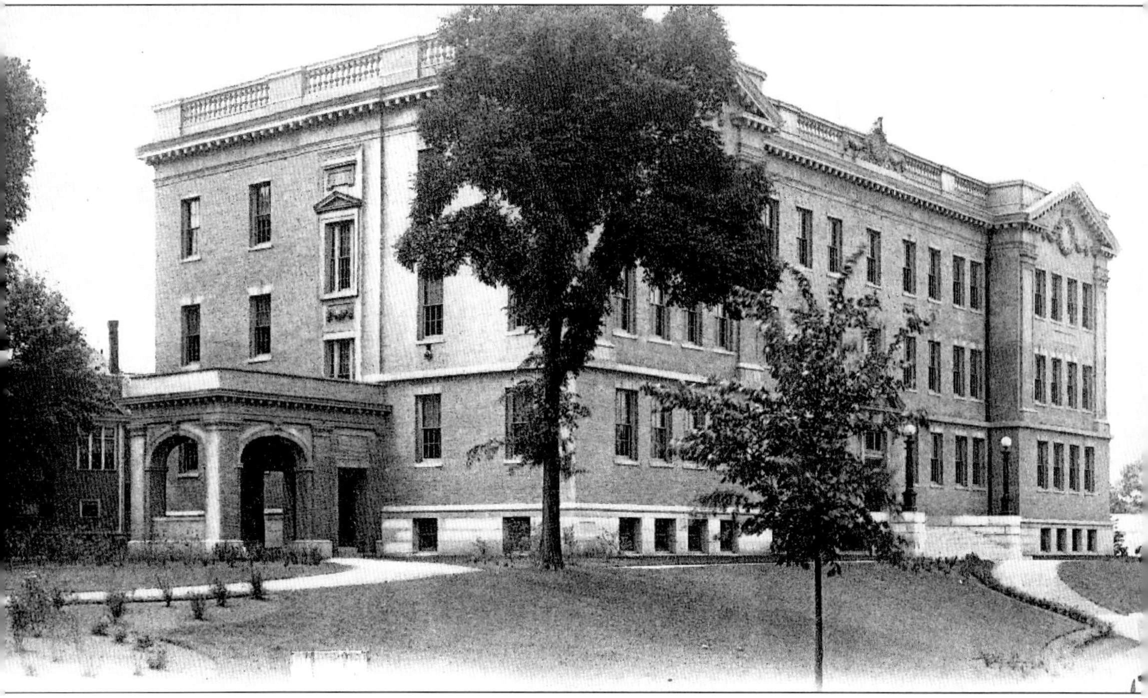

Winchester High School, *c*. 1920.

IMAGES
of America

WINCHESTER

Members of the Winchester High School
Class of 1945 including Frank H. Sleeper

ARCADIA
PUBLISHING

ISBN 978-0-7385-8843-8

Published by Arcadia Publishing
Charleston, South Carolina

Printed in the United States of America

For all general information contact Arcadia Publishing at:
Telephone 843-853-2070
Fax 843-853-0044
E-mail sales@arcadiapublishing.com
For customer service and orders:
Toll-Free 1-888-313-2665

Visit us on the Internet at www.arcadiapublishing.com

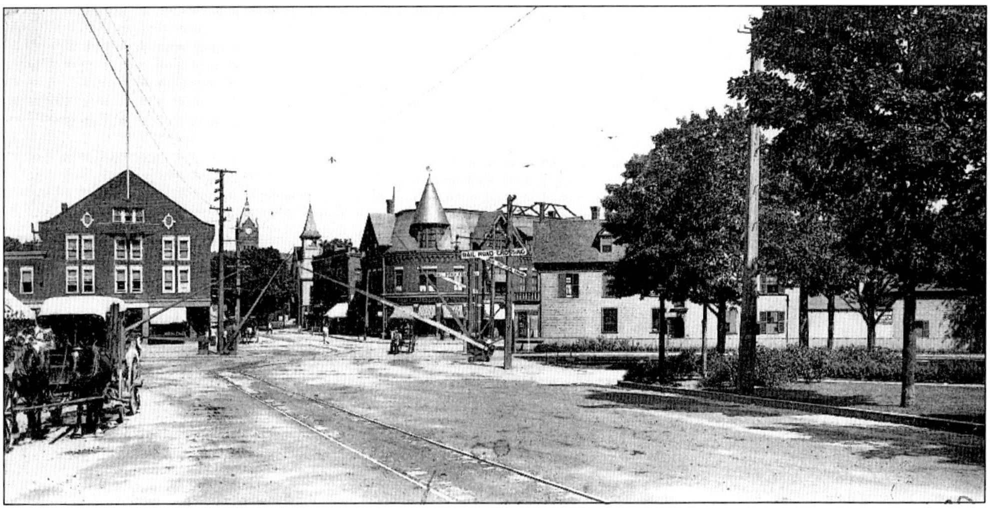

Winchester Center, c. 1890s.

Contents

Introduction		7
1.	A Comfortable Town	9
2.	Italo-Americans	35
3.	Library and Hospital	49
4.	A Sports-Loving Town	67
5.	A Scenic Town	87
6.	Doers and Shakers	107
Acknowledgments		128

Introduction

The Class of 1945 at Winchester High School had to be unusual—if only because its tenure at WHS just about covered the years the United States was in World War II. We entered as freshmen in September 1941, almost exactly three months before the Japanese attack on Pearl Harbor. We left at the start of June 1945, somewhat more than two months before the A-bombs were dropped on Hiroshima and Nagasaki. So perhaps it's not unusual for such a class to produce a book full of old photographs of Winchester as well as a painting that may end up in the Winchester Town Hall.

The author of this introduction received great cooperation from all classmates approached and from their associates (see Acknowledgments). This book would not have been possible without that cooperation. That's why the class is listed as an author.

This book does not claim to be a complete photographic history of Winchester, but it certainly updates (to 1960) the last pictorial history of the town, published in 1914. It is a series of vignettes of Winchester history as seen through the camera's eye. We see this town on the Aberjona as a comfortable town, a sports-loving town, and a scenic town. The book includes the town's doers and shakers, and is the first pictorial history of Winchester Hospital (one of the better small hospitals there is). We show the faces of Italian immigrants as they arrive and compare them to the faces of their Italian-American descendants. We have also included photographs of the Winchester Public Library, recently discovered by contractors in the walls of the library during renovations; this will give those using the larger renovated library a permanent photographic record of the older library. It is admittedly not a complete history: for instance, the arrival of the Irish immigrants, who used their abilities and energies to develop a real social mobility before the Italian immigrants arrived, is not covered in this volume (hopefully, this can be done later). Still, we feel this book has a great deal to offer.

Attendance at the Winchester Hall of Fame 5th Annual Dinner on May 11, 1995, gave this author a big leg up on the sports section. Of course, his work as a sports editor of the *Red and Black* and many years of covering Maine for *Sports Illustrated* also helped. Duplicate photographs from the Town Archives formed the basis for the section on the scenic town. All this went into the makeup of this book, a book which preserves these old photographs for posterity. The images are here for all to see, immune to loss or fire, and because of the number of books published, they will be seen forever.

We of the Winchester High School Class of 1945, at our 50th reunion, dedicate this book to all the students at Winchester High and their teachers—past, present, and future. We hope the old photographs shed a little light on the town's history. We also dedicate this book to all those who have lived, now live, or will live in Winchester.

We feel we were lucky to live and be educated in Winchester. (The author did so from 1938 to 1946, the last year of grammar school but all of junior high and high school, formative years indeed.) It's a great town in which to grow up. It's a good place for education, one of the best in Massachusetts. And it has a heritage. The Class of 1945 believes in that heritage. It wants others to know about it. Turn the pages here for a quick look. I personally think it's much better than television. I hope readers feel the same way.

For the Class of 1945
Frank H. Sleeper

One

A Comfortable Town

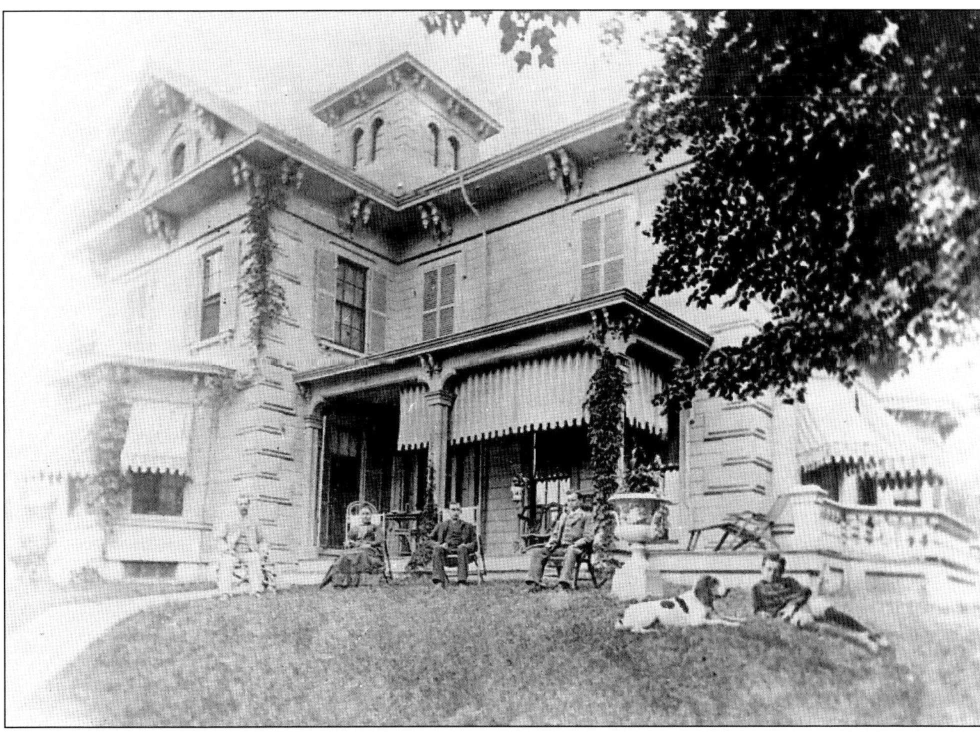

There's a look of comfort and well-being about the Rogers family in the summer of 1883 on the Rogers Estate at Washington Street on the northeast corner of Park Avenue. Mr. and Mrs. George Edwin Rogers sit with their children: Harlow Harden Rogers (left), the eldest son; the writer, fifteen-year-old Bradlee Rogers (center); and Foster Rogers (right), the youngest son.

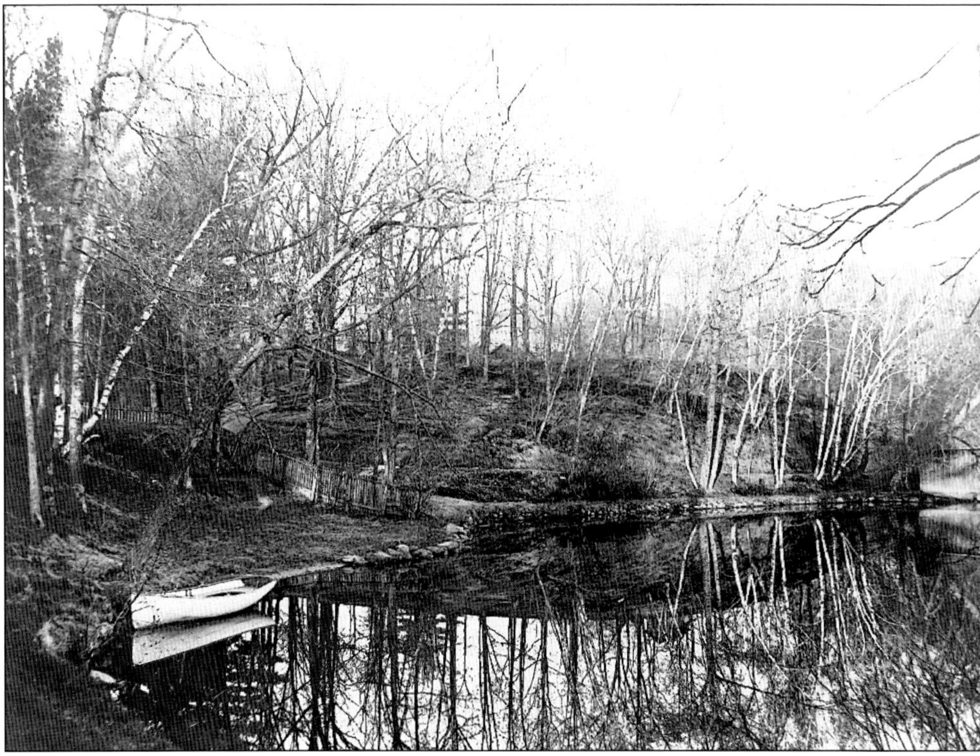

A corner of Wedge Pond, Winchester, showing the path along the bank. The photograph was taken from the rear of the Calumet Club in the late nineteenth century.

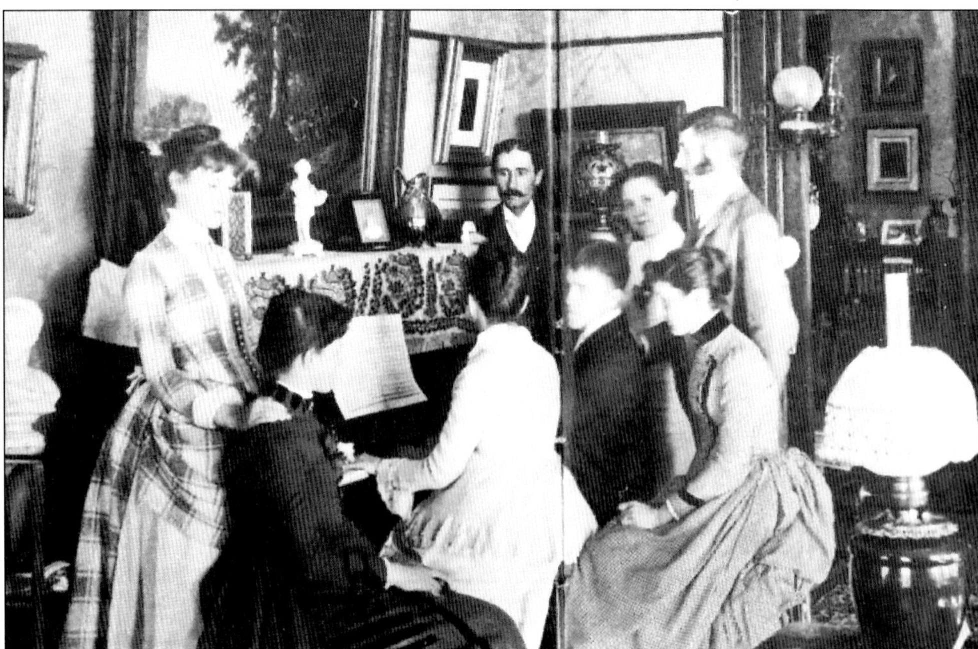

The first Winchester home lighted by electricity at 379 Main Street, *c.* 1890. It brought a new standard of comfort.

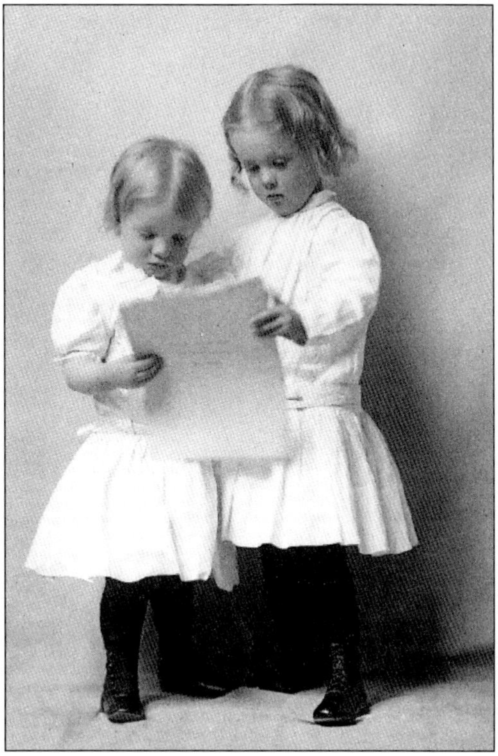

Lesley and Georgiana Brown, *c.* 1903. They do look comfortable as well as beautiful.

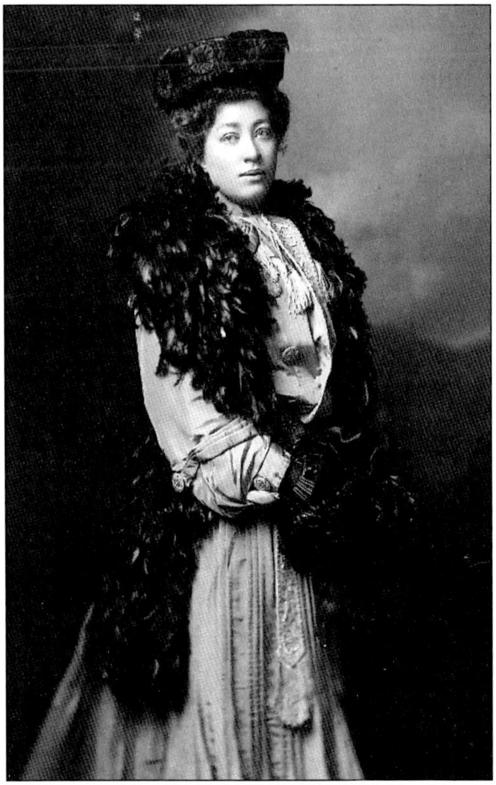

Lesley Dillingham (Bangs) Brown, *c.* 1890s. All set to ride in comfort.

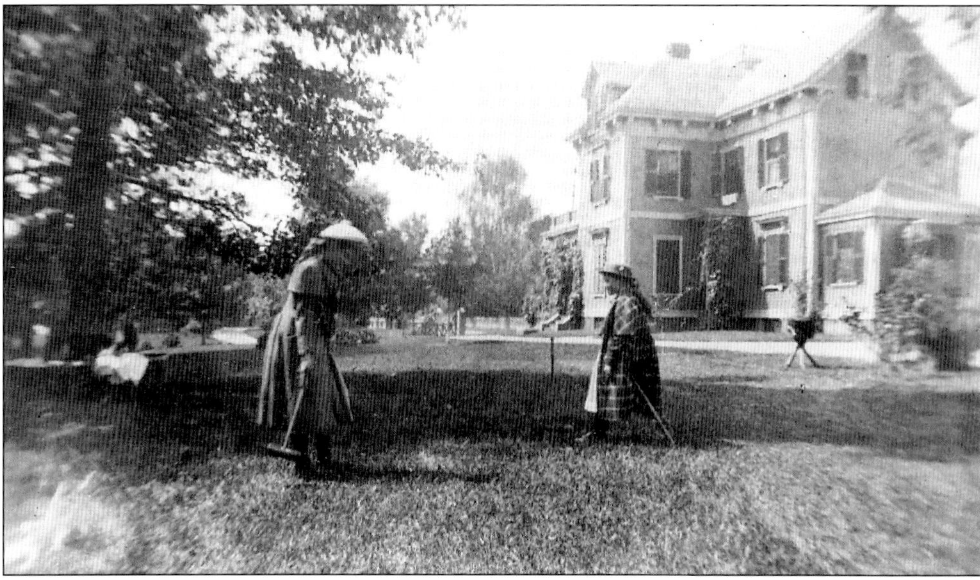

Croquet on the south side lawn of the Central Street, Bangs Estate, *c.* 1890s. The cares of the world were far away.

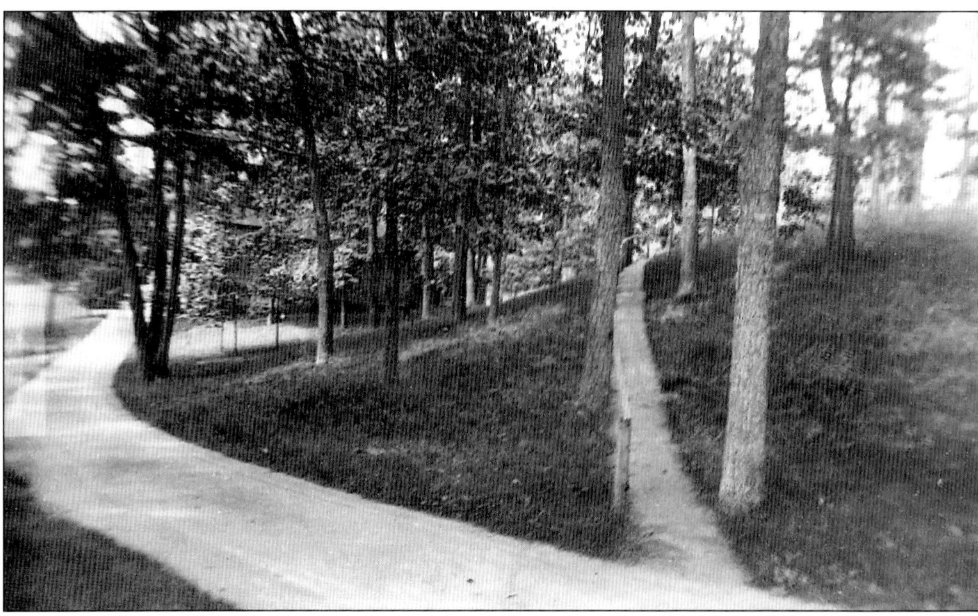

Roads, pathways, and trees in the Skillings' Rangeley development, *c.* 1890s. Plenty of green space for whatever environmentalists there were in those days.

Aunt Mamie (Mary) Sanborn (Skillings), c. 1914–15. She was a member of the first class at Vassar College in 1865 and lived on Church Street, on the corner of Wildwood Street.

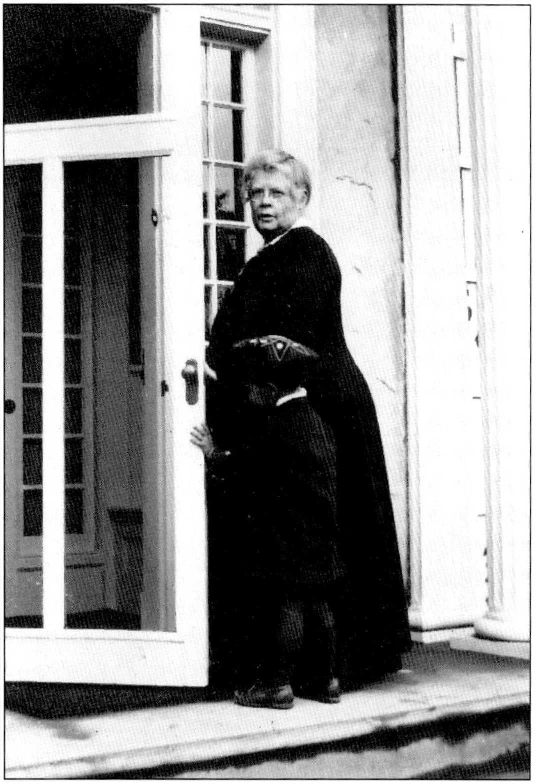

Walter J. Brown and a friend are on a serenading spree to his future wife (Lesley D. Bangs) in 1892. Brown is the taller man on the right.

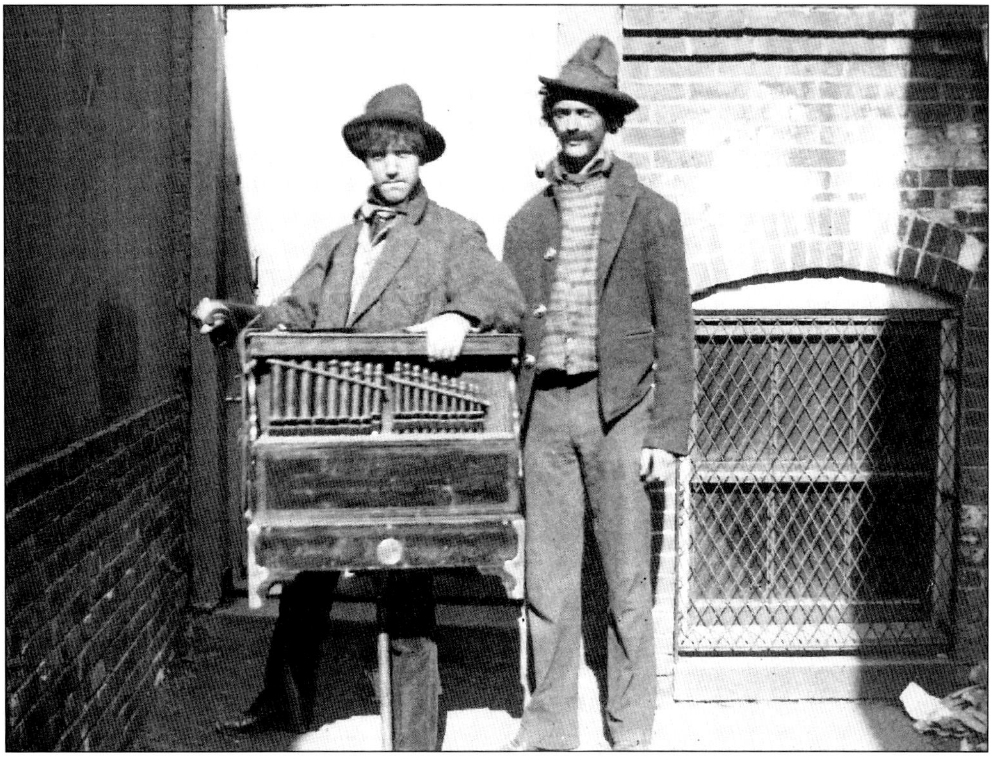

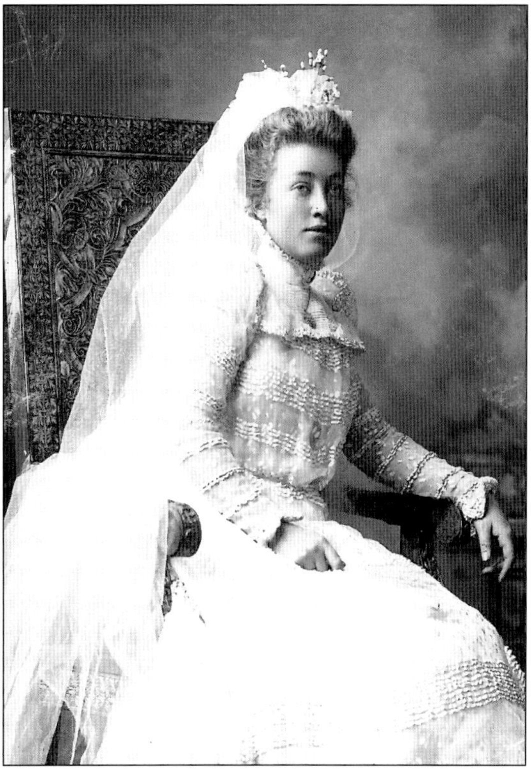

Lesley Bangs Brown was married December 27, 1897, in a Winchester ceremony. However, this shot was taken in comfort, in September 1898.

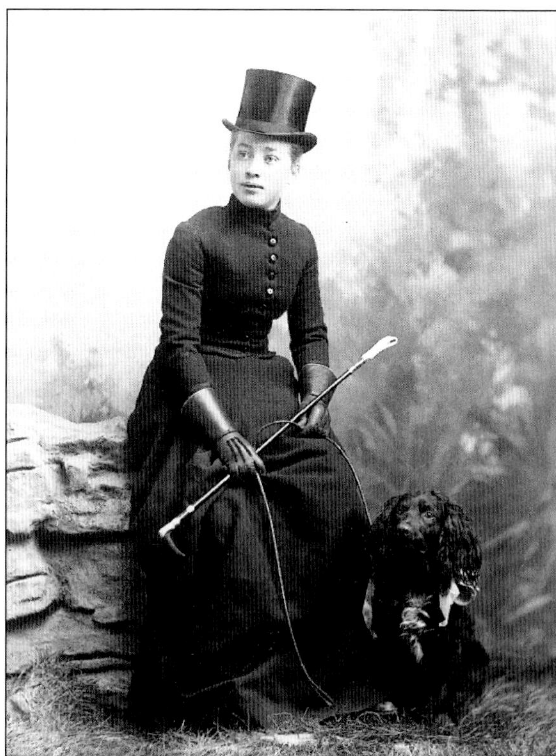

Lesley Dillingham Bangs is in her riding habit with her poodle in the early years of the twentieth century.

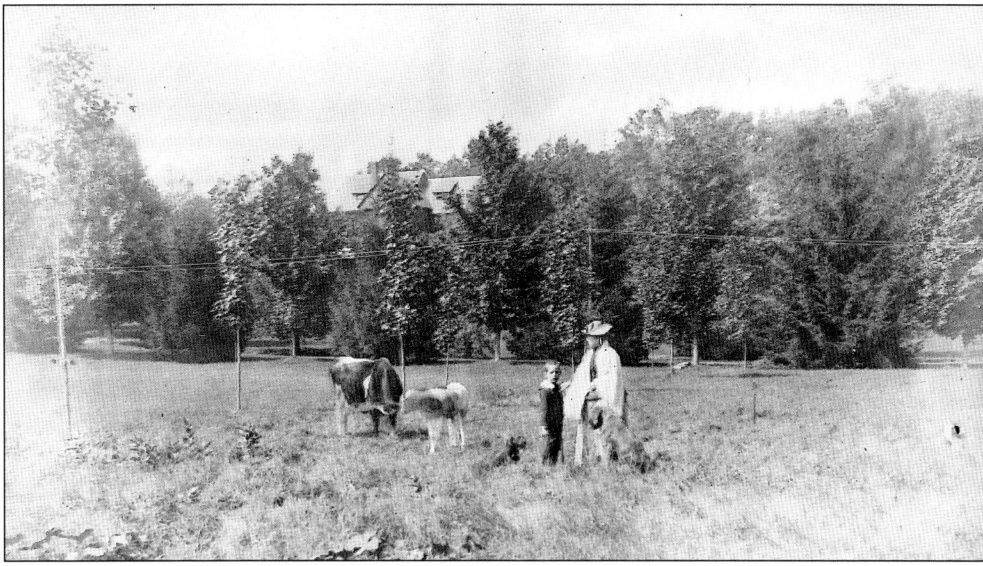

A peaceful and comfortable meadow in the Rangeley development, *c*. 1890. Note the cow, calf, three dogs, woman, and boy, all unidentified.

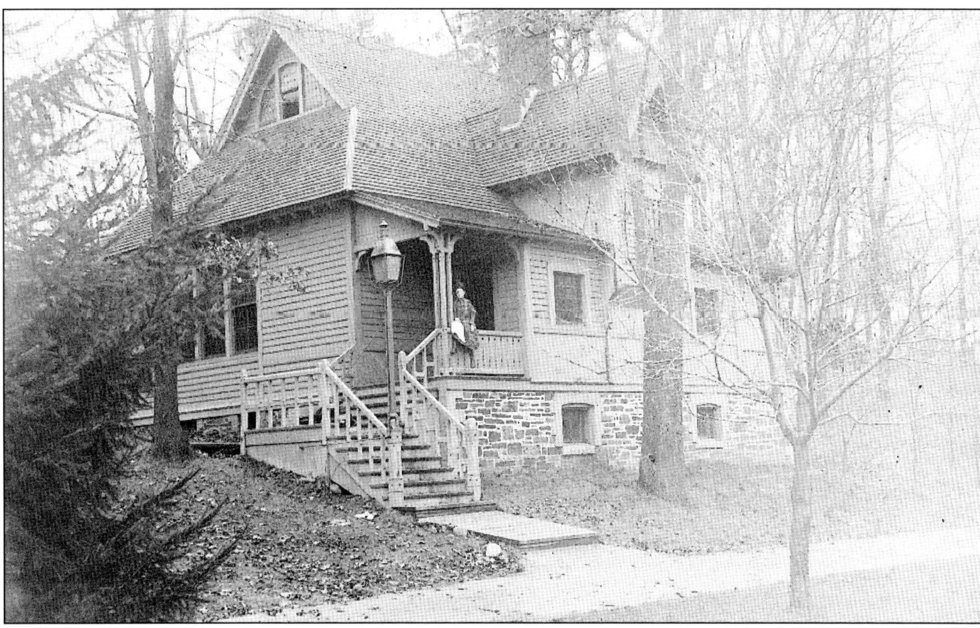

Rangeley Hall was built by David Nelson Skillings, who hailed from one of Winchester's first families, on the lower side lawn of the E.D. Bangs Estate. The hall was built as a community schoolhouse and social hall. Miss Mary Pickard Winsor, founder of the Winsor School in Brookline, Massachusetts, was the teacher. The structure was torn down *c*. 1905–06. The girl on the railing is probably Lesley Bangs.

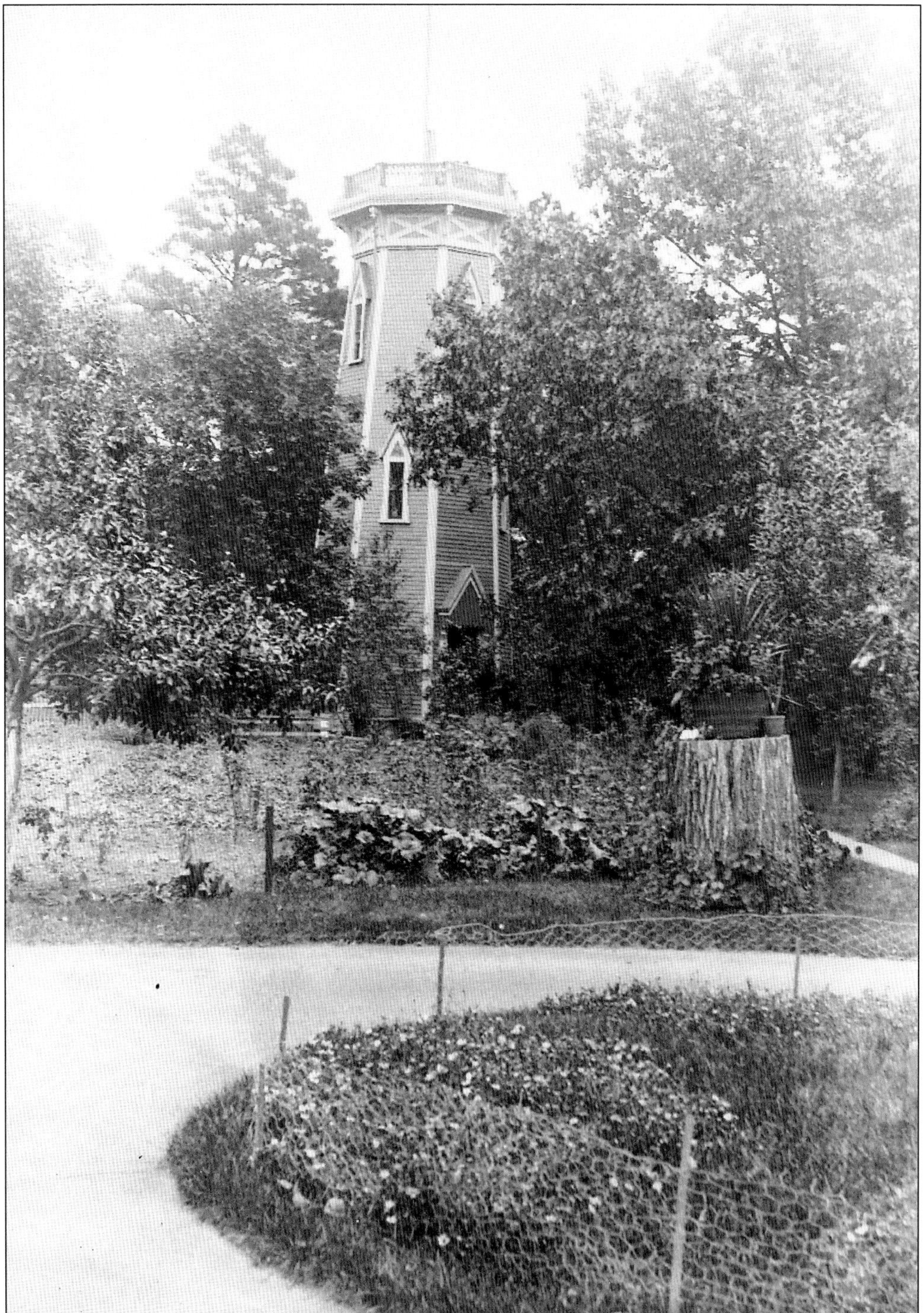

The water tower on the E.D. Bangs Estate at the extreme easterly edge of the Central Street Estate. It was converted to a sunken herb garden in the stone foundations by Bangs' widow, Georgianna Skillings Bangs, in 1889. This was, of course, one of Winchester's most prominent early families.

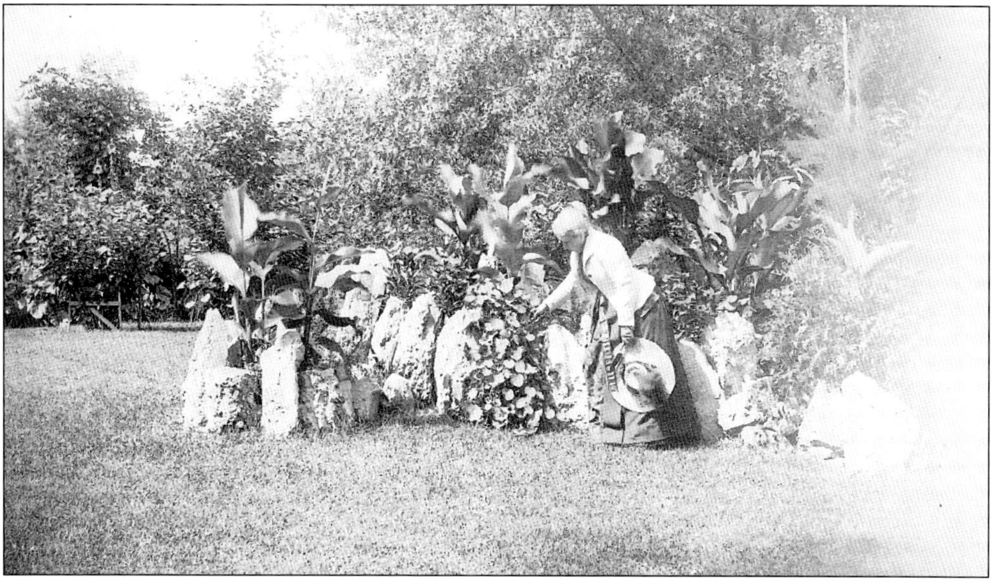

A fern rockery with Georgianna (Skillings) Bangs at Central Street in the Rangeley development, *c.* 1890s. Wonderful gardens were part of the comfortable life in much of Winchester during this time.

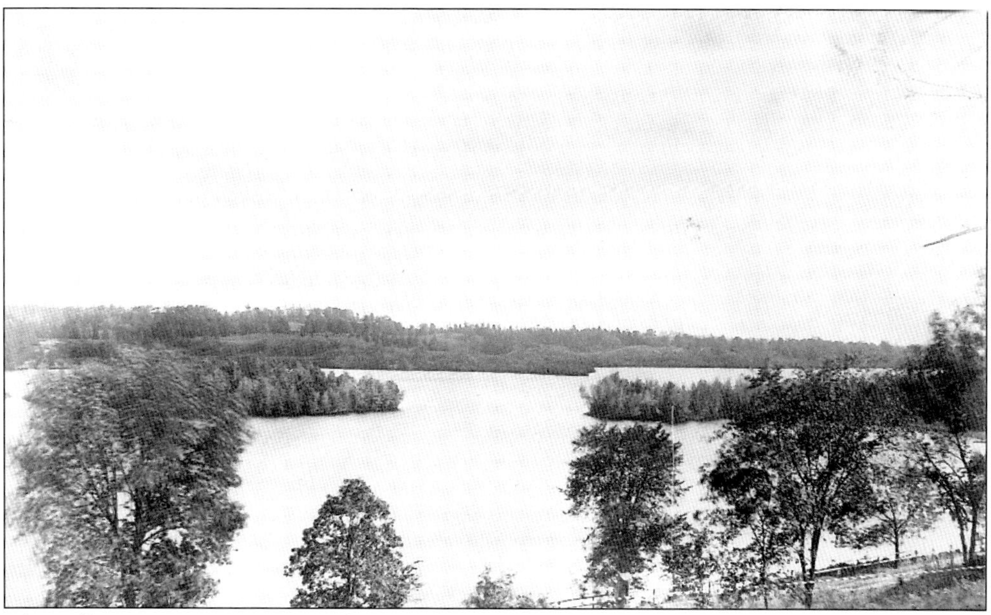

The Fells Reservoir, *c.* 1890s. The wooded Fells area remains preserved today. It has always been part of the comfort of Winchester life.

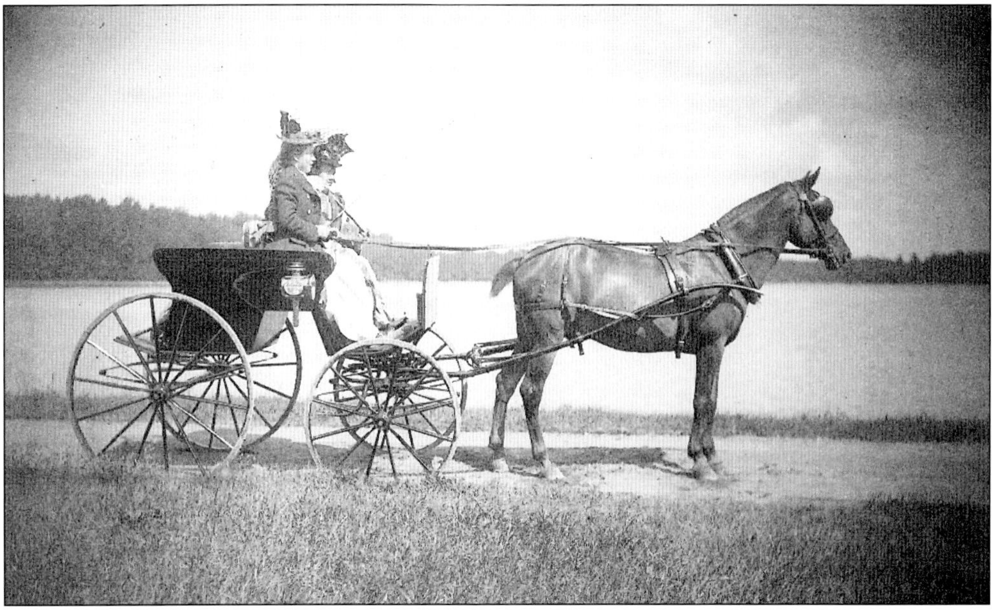

Lesley Dillingham Bangs at the reins at the Winchester Reservoir, Middlesex Fells, *c.* 1890s.

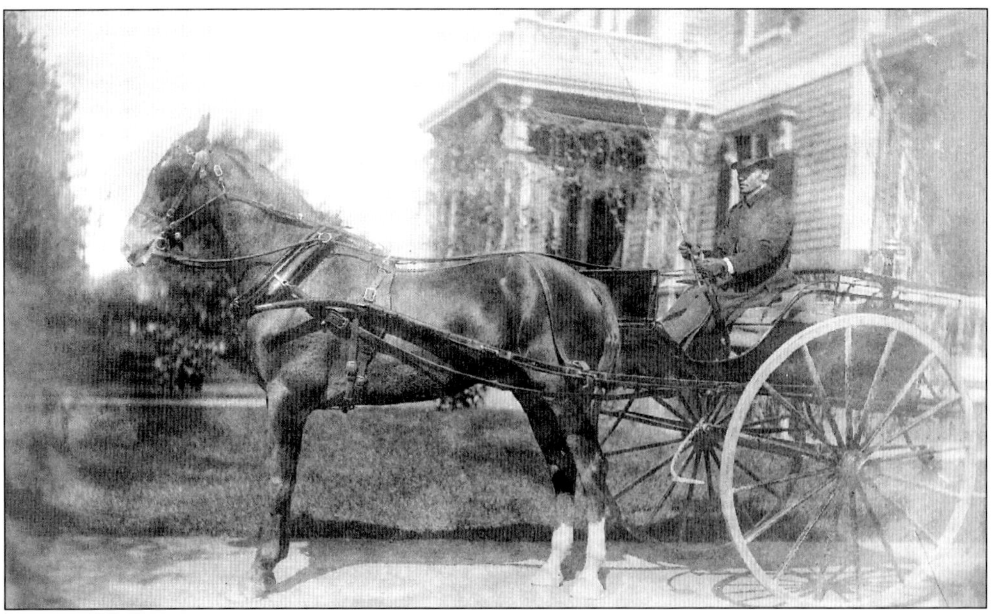

The E.D. Bangs coachman at the Central Street Estate, *c.* 1890s. It was all part of this good, comfortable life.

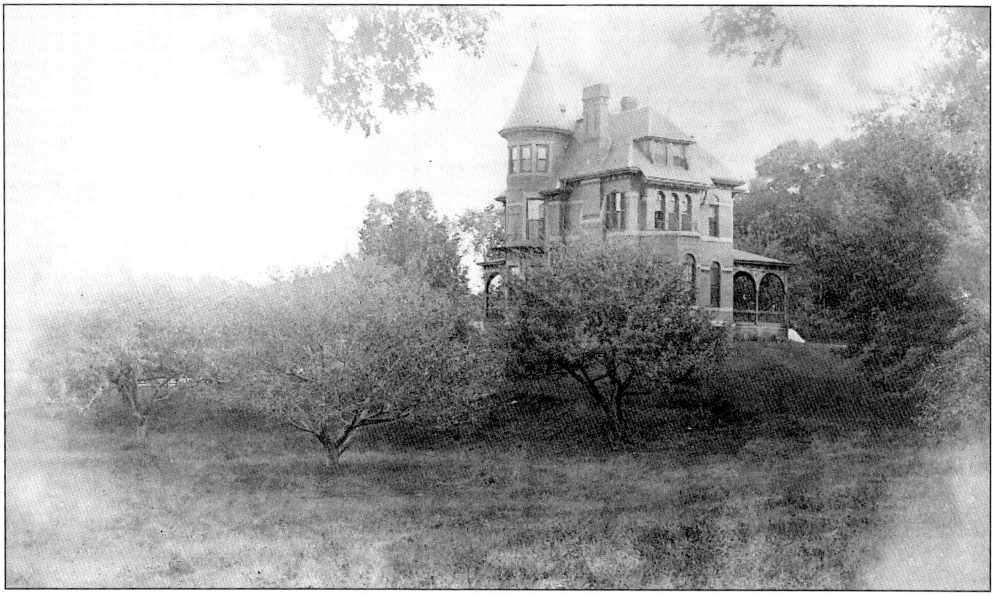

This imposing home with turret was built by David N. Skillings on Rangeley Ridge for friends. It was generally rented and was torn down, *c*. 1890s.

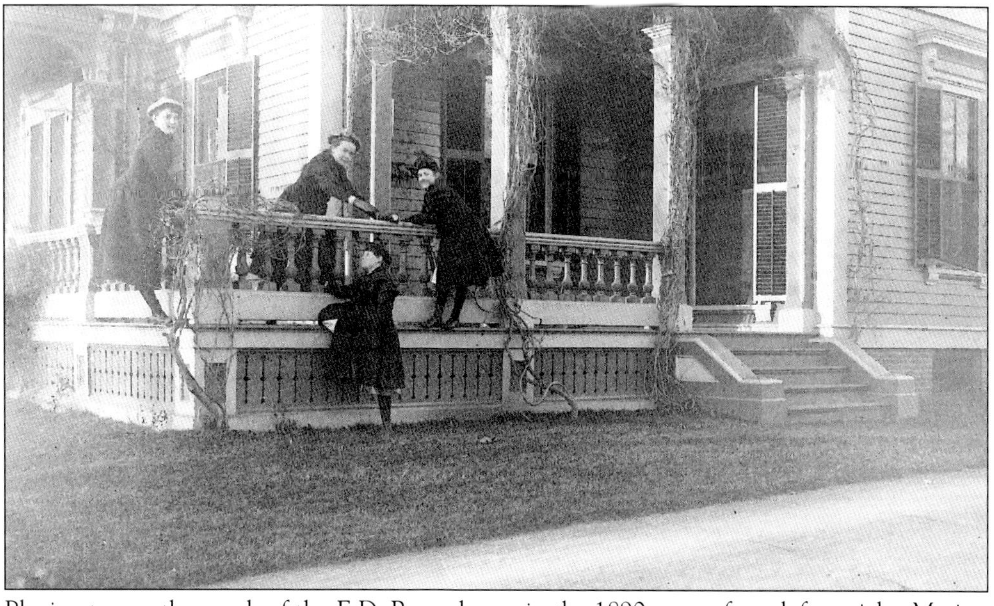

Playing tag on the porch of the E.D. Bangs home in the 1890s were, from left to right, Marion X, Rhoda Skillings, Alice Skillings, and Isabel X.

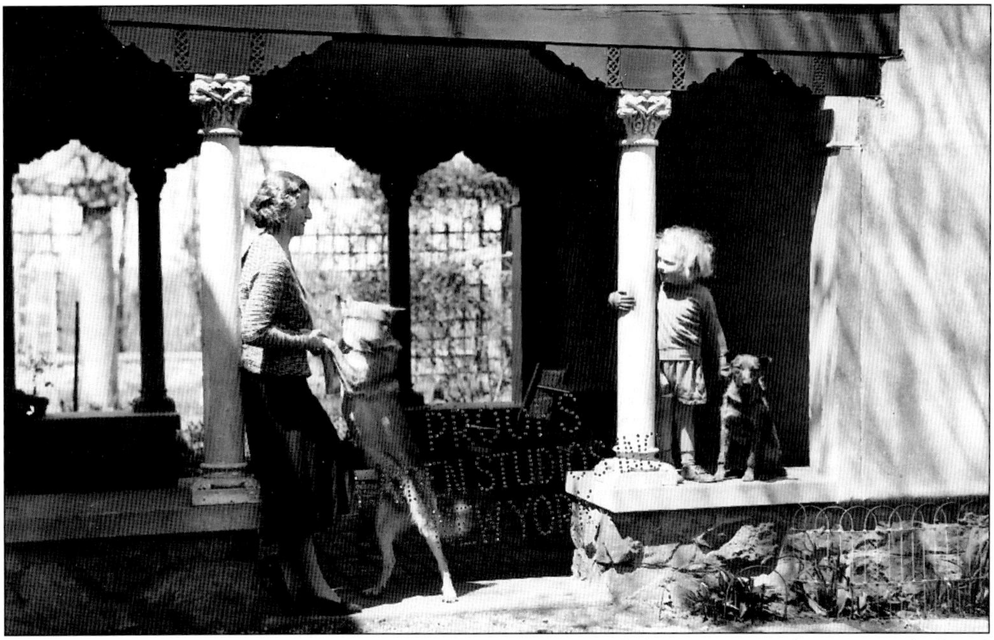

Peace, calm, and comfort existed in Winchester far beyond the 1890s. Carlene Samoiloff and her son Alexander are in their house on Highland Avenue, *c.* 1932.

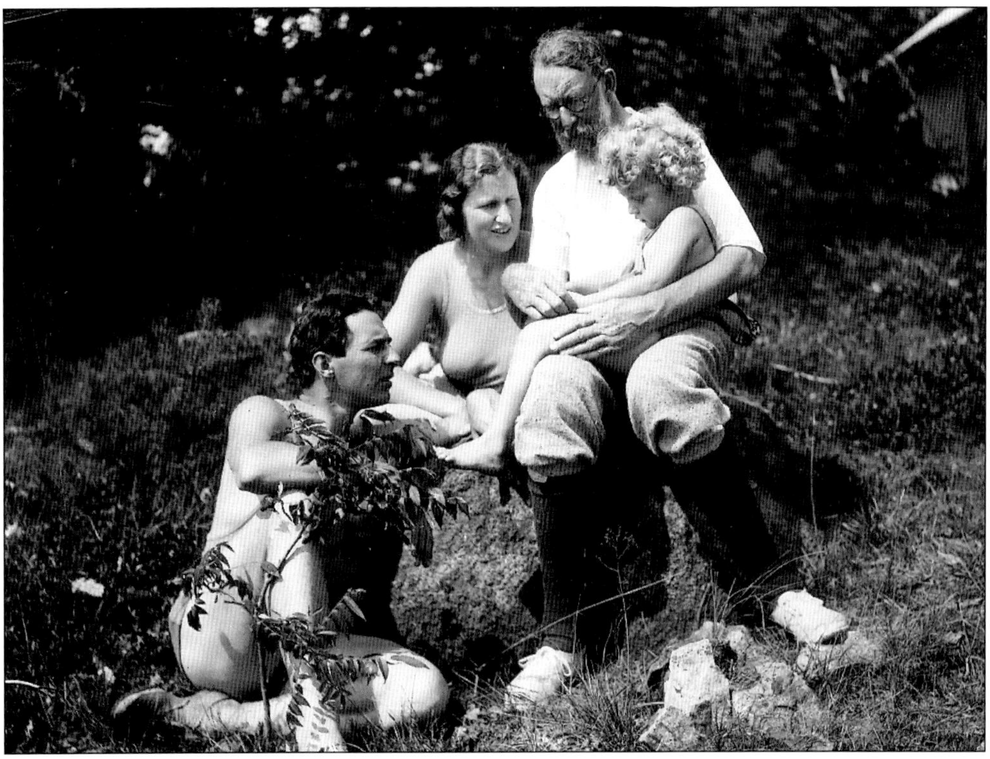

Another example of family life in Winchester, *c.* 1931, during the Depression. From left to right are Alexander Samoiloff, Carlene Murphy Samoiloff (Alexander's wife), Herman Dudley Murphy (Carlene's father, and a famed artist and canoeist), and Alexander Samoiloff Jr.

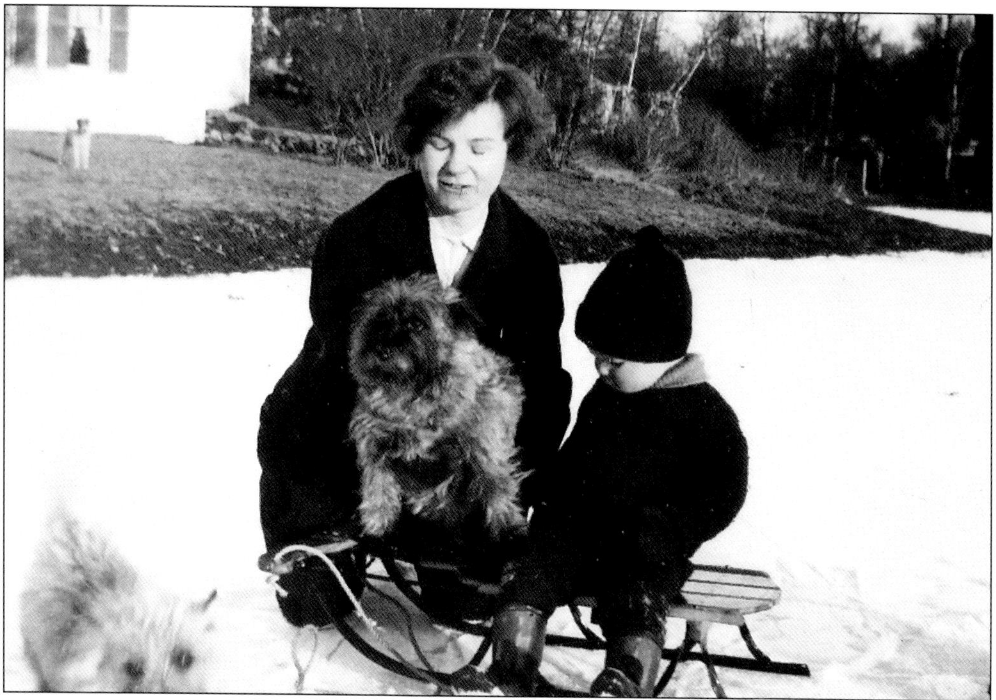

Life was often still comfortable in Winchester during the Depression as this 1934 photograph shows. Lois Hersey is with her son Elliott, who is on the sled with Molly, one of the dogs. Barker is the other dog. All are on Big Winter Pond.

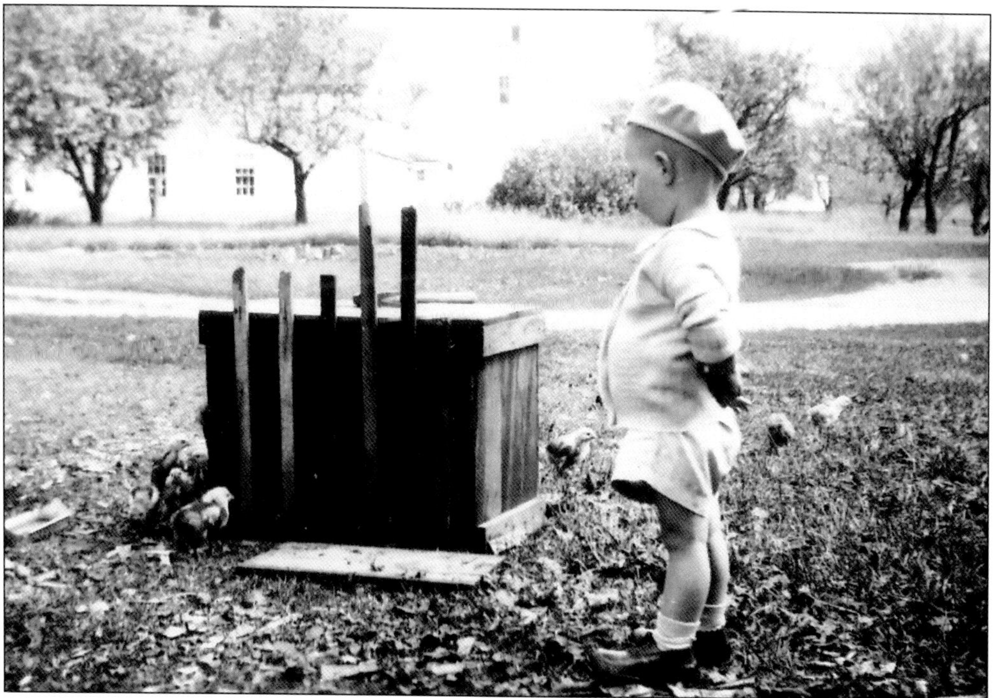

Ah, the peace, quiet, and comfort that could come even in the Depression. In 1934, Elliott Hersey looks at the box which once contained the chicks in the photograph.

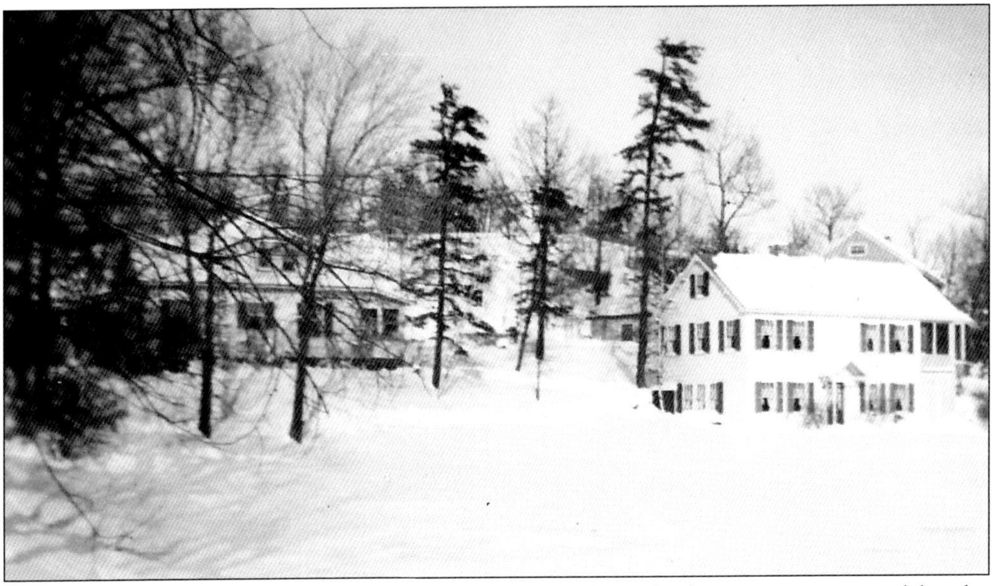

Houses on Big Winter Pond in the 1930s. On the left is the home now occupied by the Shirley family, while at the right is the house of Sara Hersey, the grandmother of Althea Hersey Shirley.

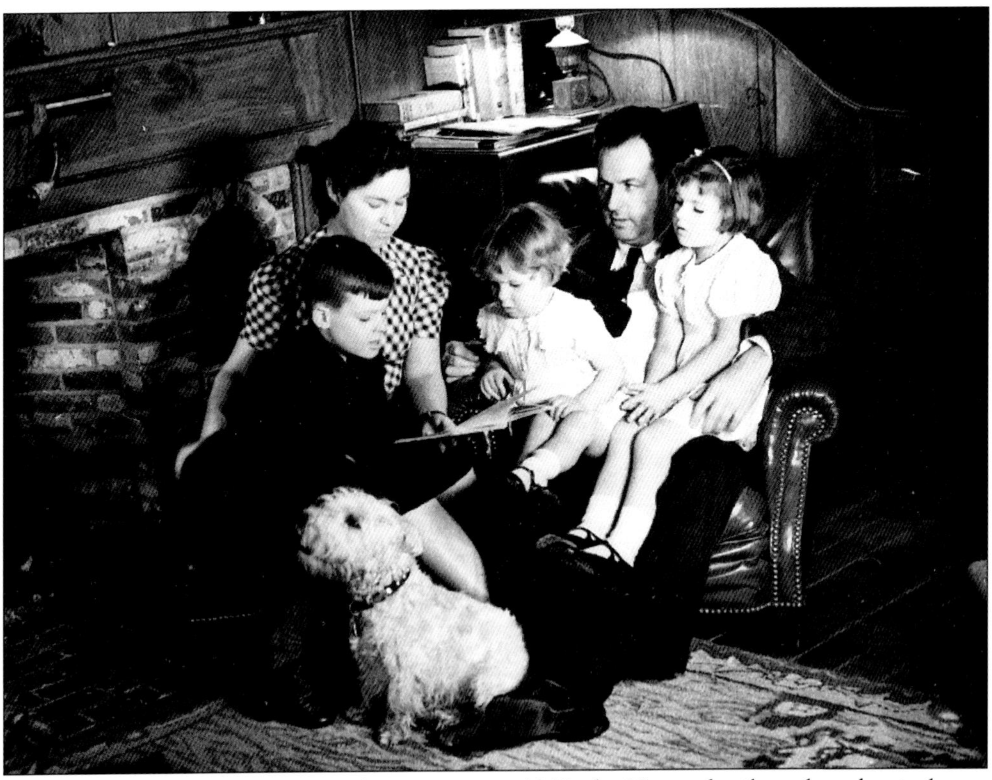

Just before World War II came to this country, in 1940, the Hersey family gathered at its home on Woodside Street. From left to right are: Elliott Hersey; Lois Hersey, the mother; Alison Hersey (Risch); Walden (Bradbury) Hersey, the father; and Althea Hersey (Shirley).

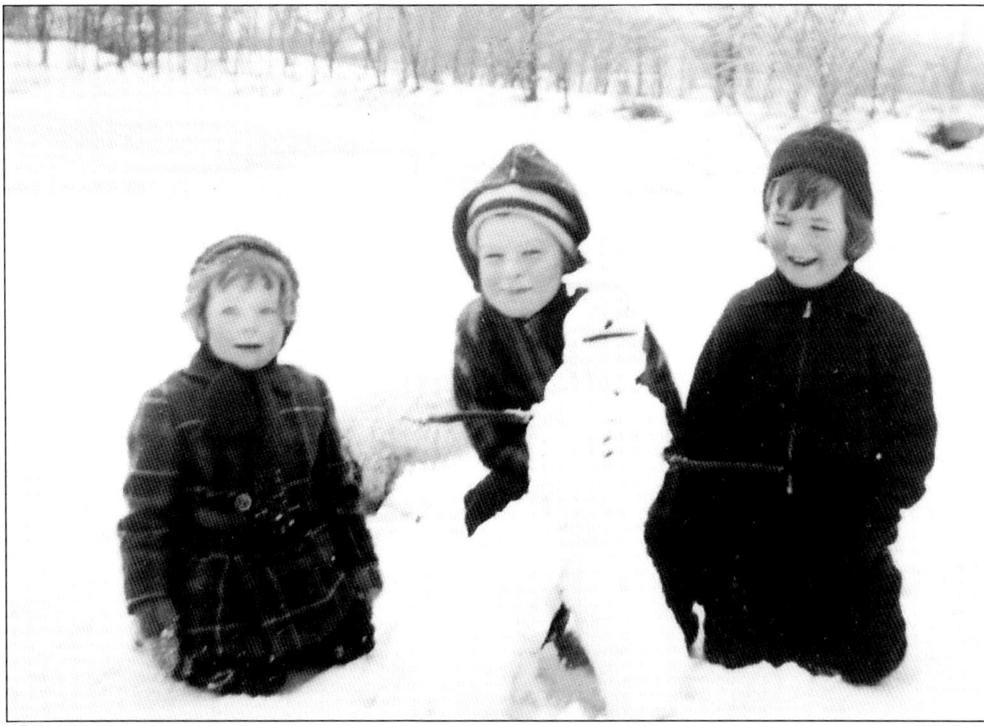

There's a snow man on Little Winter Pond in this 1940 Christmas card along with, from left to right, Alison Hersey (Risch), Elliott Hersey, and Althea Hersey (Shirley).

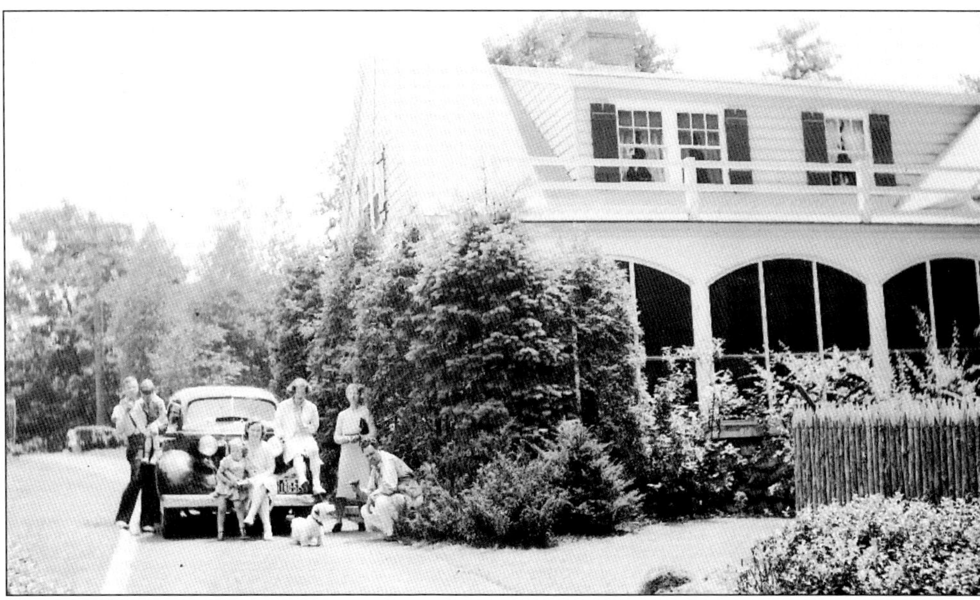

Sitting on or by a car, c. 1939. At their home on Woodside Street were, from left to right, Rod Elliott, Elliott Hersey (sitting), Althea Hersey (Shirley), Lois Hersey, Mrs. Ruby Elliott, Alice Josephson, and Brad Hersey. The Elliotts were neighbors.

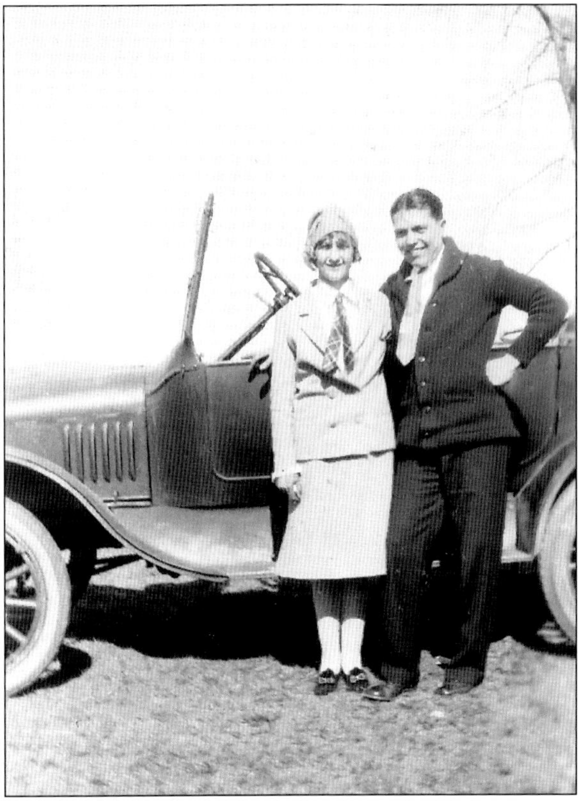

Harry Chefalo and his sister-in-law Anne Nelson with a Ford on the Woburn Parkway in April 1927.

More comfort and joy during the Depression. Sisters Alice and Marilyn Chefalo are at the Flume in Franconia Notch, New Hampshire, in the 1930s.

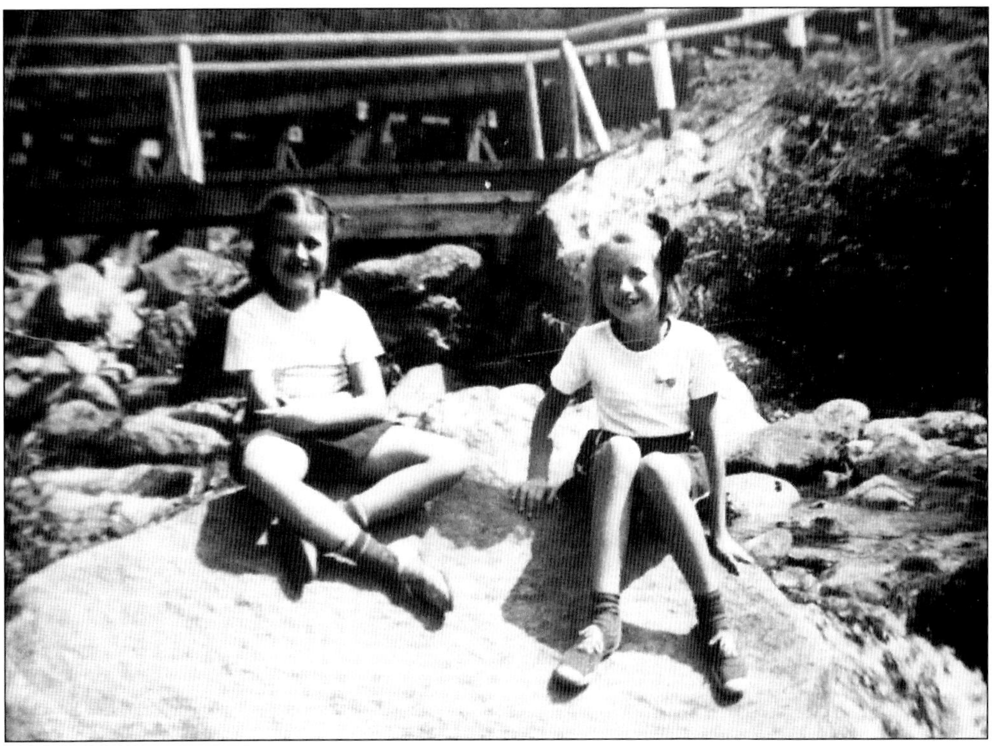

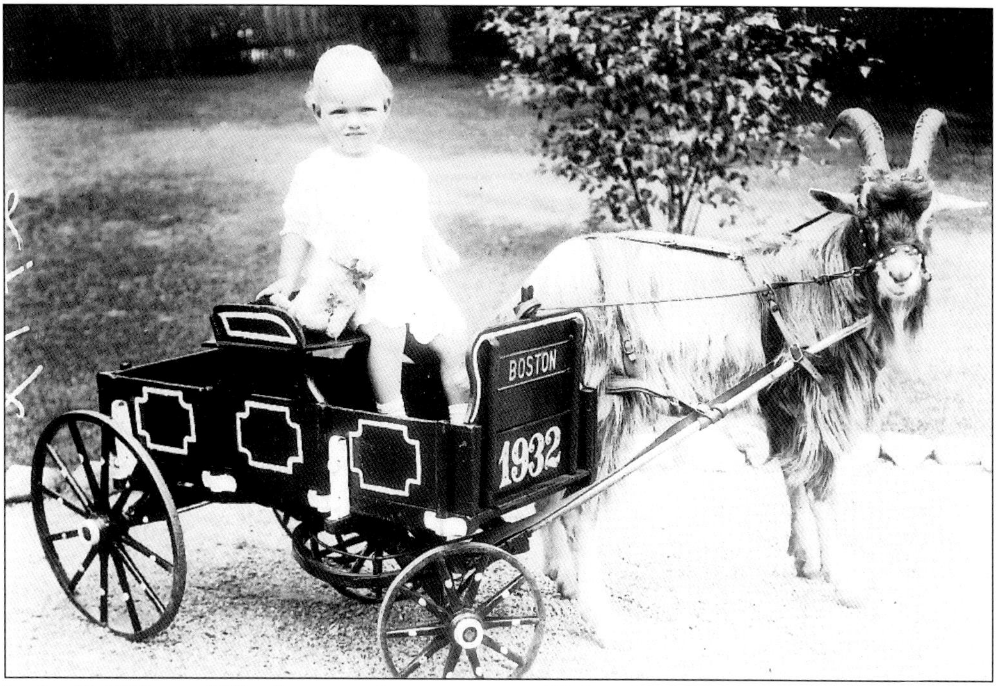

Lesley D. Wilcox of Winchester with a goat cart in Waban, Massachusetts, in 1932.

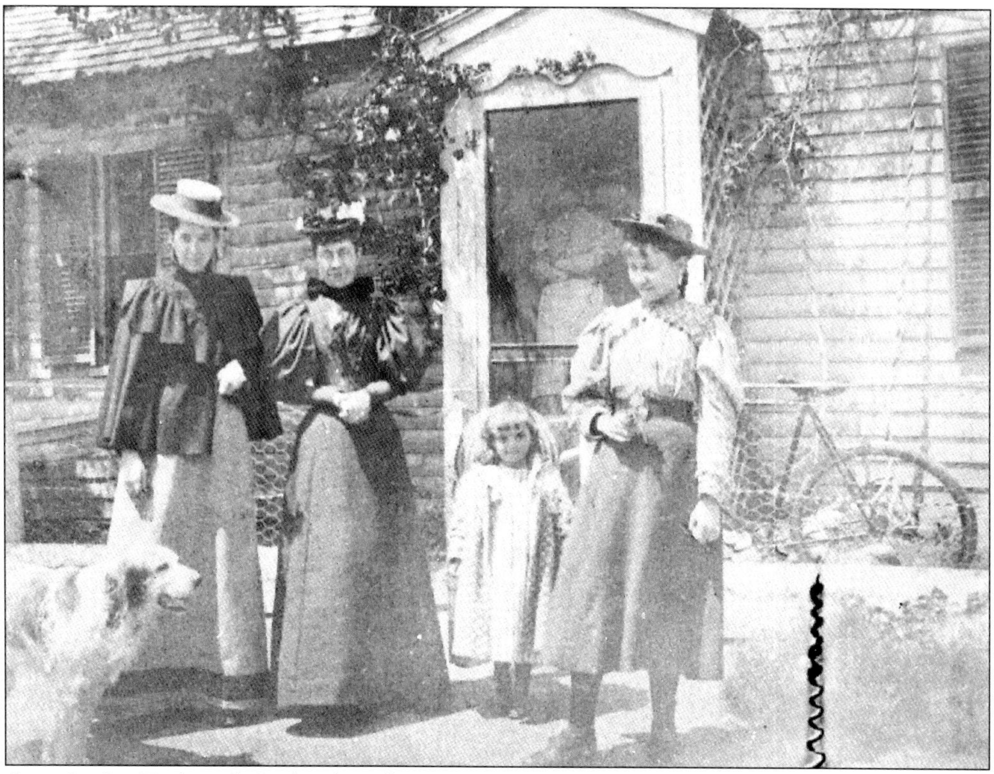
Outside the Zachariah Richardson house, 607 Washington Street, *c.* 1889, was Laura Bird Tolman, who was born in 1882.

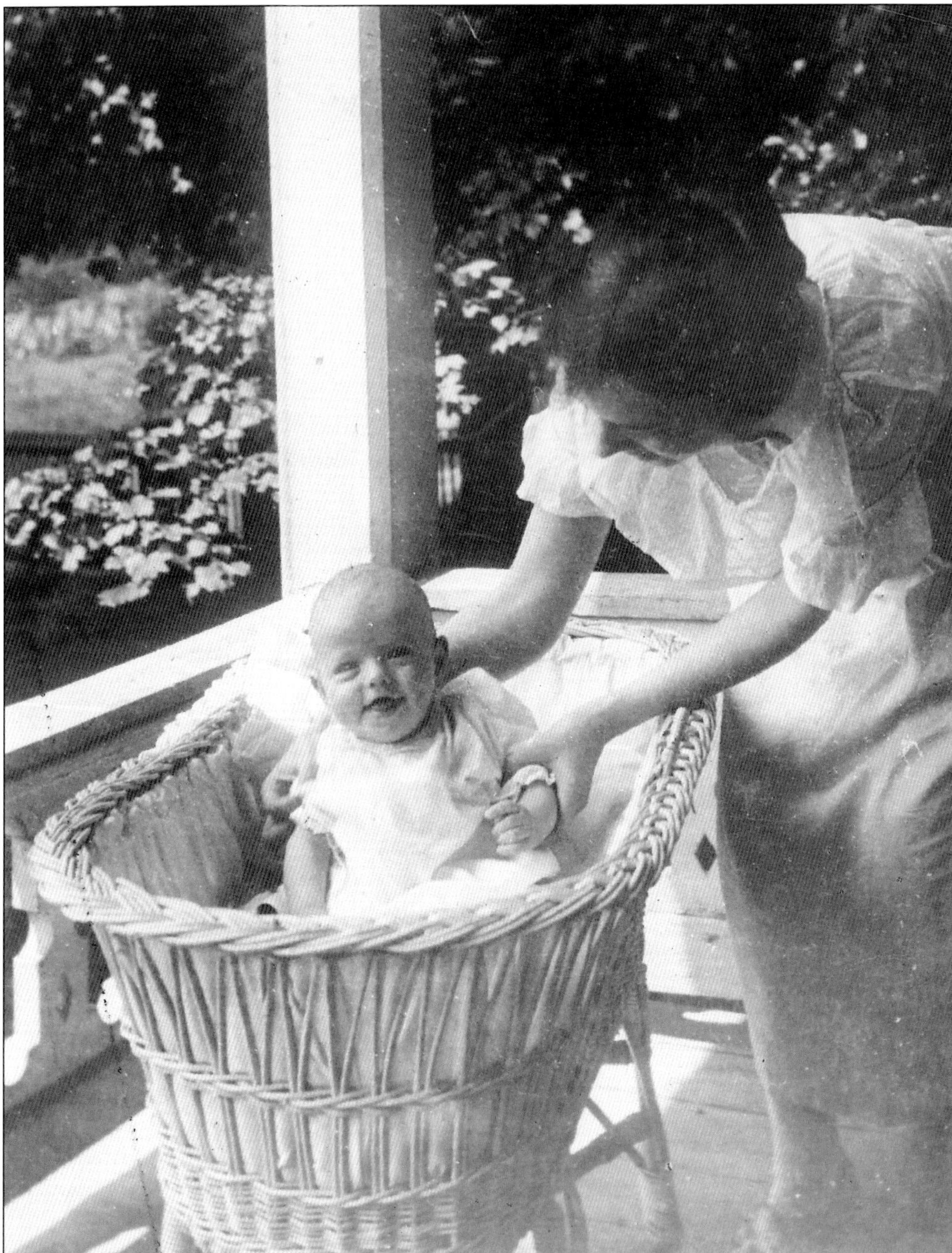

William Sherburne, about six months old, looks up from his bassinet at his home on Highland Avenue as his mother, Barbara Blank Sherburne, supervises, *c.* 1923.

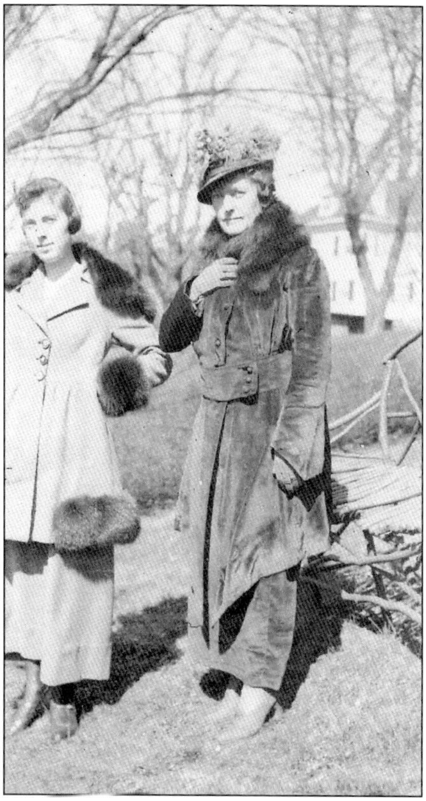

Barbara Blank (Sherburne), at left, and her mother Grace Belle Manning Blank, *c.* 1910s, at Highland Avenue, Winchester. The Blanks were one of the wealthiest families in Winchester at that time.

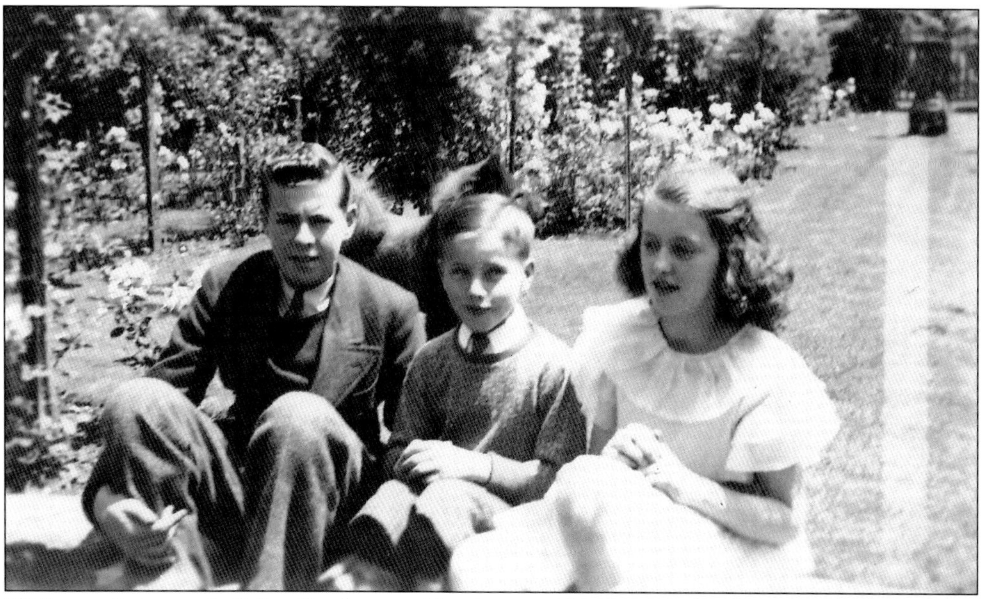

William, Dale, and Sally Sherburne (Finn), *c.* 1930–31, in the Downs rose garden at 1 Arlington Street, generally considered then the most beautiful garden in Winchester.

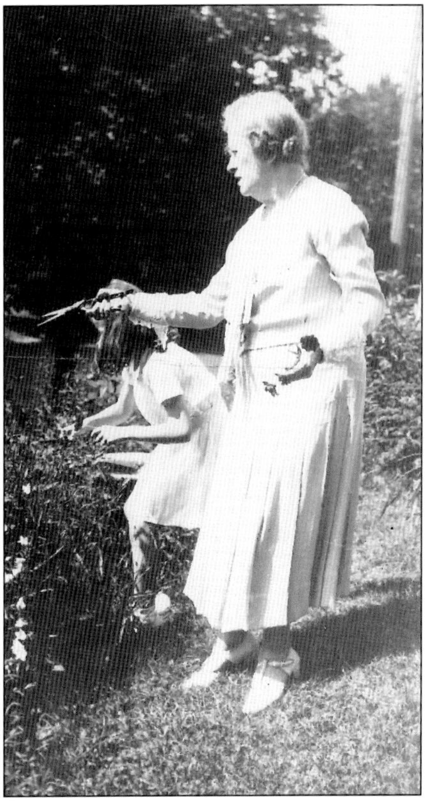

Sally Sherburne (Finn), at left, in the garden with her grandmother Grace Belle Manning Blank, *c.* 1931.

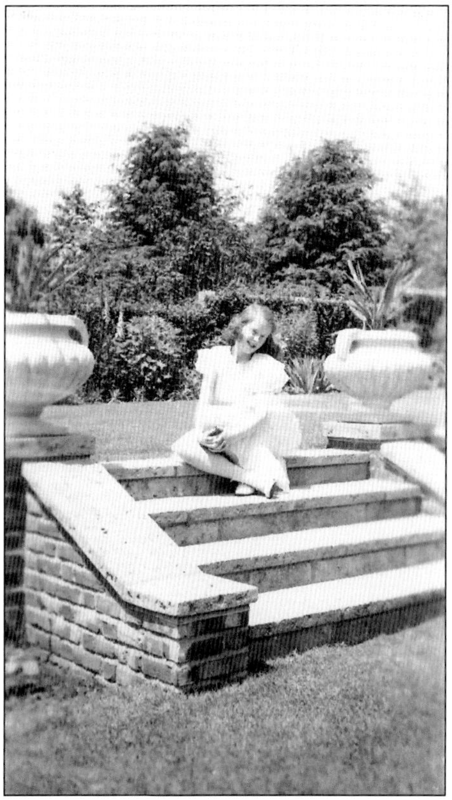

Sally Sherburne (Finn) sits in the Downs rose garden, *c.* 1935. Again, there was beauty and comfort during the Depression.

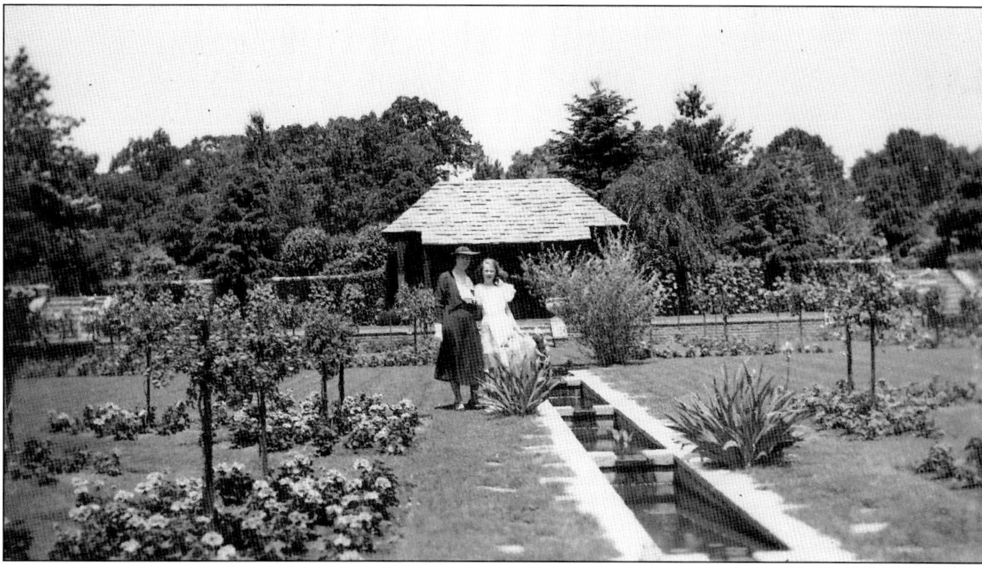

Sally Sherburne (Finn) and her grandmother Grace Belle Manning Blank stand in the English formal garden section of the Downs garden at 1 Arlington Street, *c.* 1935.

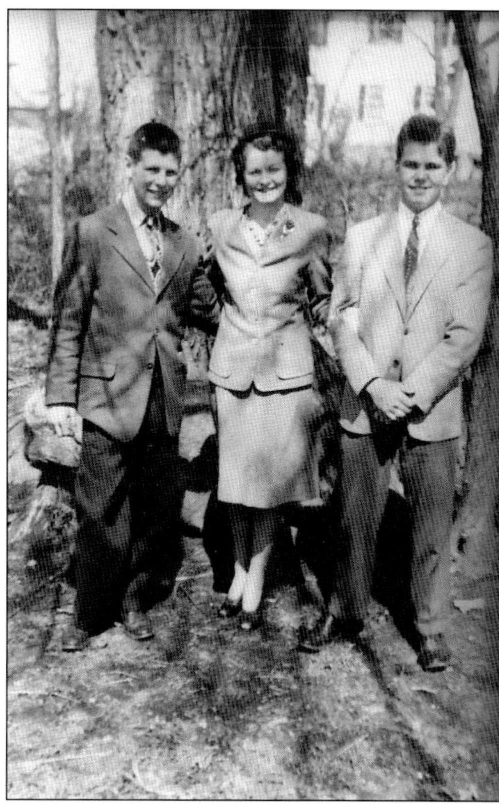

There was still plenty of comfort in Winchester after World War II. From left to right are Bob Quine, his mother, and Jimmy Quine (his brother) in 1947 at the Quine Grayson Road home.

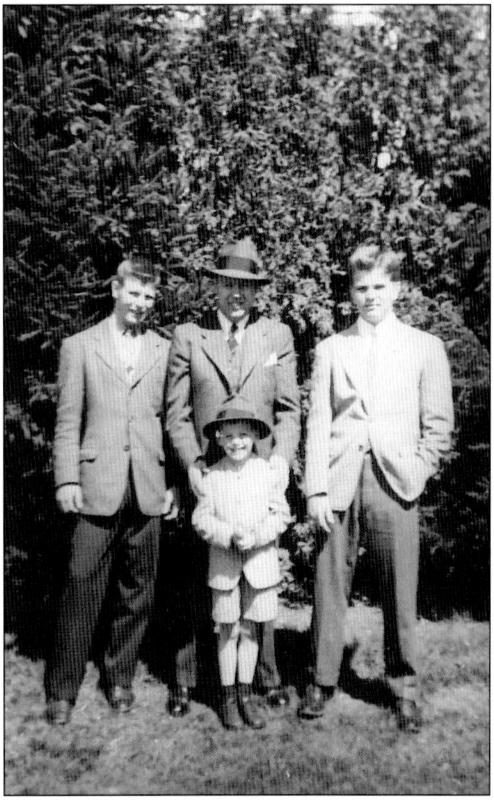

Another photograph at the Quine Grayson Road home in 1947 with Bob, Frank (his father), Jimmy, and Peter Quine, who died in 1959.

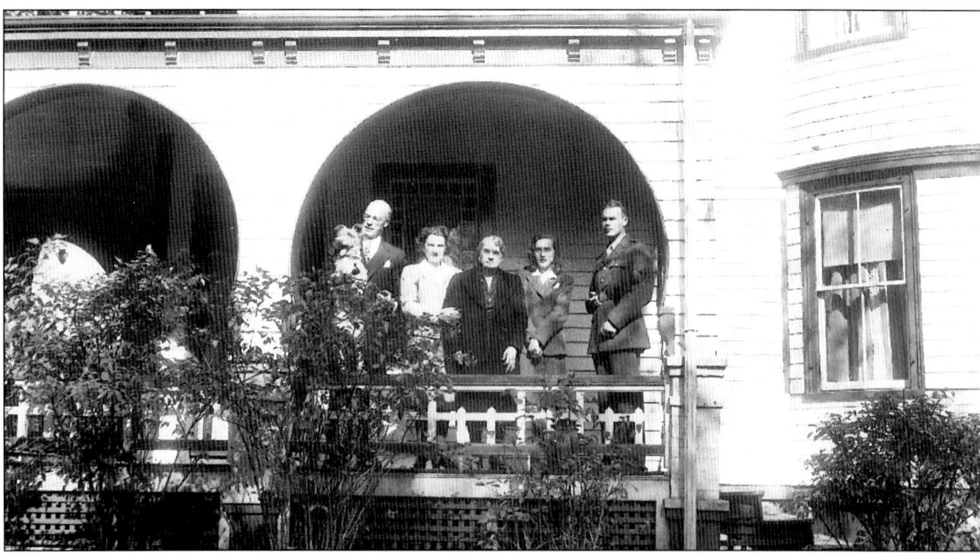

Another home picture illustrating the relative comfort of Winchester life, even during World War II. The Crandall family is at 25 Wildwood Street in 1943 when son Courtney was home on furlough. From left to right are: Rex Crandall, Courtney's father; Ola Crandall, Courtney's mother; Kate Long, Courtney's grandmother on his mother's side; Cara, Courtney's sister; and Courtney himself.

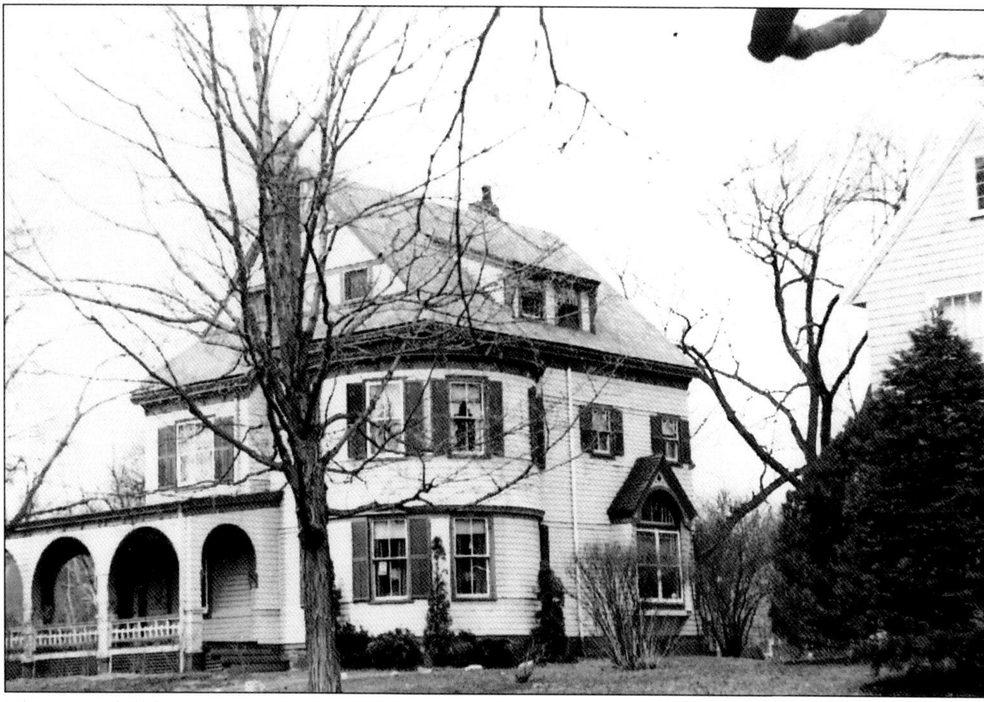
The Crandall home at 25 Wildwood Street in the 1940s. It was a comfortable place to live.

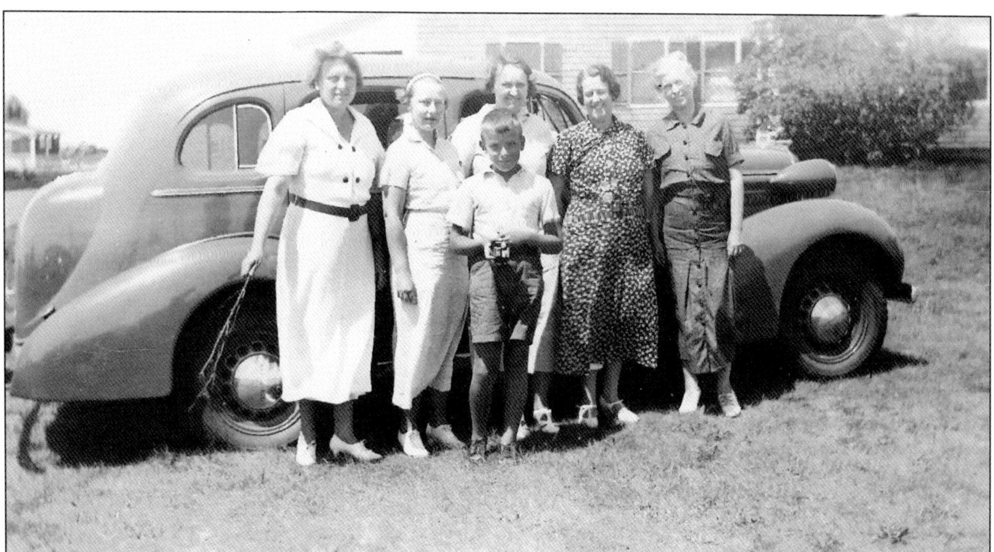
Members of the bridge club sponsored by Barbara Blank Sherburne in the late 1930s or early 1940s. From left to right are Ruth French, unknown, Edith Harris, Charlena Locke, Dorothy Wills, and Richard Wills (the boy in front).

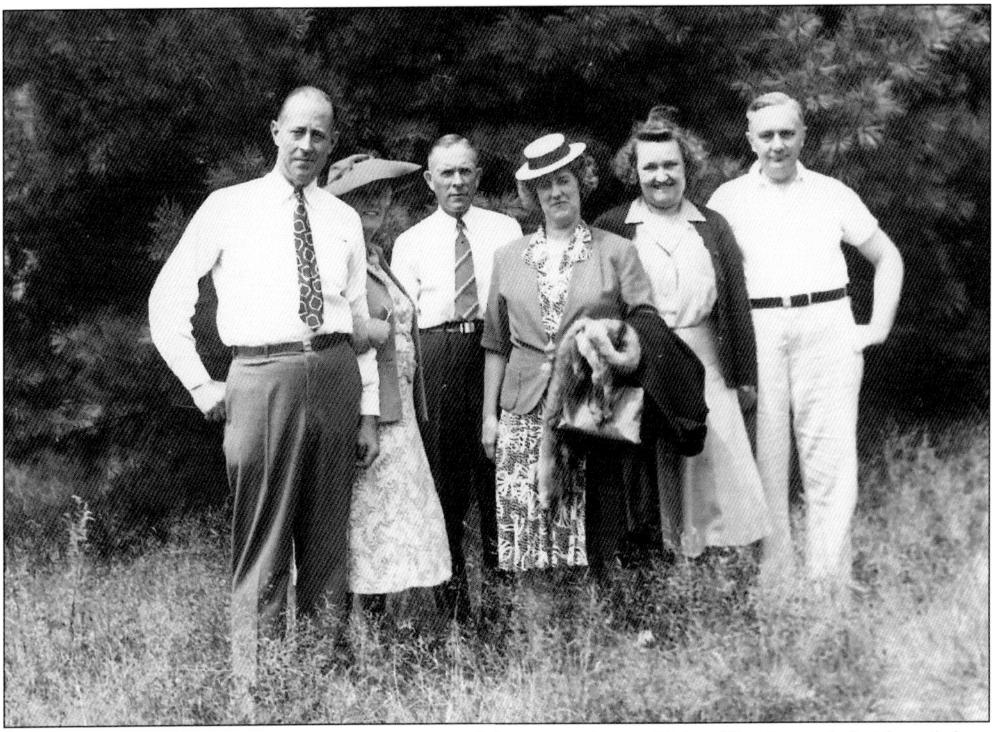

More members of Mrs. Sherburne's bridge club in the late 1930s or early 1940s. From left to right are: Willard Hudson; his wife, Pauline Hudson; Harry Dexter Locke; Harry's wife, Charlena Locke; Edith Harris; and Edith's husband, Arthur Sanders Harris.

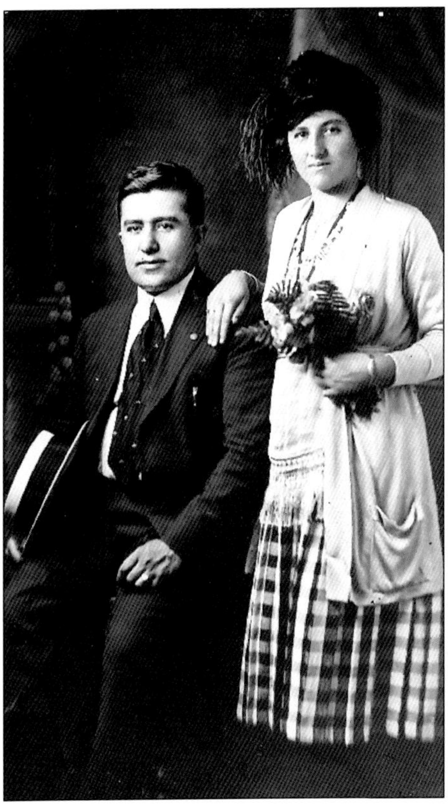

The wedding picture of Krikor (Koko) and Herpisme Boodakian at the Holy Trinity Armenian Orthodox Church in 1920. Koko came from Aintab in what is now Turkey before World War I. He came to Simsbury, Connecticut, and served in World War I with the Americans, moving to South Boston, Massachusetts, after the war. His wife lived in Killis, Turkey, and came to this country when Koko sent for her. It was an old country tradition.

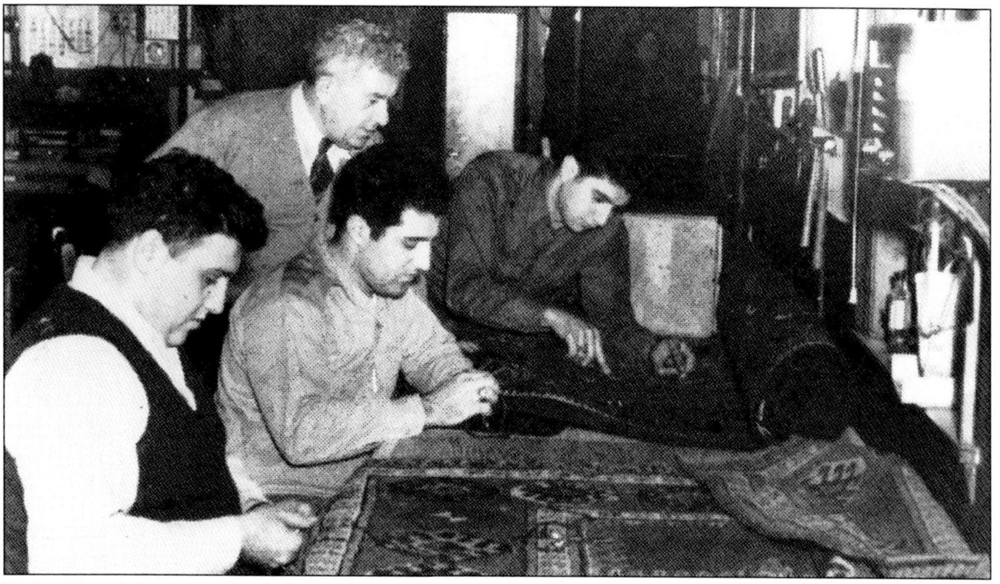

Koko Boodakian worked for Adalian Brothers, a Boston oriental rug firm, for twenty-five years. He and his family moved to Winchester in 1927 and he started his own oriental rug cleaning and repairing business at his home at 14 Lochwan Street, October 1, 1938. Rugs were washed in the front of the house and dried on the lawn. In 1941, a separate building was constructed behind the house and is still used as the cleaning plant. Shown in that building *c.* 1950 are Koko Boodakian (standing at the rear), and, from left to right, his sons Leo (Levon), Harry, and Michael.

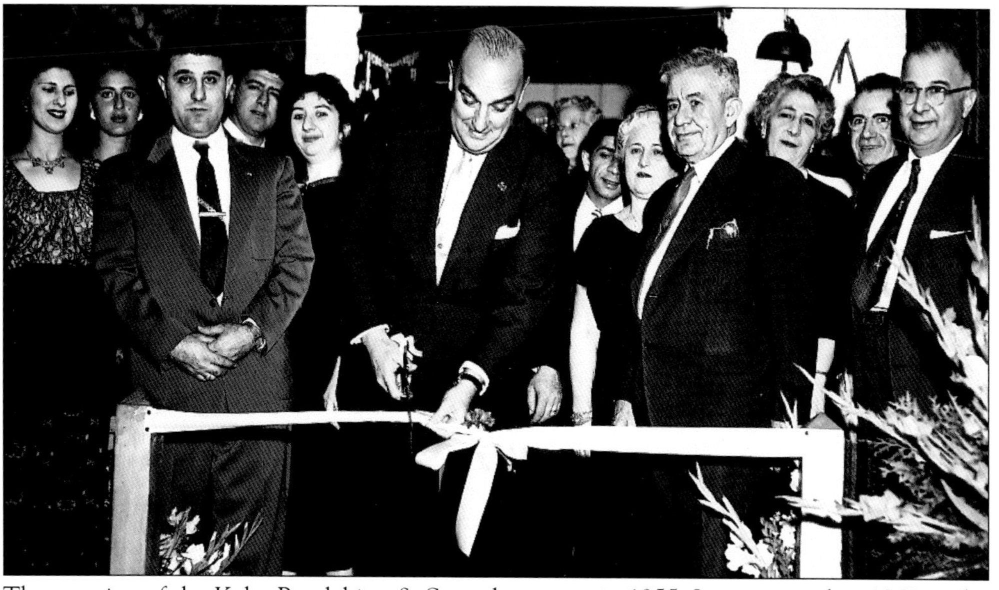

The opening of the Koko Boodakian & Sons showroom in 1955. It was moved in 1961 to the present location on Main Street, Winchester, not far from the Woburn town line. From left to right are: Mrs. Harry Boodakian (Dolores); Mrs. Michael Boodakian (Mary); Harry Boodakian; Michael Boodakian; Mrs. Leo Boodakian (Leona); Massachusetts Attorney General George Fingold; George Tashjian, a cousin; Mrs. Koko Boodakian (Herpisme); Koko Boodakian; Mrs. Tapjian, mother of Leona Boodakian; and Charles Sulahian, uncle of Leona Boodakian.

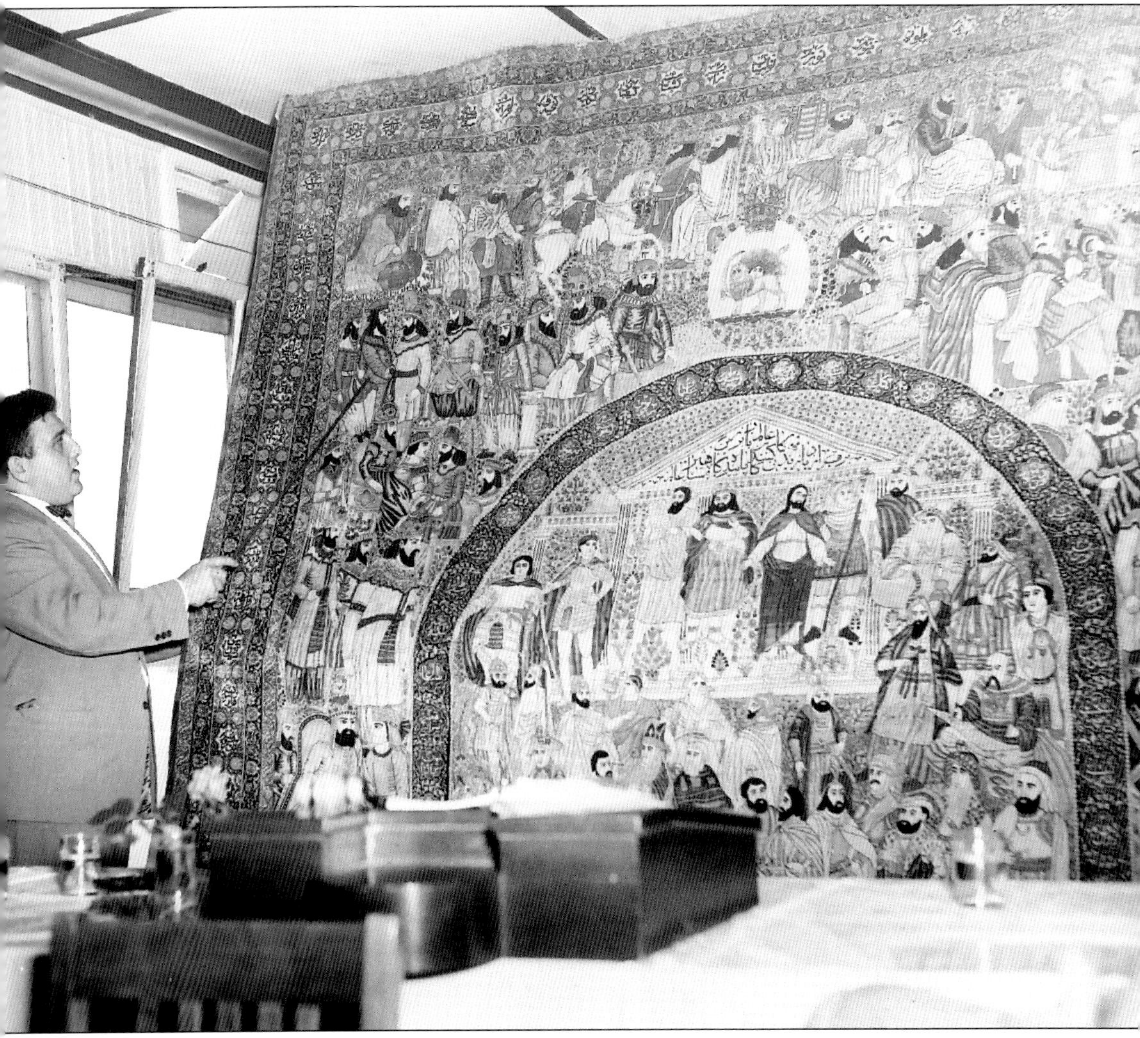

The Boodakians were the third Armenian family to move into Winchester. There are now about forty Armenian families in the town. The first two families were those of Dr. Baghdoyan and of Aram Mouradian. The Mouradians and Boodakians were friendly competitors in the oriental rug business many years. In the above photograph, Leo Boodakian points to some of the 165 figures on the "Rug Of Civilization," owned by Koko Boodakian & Sons Inc. It took nearly twelve years to complete. There are nearly 1,000 knots per square inch (compare that to the 100 knots per square inch decreed by Ayatollah Khomeini in Iran). The estimated value of the rug is about $1 million. It was presented to Shah Ahmed Mirza Kajar of Persia on his accession to the throne in 1905 and was eventually sold by the Shah.

Two

Italo-Americans

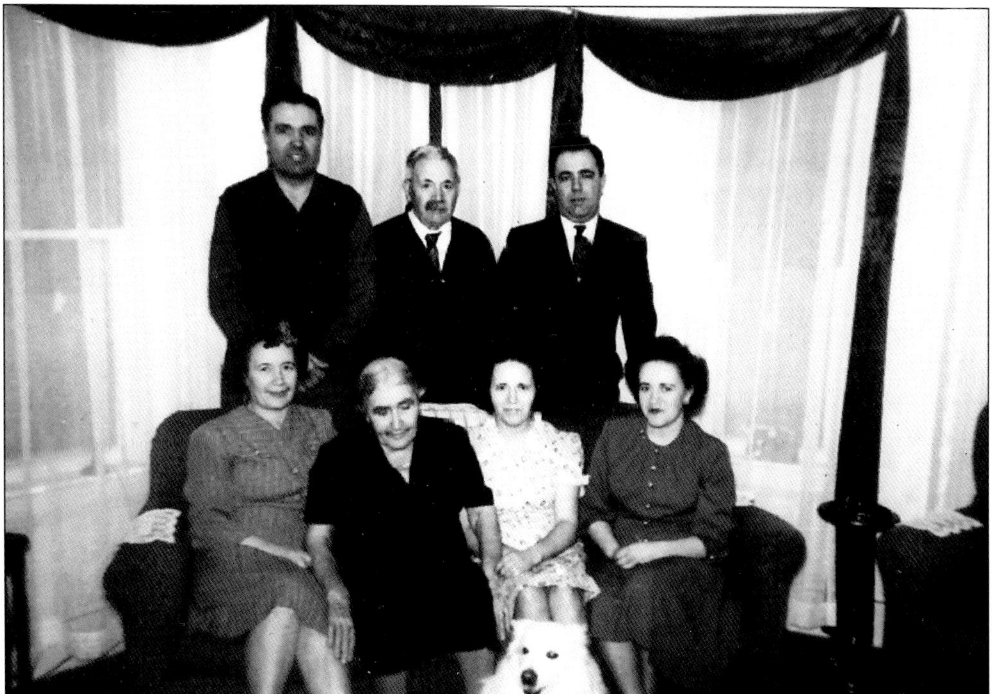

A 1960 photograph of the Cefalo (Chefalo) family. From left to right are: (front) Josephine (the oldest sister of Harry), Theodora, Susie, and Camilla; (back) Harry, Vincenzo, and Tony. As the Boodakian family increased the comfort of Winchester through its oriental rug services and, thus, became comfortable economically itself, so Harry Chefalo supplied plumbing services and became comfortable himself.

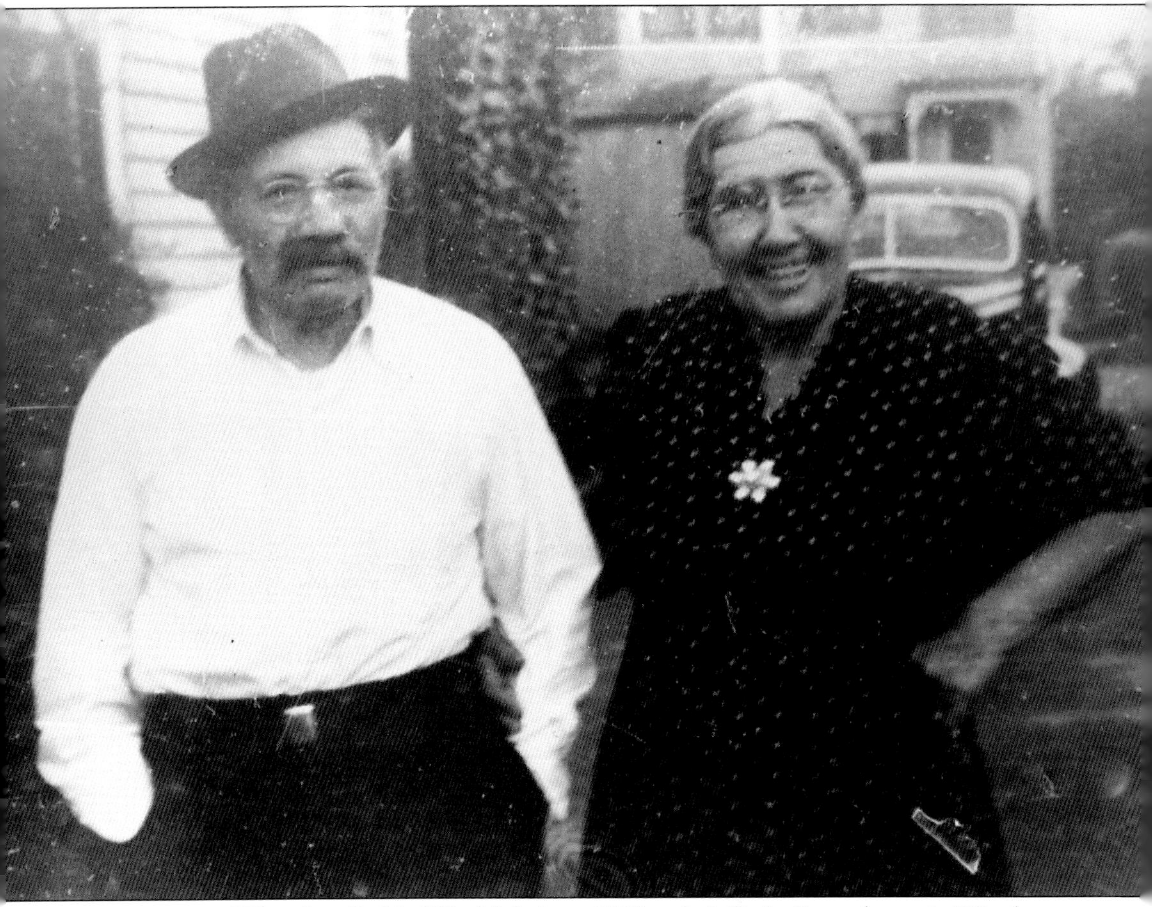

Vincenzo and Theodora Cefalo (Chefalo) about 1960 at their Cedar Street home in Winchester. Vincenzo came in 1902 from a small town near Naples. He left because his sister was going to marry a man he didn't like, according his son, Harry Chefalo, now eighty-eight years old himself. Vincenzo never went back to Italy. He died at age seventy-six, and Theodora died at age ninety-two. Vincenzo worked at the J.O. Whitten Co., which made gelatin and jells. He retired at a relatively old age. There were very few Italians in Winchester when he came in 1902.

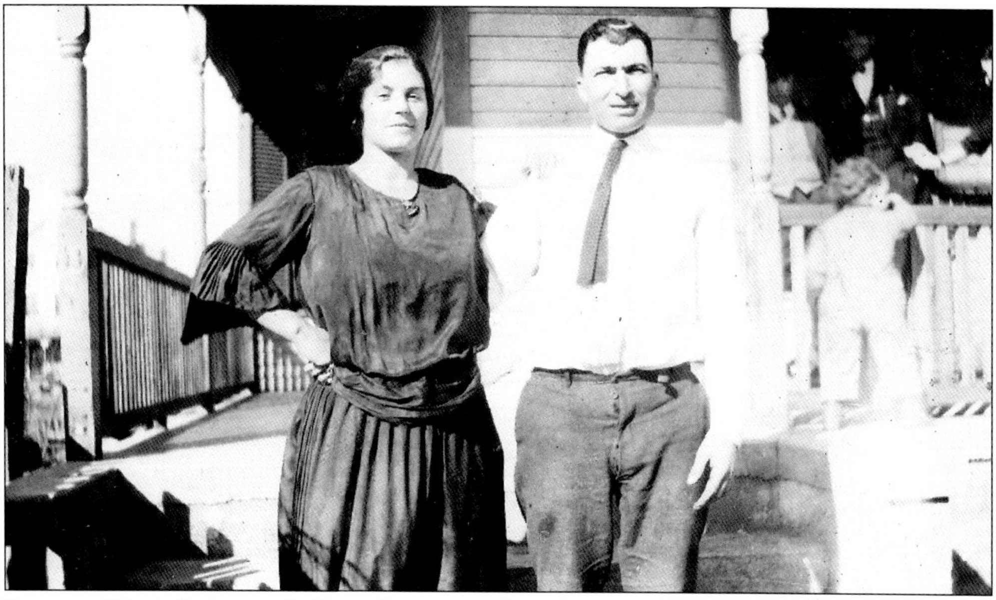

Frances Crimi Errico and Fiore Errico at their home on Harvard Street, Winchester, c. 1923–24. The following year, the house at 398 Washington Street was built and the family moved in. Both homes were in the section of Winchester known as "The Plains," where many Italo-Americans lived after they first came to the town. In recent years, many have moved to other parts of Winchester.

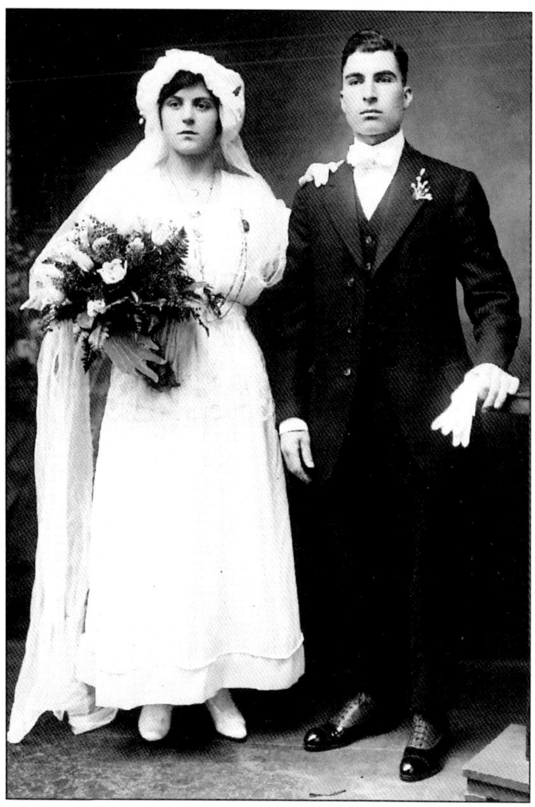

The wedding picture of Fiore and Frances Crimi Errico, October 21, 1917, at St. Mary's Church, Winchester. Fiore was born in 1893 at Monte Fusco, Italy, and came alone to the United States in 1907. Frances was born in 1901 in Marsala, Sicily. She came to Winchester in 1911 with her mother and father. The two met in Winchester, where Fiore was a contractor.

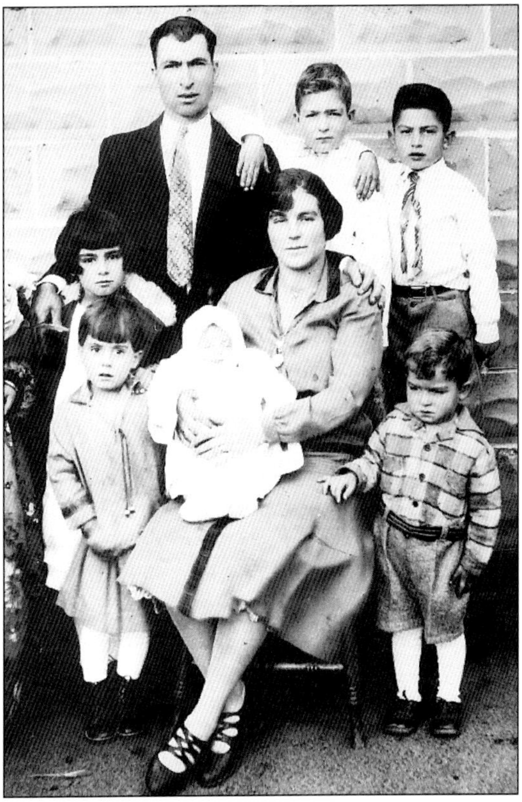

The Errico family in 1927 by the garage wall at the Washington Street home. From left to right are: (front) Loretta (with Anne in front of her), Joe (the baby), Frances (the mother), and Jack; (back) Fiore (the father), Louis, and Vincent.

The Errico family in the early 1950s during the Korean War. World War II and the Korean War increased the social mobility of many by providing new skills, as well as money (via the GI Bill) for future education. From left to right are: (front) Gerald, Joe, and Jack; (middle row) Richard, Loretta (Dube), Anne (Rallo), and Frank; (back) Vincent (now dead), Fiore (Frank), Vincent (Vincenzo) Crimi, Frances, and Louis. Richard and Frank were both serving in the Korean War at the time.

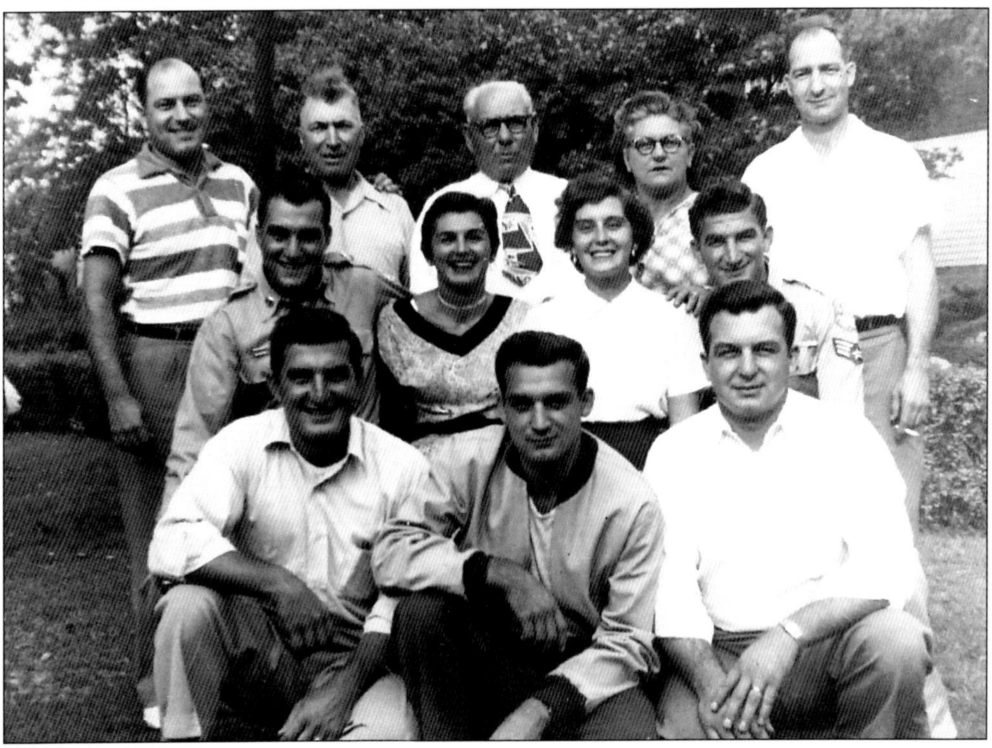

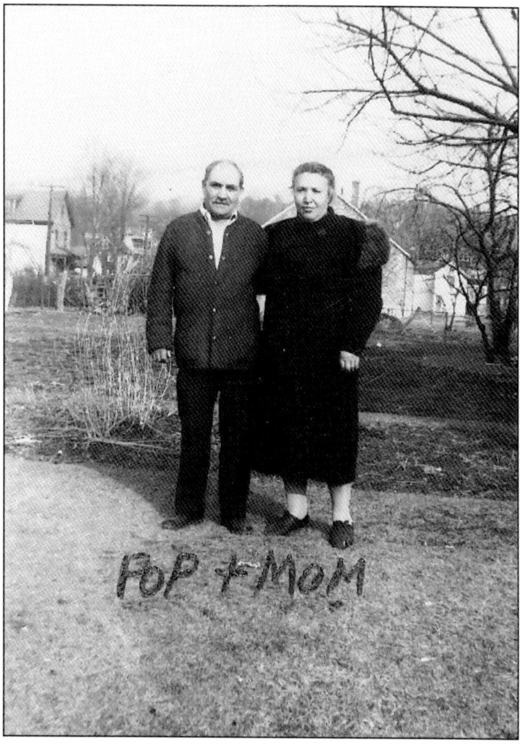

Peter and Mary Provinzano came to Winchester in the early 1920s, probably from Pennsylvania. Both originally were from Calabria in Italy. Peter worked in the gelatin factory. This is a *c.* late 1920s photograph.

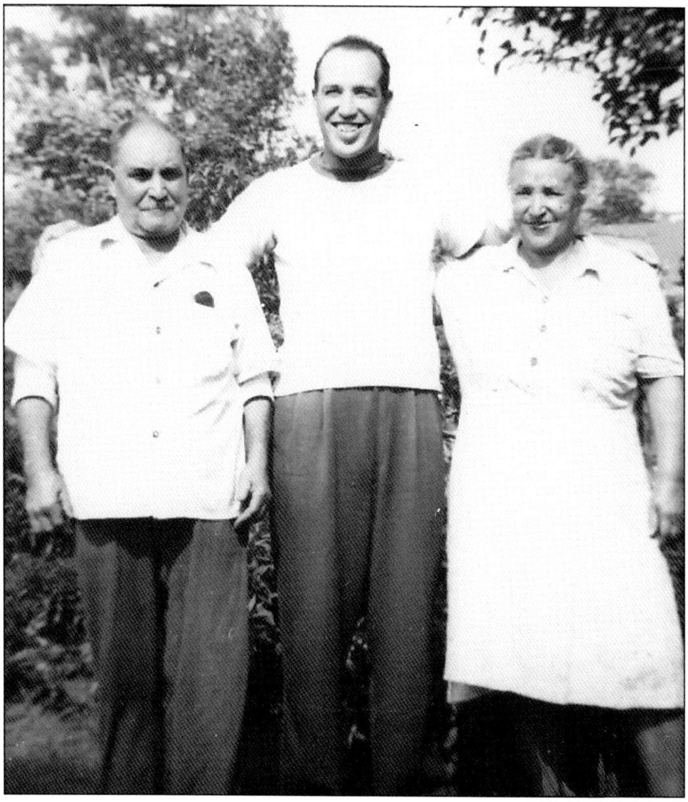

Peter and Mary Provinzano stand with one of their sons, Peter, during World War II. Peter, a star football and baseball player at Winchester High, later became the head trainer for Harvard College athletic teams for more than thirty years.

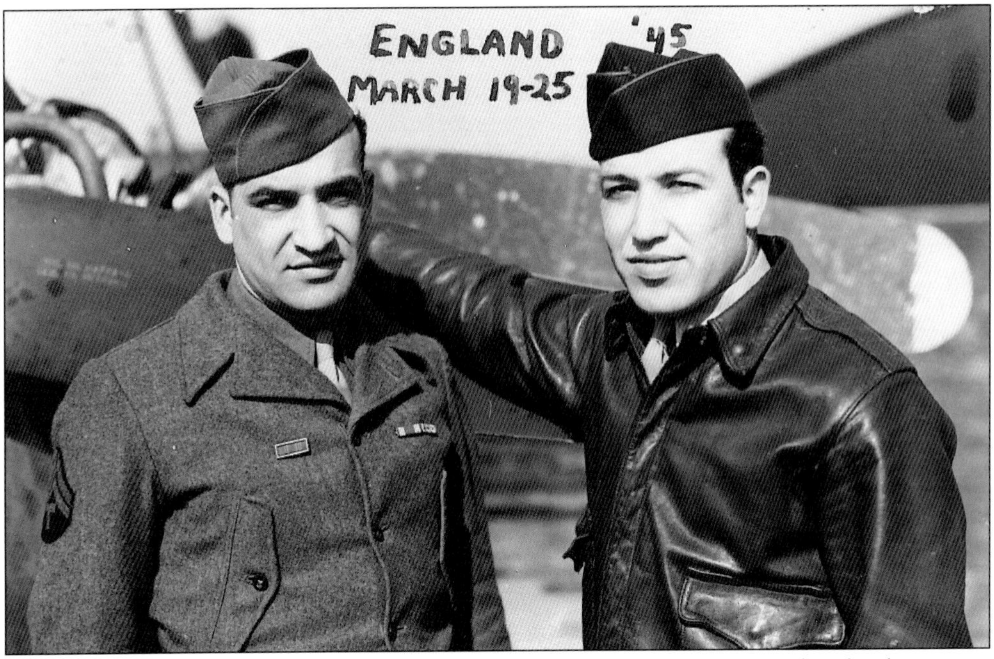

Frank and Peter Provinzano, brothers from Winchester, hadn't seen each other for three years and one month before a seven-day joint leave March 19-25, 1945. Frank, who died in 1980, was called back to Winchester High by Henry Knowlton as an assistant football coach in 1951. He also was varsity basketball coach. Frank moved to Lynch Junior High in 1961, handling the physical education program there.

FOR SELECTMAN

HARRY E. CHEFALO

Native and Life-Long Resident of Winchester.

Graduate of Winchester Schools and Wentworth Institute.

Two Children, Graduates of Winchester Schools.

Established in Plumbing and Heating Business twenty years.

Substantial Tax-Payer.

Three Years on Finance Committee.

I Will Appreciate Your Support March 6.

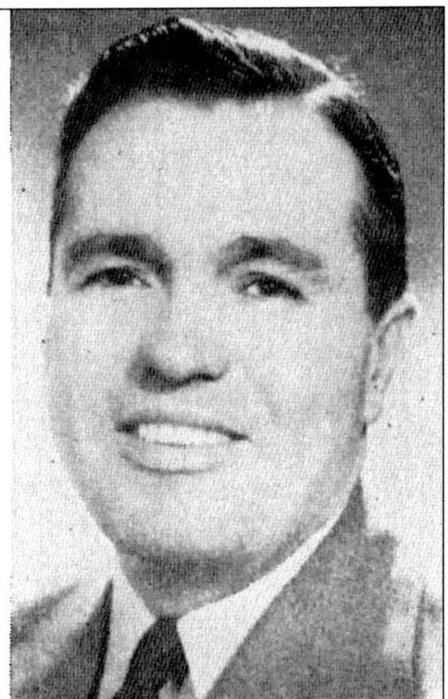

It was a milestone for Winchester's Italo-Americans when Harry E. Chefalo became the first Italo-American elected to a selectman's post in 1950. He was elected again in 1976. When a leading Democrat pointed out to Chefalo that "You won't be elected because you're Catholic," Harry turned on his heel and campaigned harder than ever.

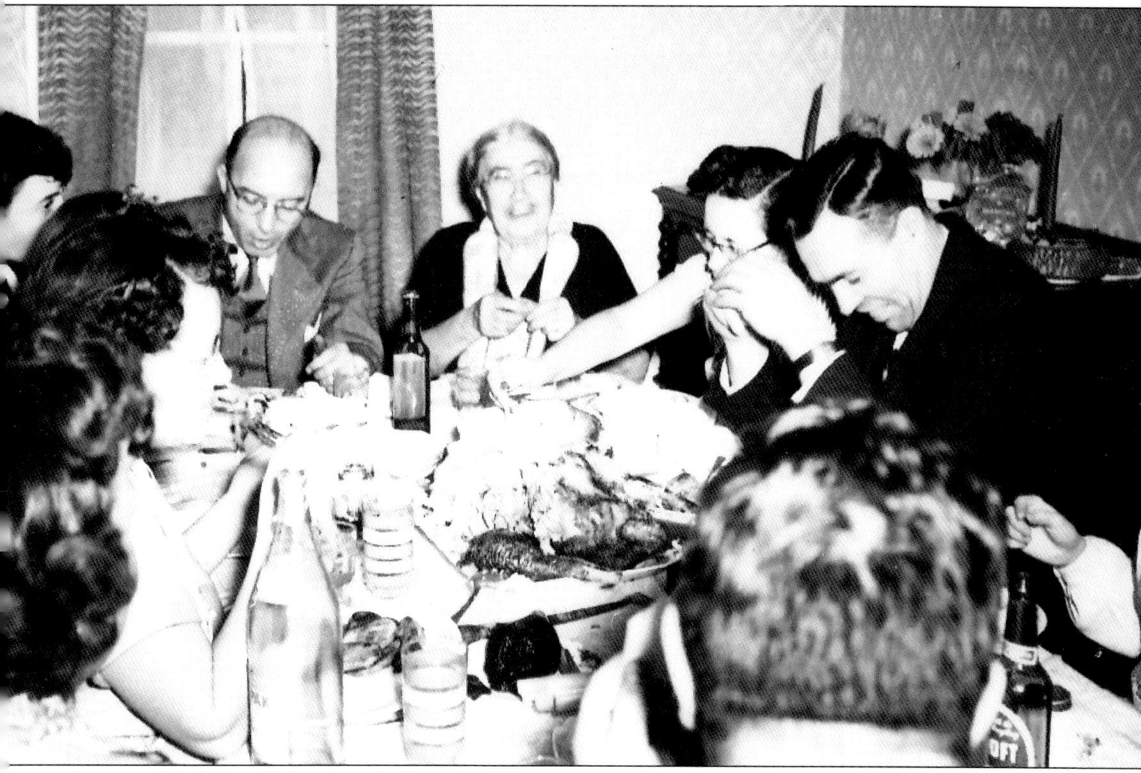

A typical Italian celebration feed in the 1940s in Winchester. Theodora Chefalo is in the back; also in the photograph are her daughter Susie and her son Harry. Italian food, of course, was an important element of Italo-American culture. There's an excellent Italian restaurant in Winchester Center right now.

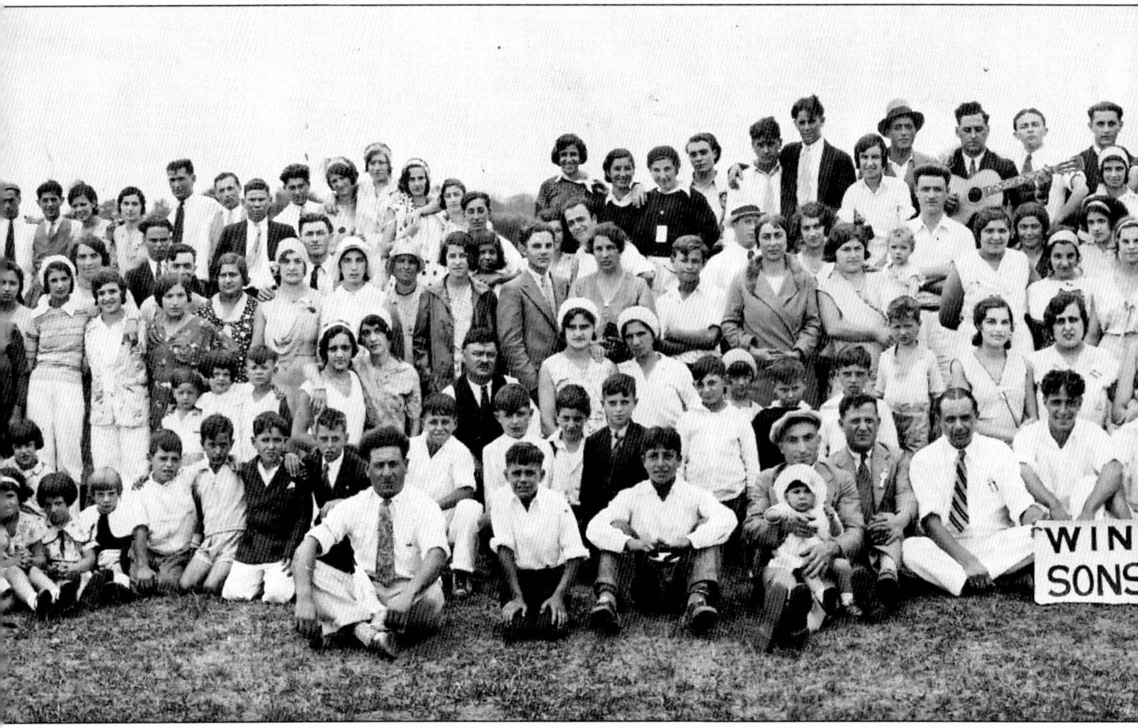

The Winchester Sons of Italy was founded in 1930. This is the charter group, photographed that year. The Sons of Italy, with a clubhouse on Swanton Street, had much to do with the increase in social mobility of the town's Italo-Americans. As Harry Chefalo explains, some

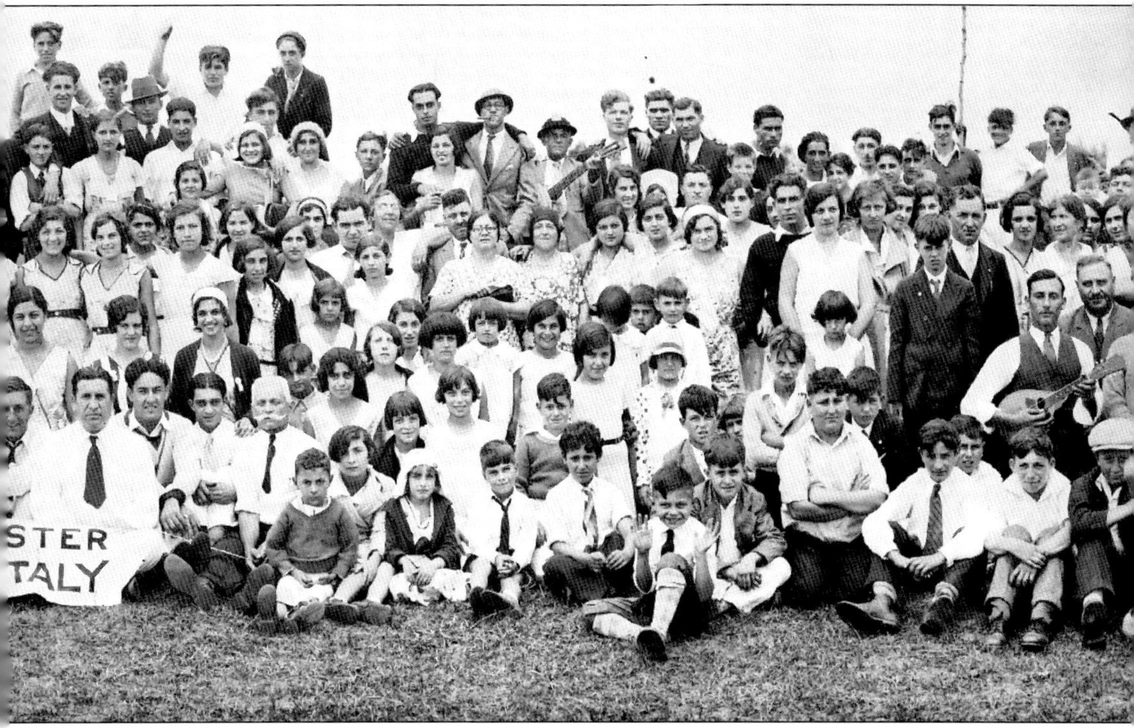

form of organization brings more power and that's exactly what happened as a result of the formation of the group.

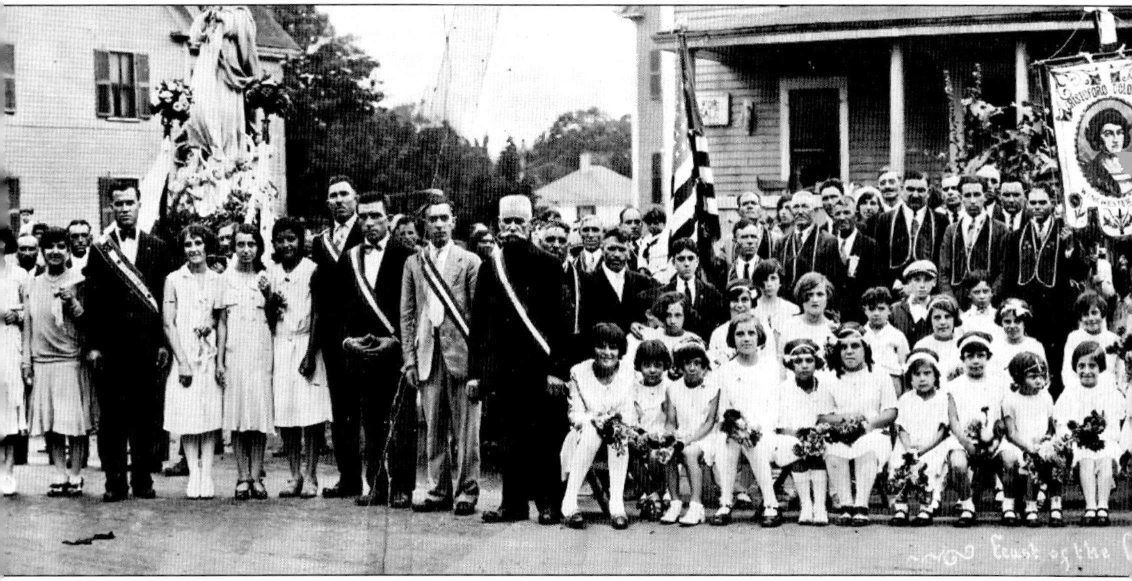

Every August, Winchester Italo-Americans celebrate the Feast of the Assumption. There used to be a parade through part of the town after Mass and fireworks for the public at Manchester

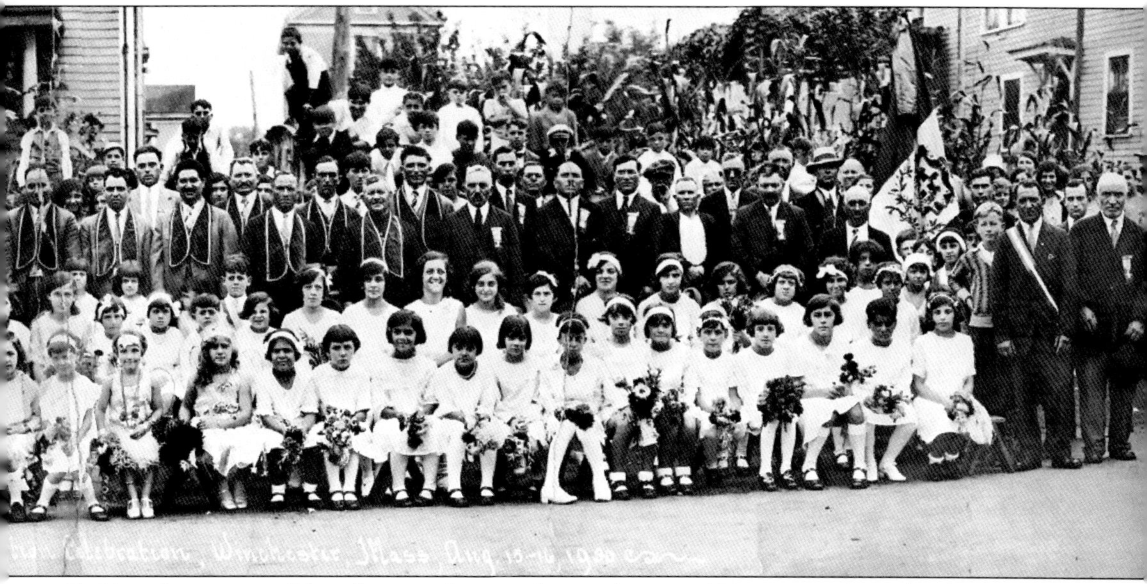

Field in the evening. This photograph was taken in August 1930. Missing from the photograph was the statue, a feature of the parade.

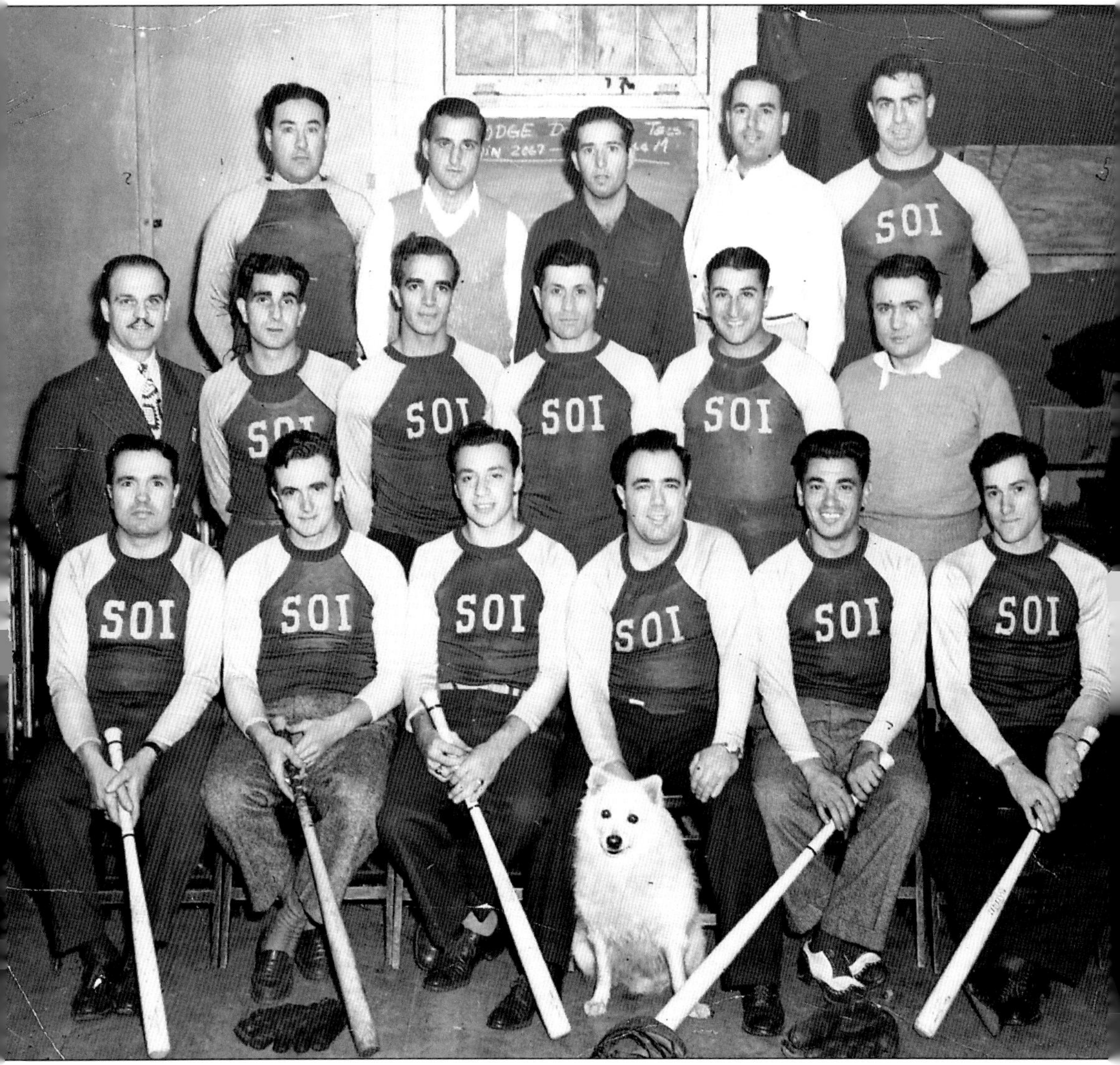

The Winchester Sons of Italy softball team in 1930. From left to right are: (front row) Harry Chefalo, unknown, unknown, Tony Chefalo, Ralph DiMambro, and Melligan Fiore; (middle row) unknown, Gaspar Morraco, unknown, Hockie Procopio, Bob Del Grasso, and Dippy Diapella; (back row) Muskie Tofiore, Tony Saraco, Al DiMinico, another DiMinico, and Dynamite Lentine. The dog was Jerry. Jerry disappeared once for two weeks. He was spotted by a Winchesterite who knew him on Dorchester Avenue in Dorchester. He called "Jerry" and the dog came right over. The animal was probably on his way home.

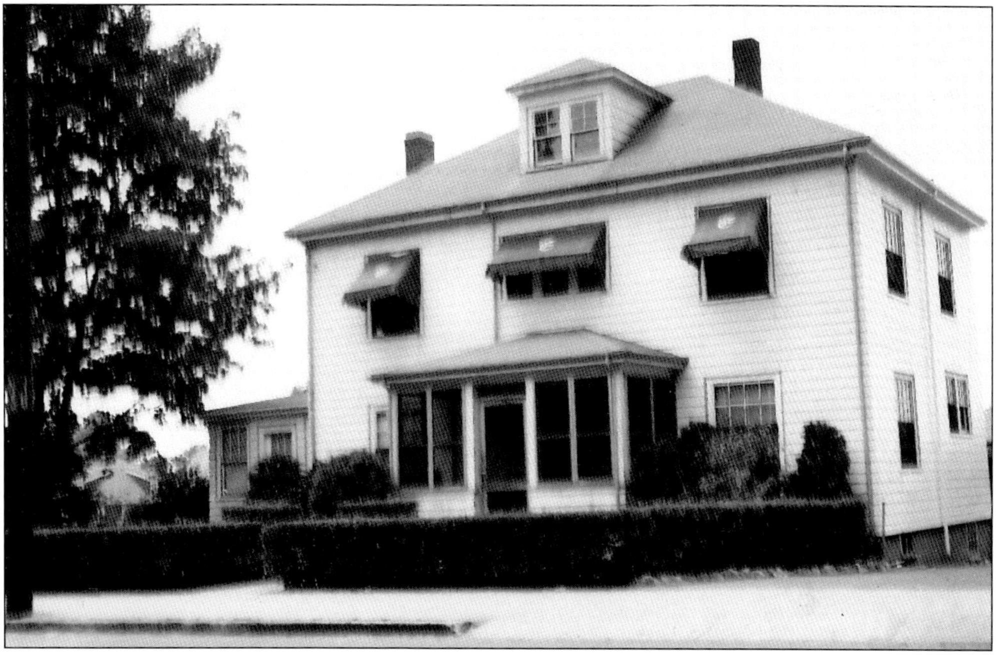

The Errico homestead at 398 Washington Street, *c.* 1950s.

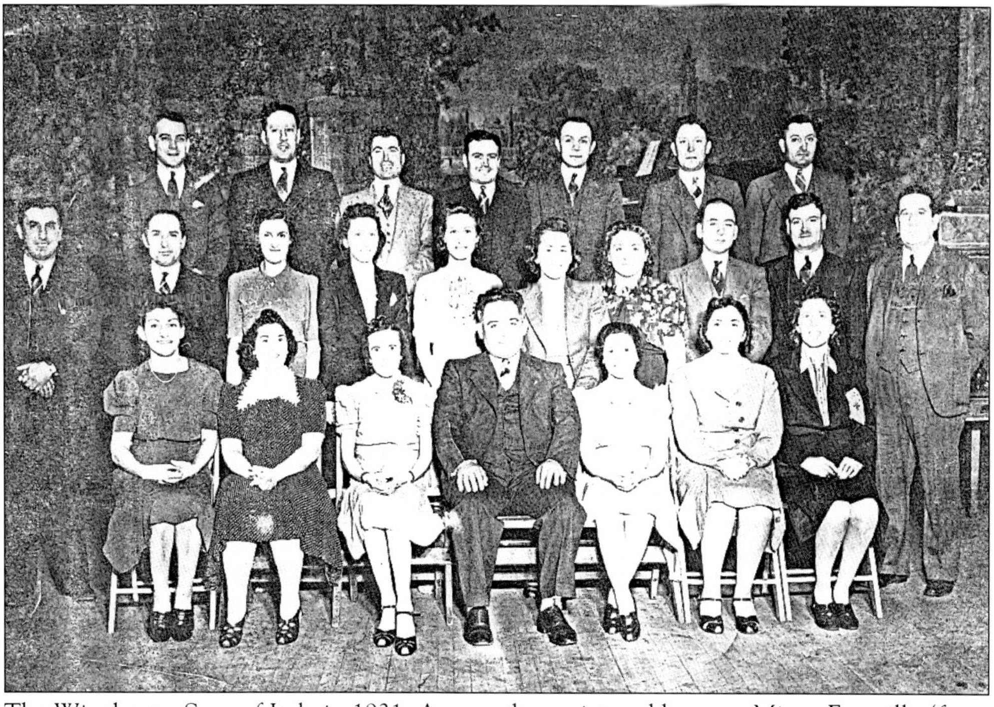

The Winchester Sons of Italy in 1931. Among those pictured here are Mingy Frongillo (front center) and Fiore Errico (back, third from the left).

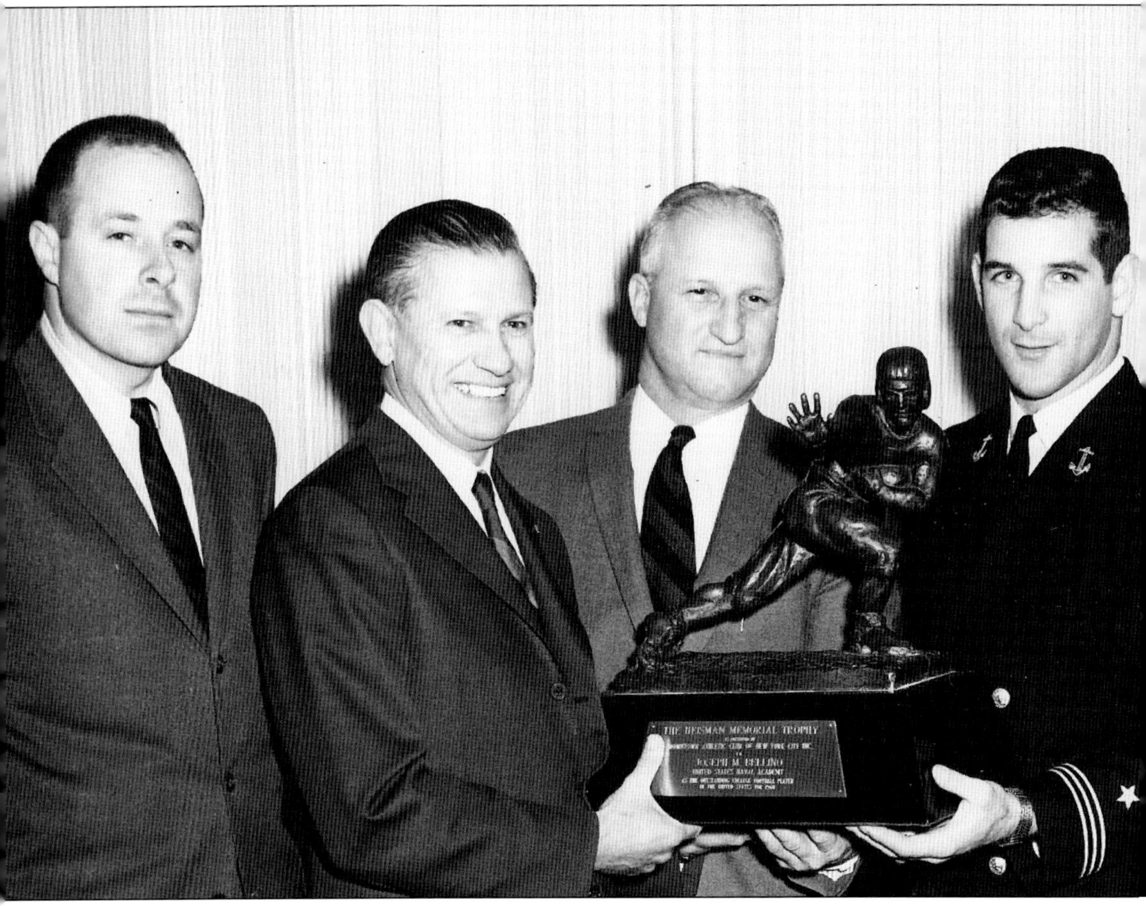

Two ingredients that made 1960 one of the peak years of Italo-American power and influence in Winchester. Joe Bellino (right) shows his Heisman trophy at a coming home party in Winchester, December 17, 1960. From left to right are: Sherman Saltmarsh, chairman of the party; John Volpe of Winchester, elected governor of Massachusetts in the November, 1960, election but not yet actually in office; and Henry Knowlton, long-time Winchester High football coach who was Bellino's high school coach. Volpe, an Italo-American, was three times the governor of Massachusetts. The only other person to be Massachusetts governor three times was Samuel McCall, much earlier, also from Winchester.

Three

Library and Hospital

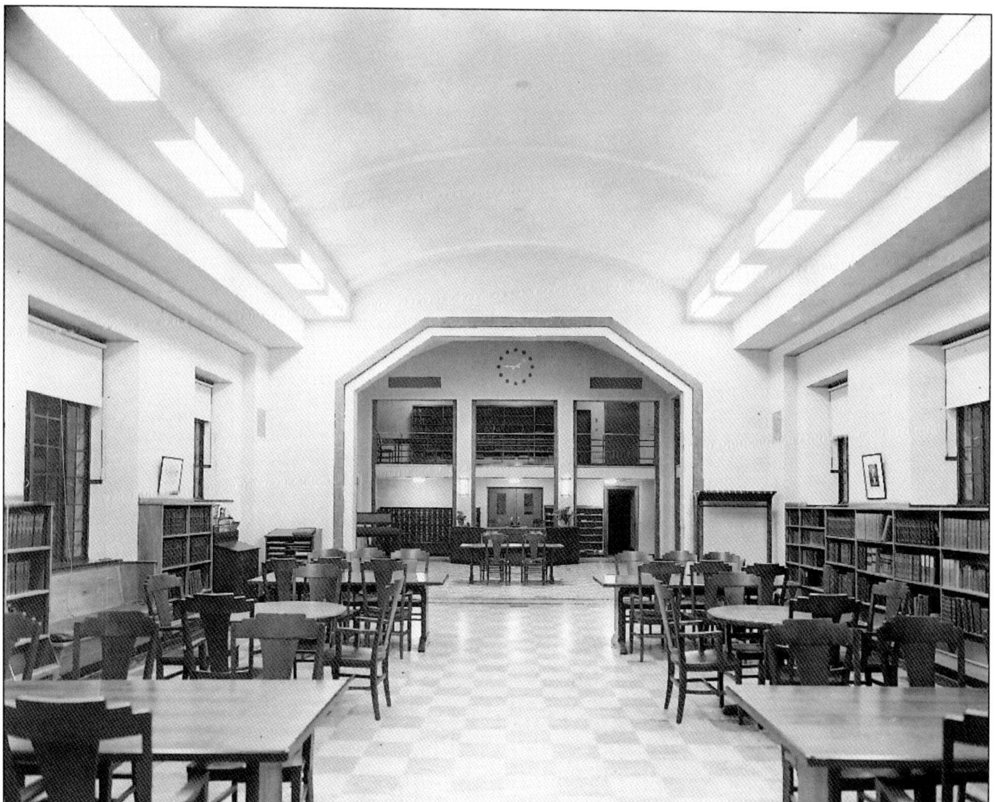

The reading room in the Winchester Public Library in the 1930s. The library, always heavily used, increased social mobility through education from reading and helped keep people in town. The excellent hospital also kept people in town because of its facilities.

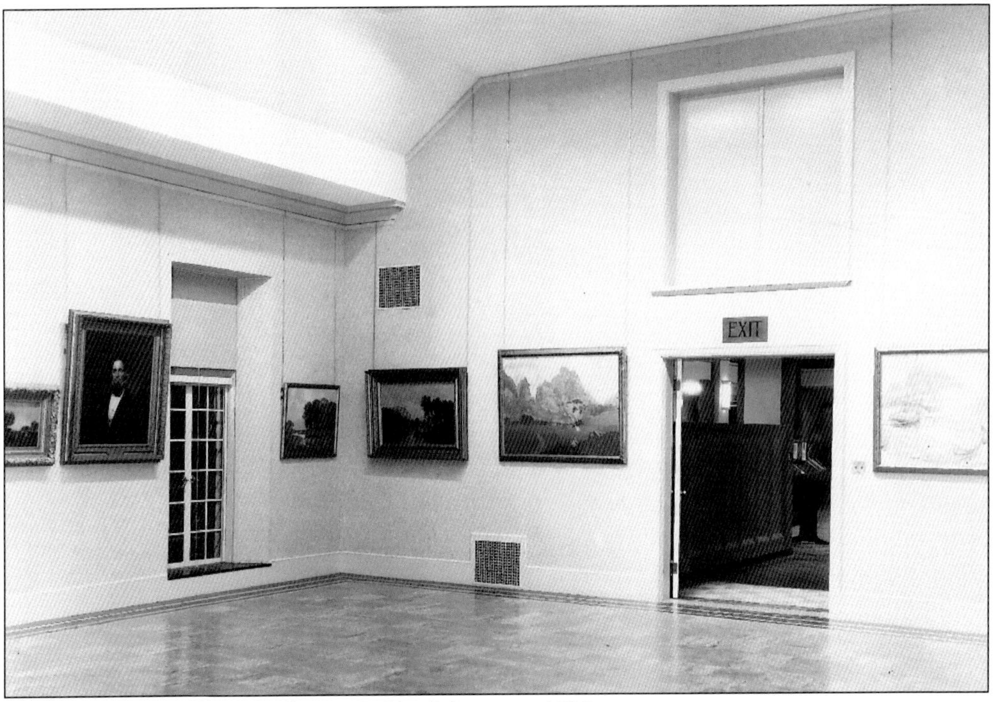

The art gallery in the Winchester Public Library, *c.* 1930s.

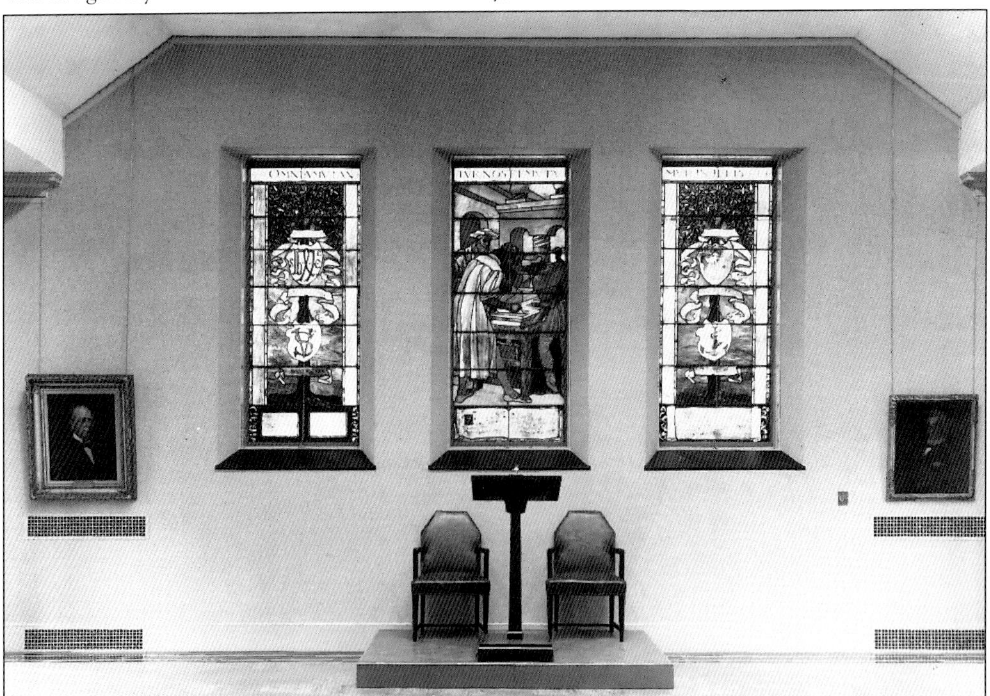

Windows of Tiffany painted glass in the gallery at the library. They were given in memory of Joseph H. Tyler, who was for years the Register of Probate of Middlesex County and a library trustee.

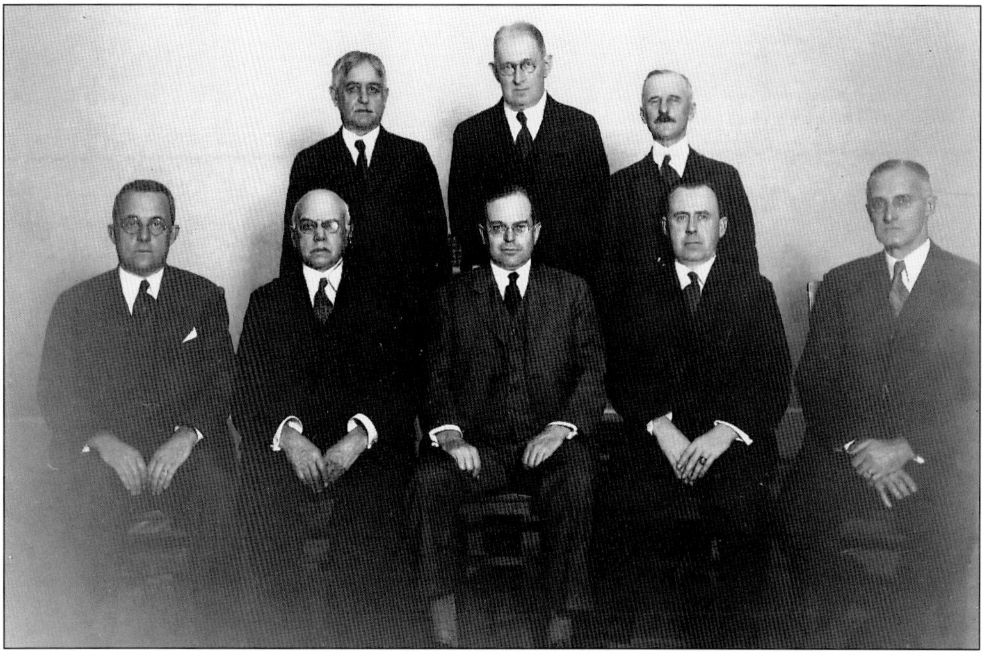

The Winchester Public Library Building Committee and architects, c. 1930–31. From left to right are: (front) Carl F. Woods, Edgar J. Rich, Ralph T. Hale (chairman), M. Walker Jones (secretary), and James Nowell; (back) Robert Coit (architect), Walter H. Kilham (architect); and Fred C. Alexander (builder). The new library, by the town hall, was dedicated December 5, 1931. The cost of the library, now being renovated and expanded, was $173,000.

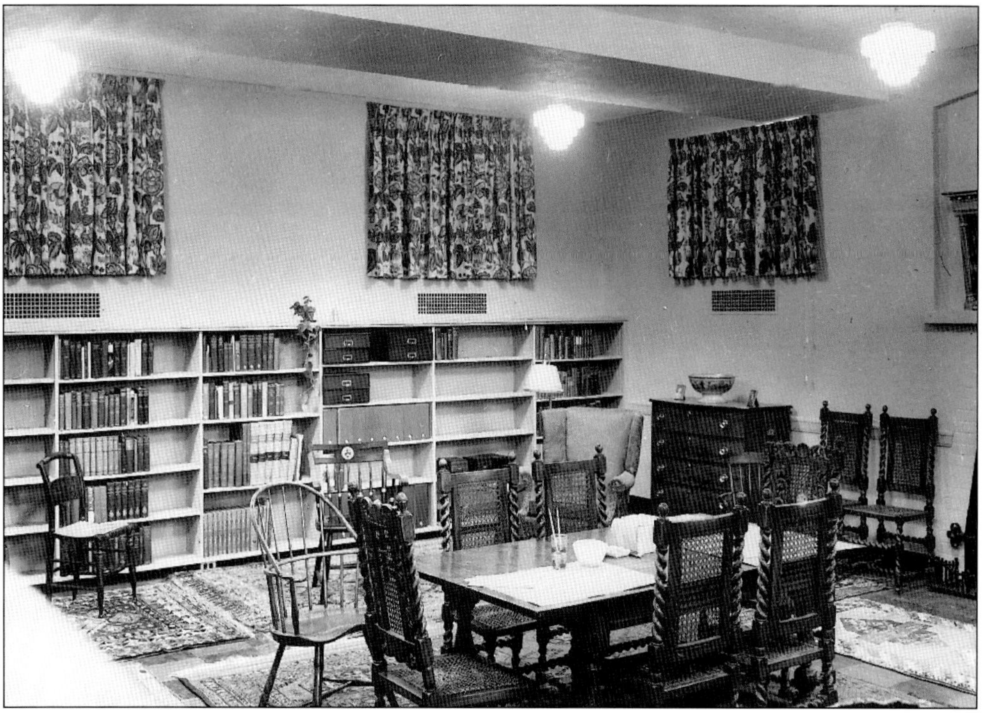

The Rich Meeting Room in the Winchester Public Library, 1952.

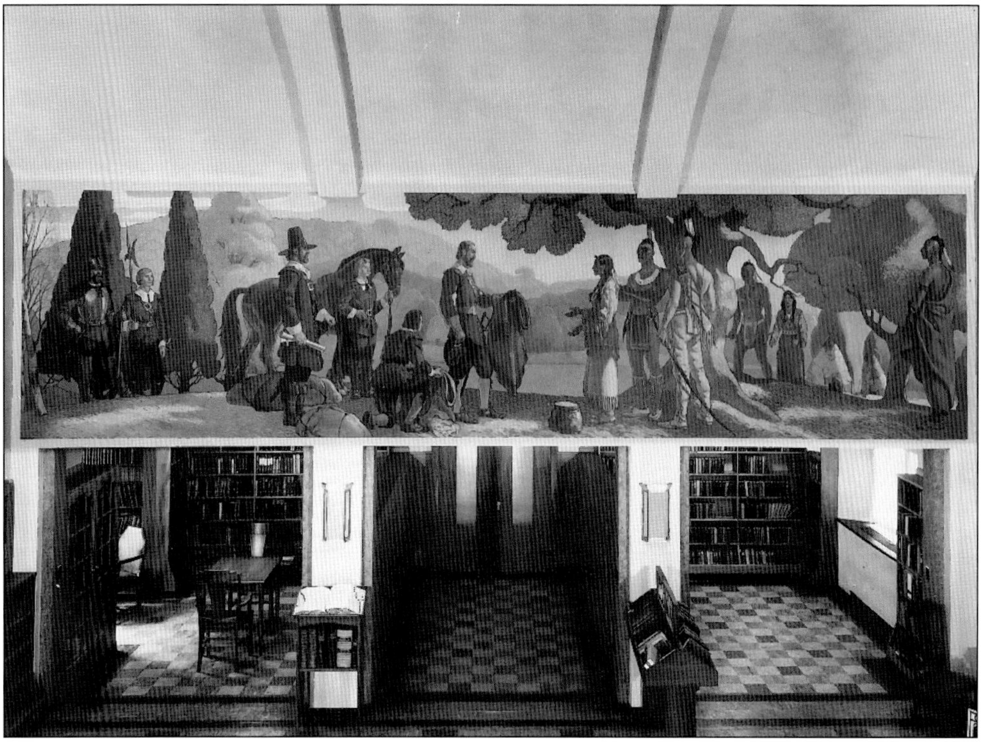

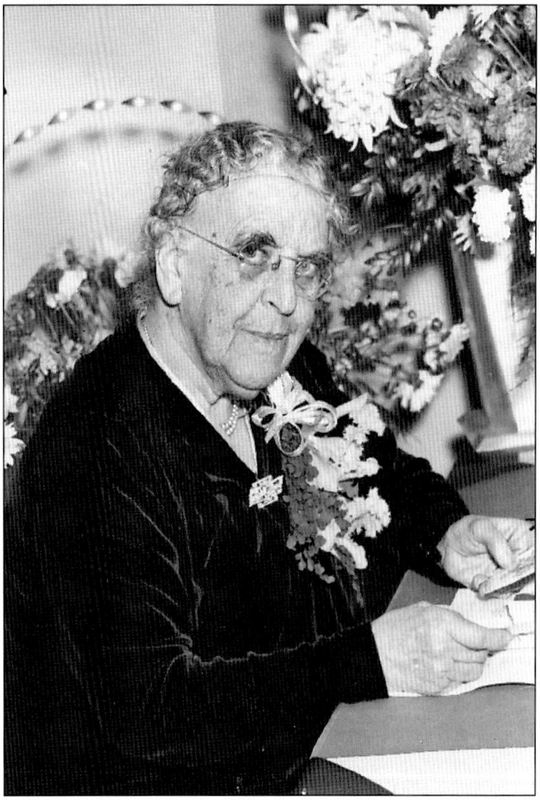

The Squaw Sachem mural in the Winchester Public Library painted by Alden Lasalle Ripley of Lexington. It was completed in June 1934 and is opposite the library front door. Ripley taught water color painting at the Harvard School of Architecture. The mural shows the sale of lands including the largest part of Winchester by the Indian queen of the Pawtuckets, Squaw Sachem, to white men from Charlestown in 1639.

Miss Cora A. Quimby retired in 1940 after serving fifty-one years as head librarian of the Winchester Public Library. This picture was taken in December 1938. She became head librarian in 1888.

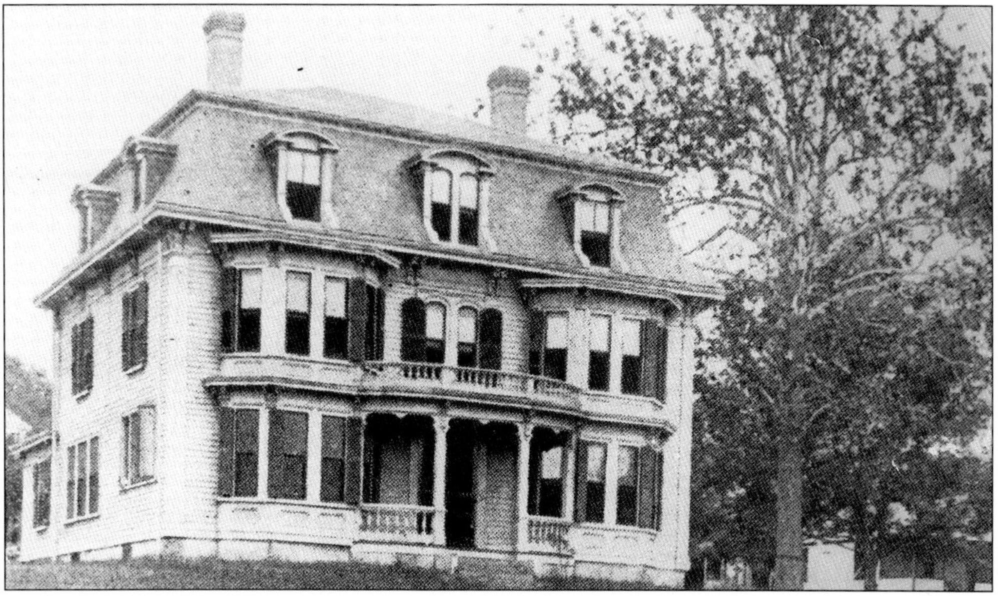

The first Winchester Hospital, the twelve-bed Cottage Hospital, opened in the former Todd House at the corner of Washington and Lincoln Streets, March 11, 1912. It was started by the Visiting Nurses' Association. An immediate success, it led to the purchase of 5.5 acres of land on Highland Avenue, Valley Road, and Maple and Fairmont Streets. On May 28, 1917, the first patient was admitted to the forty-four-bed hospital.

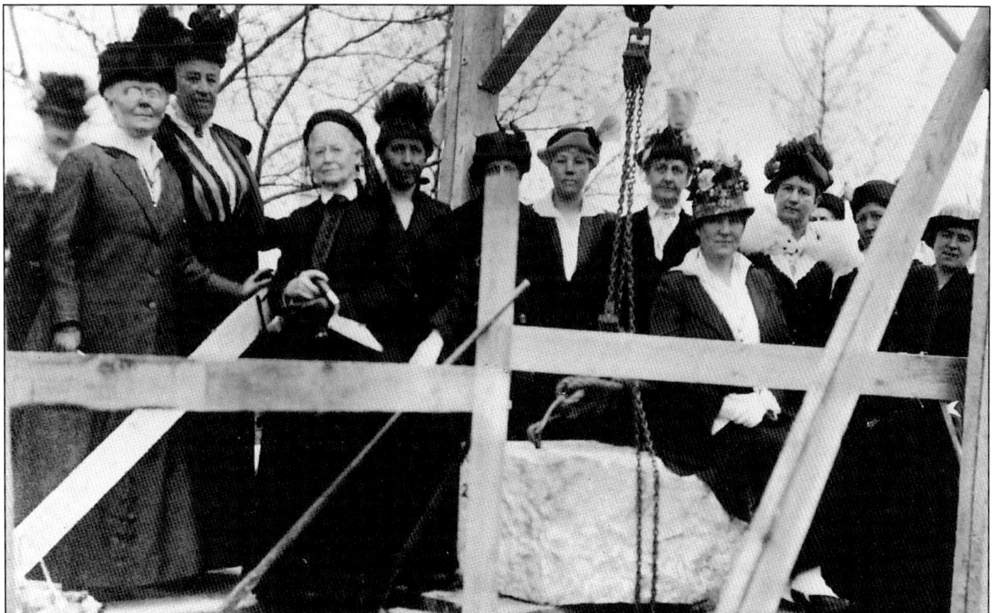

At the laying of the corner stone of the Winchester Hospital on May 18, 1916, were officers and committee of the Visiting Nurses' Association who raised the $100,000 for the land and building. Included were Miss Kate Pond, Mrs. Ellen Metcalf, Mrs. Joshua Coit, Mrs. Henry L. Houghton, Mrs. Edwin C. Gilman, Mrs. Mott A. Cummings, Miss M. Alice Mason, Mrs. Oren C. Sanborn, and Mrs. William I. Palmer.

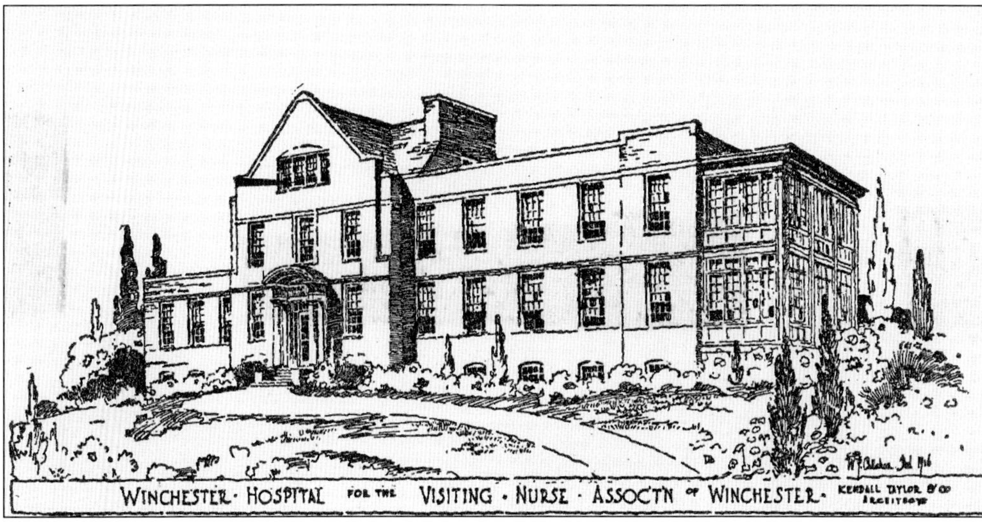

The second Winchester Hospital on its present site, dedicated June 17, 1917, with accommodations for forty-four patients. The enlarged and remodeled hospital, ready in the fall of 1951, had 104 adult beds and 40 bassinets.

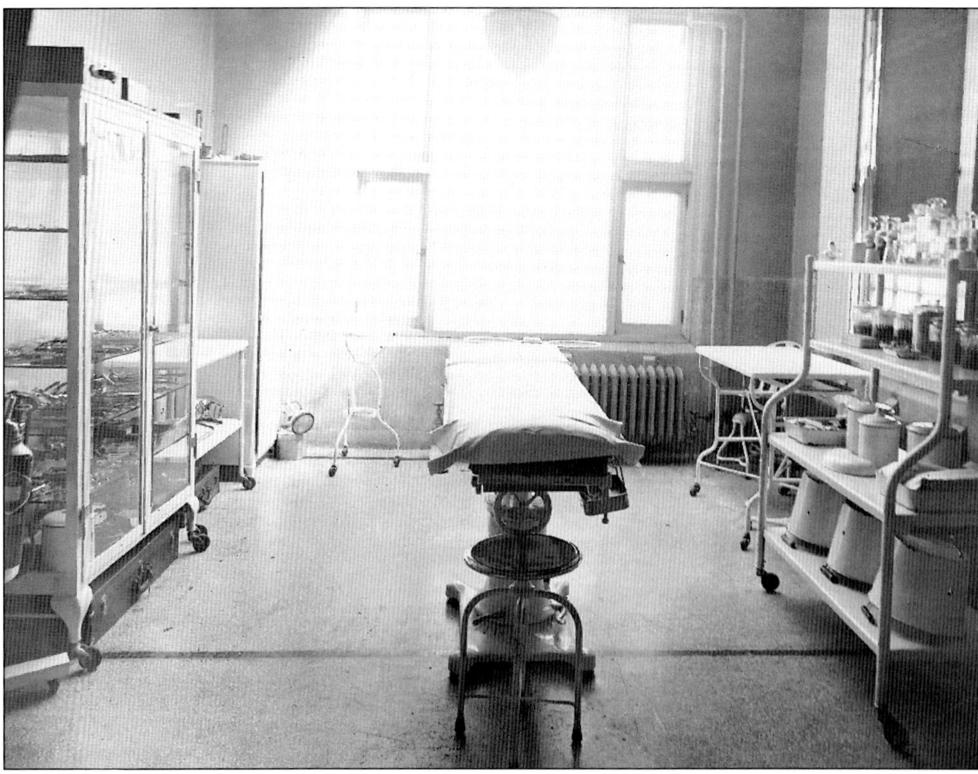

The operating room at the Winchester Hospital, August 1926.

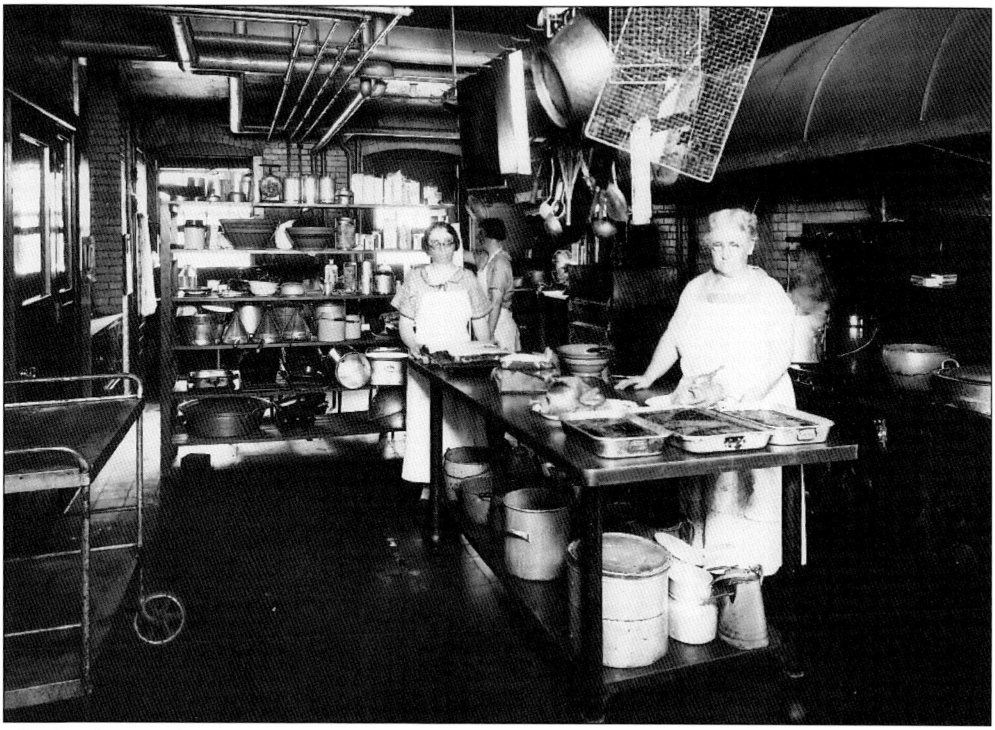

The kitchen at the Winchester Hospital, August 1926.

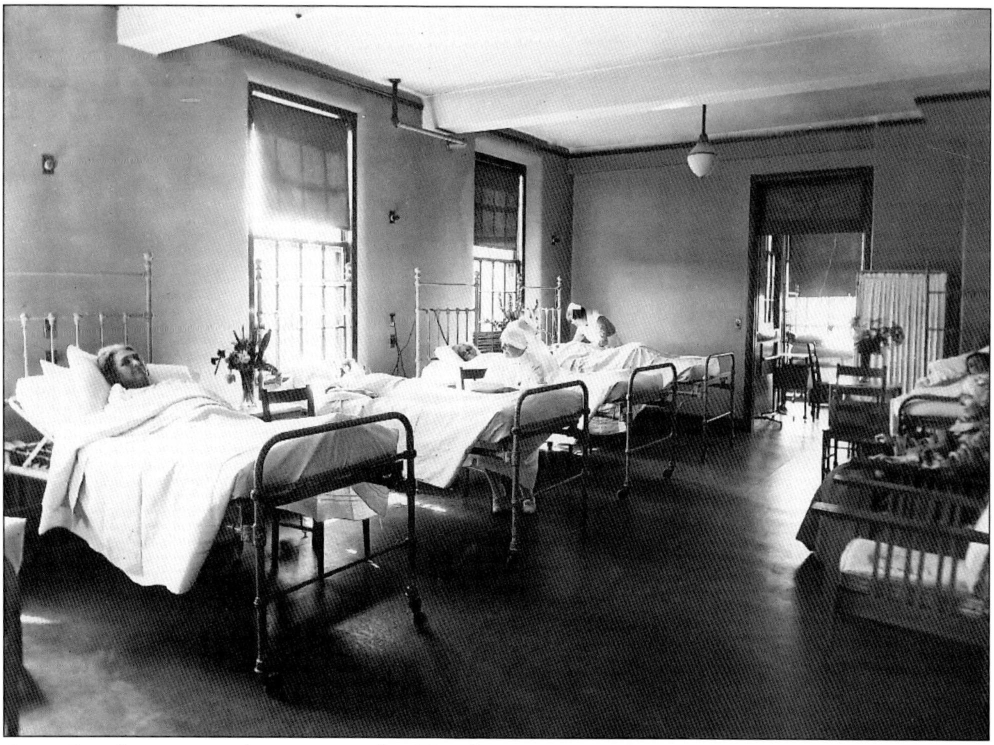

A ward with nurses and patients at the Winchester Hospital, August 1926.

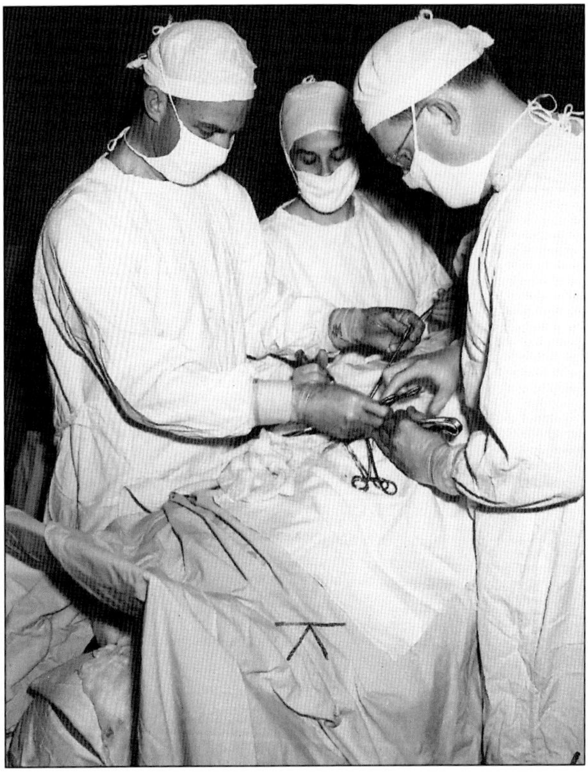

Dr. George A. Marks, Dr. Ernest C. MacDougall, and Nurse June Parman during an operation at the Winchester Hospital, November 22, 1946.

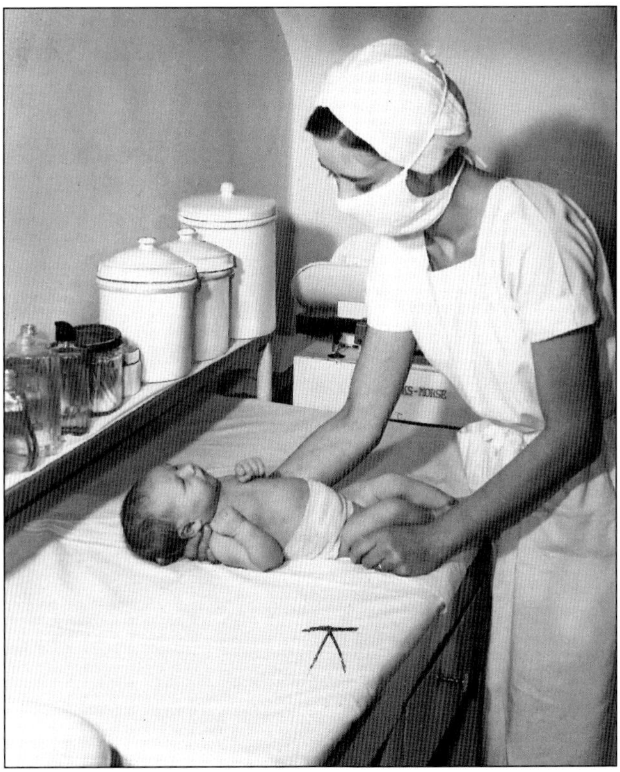

The Van Gelder baby on a weighing table at the Winchester Hospital, November 22, 1946. The nurse is Mrs. Helen Dacey.

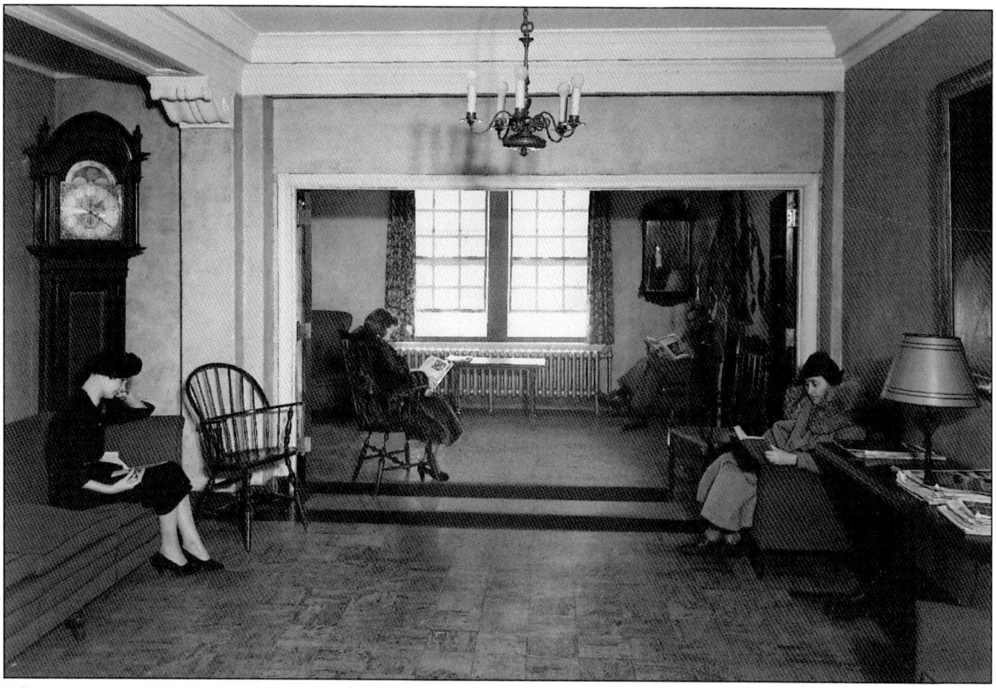

The reception room at the Winchester Hospital, November 22, 1946.

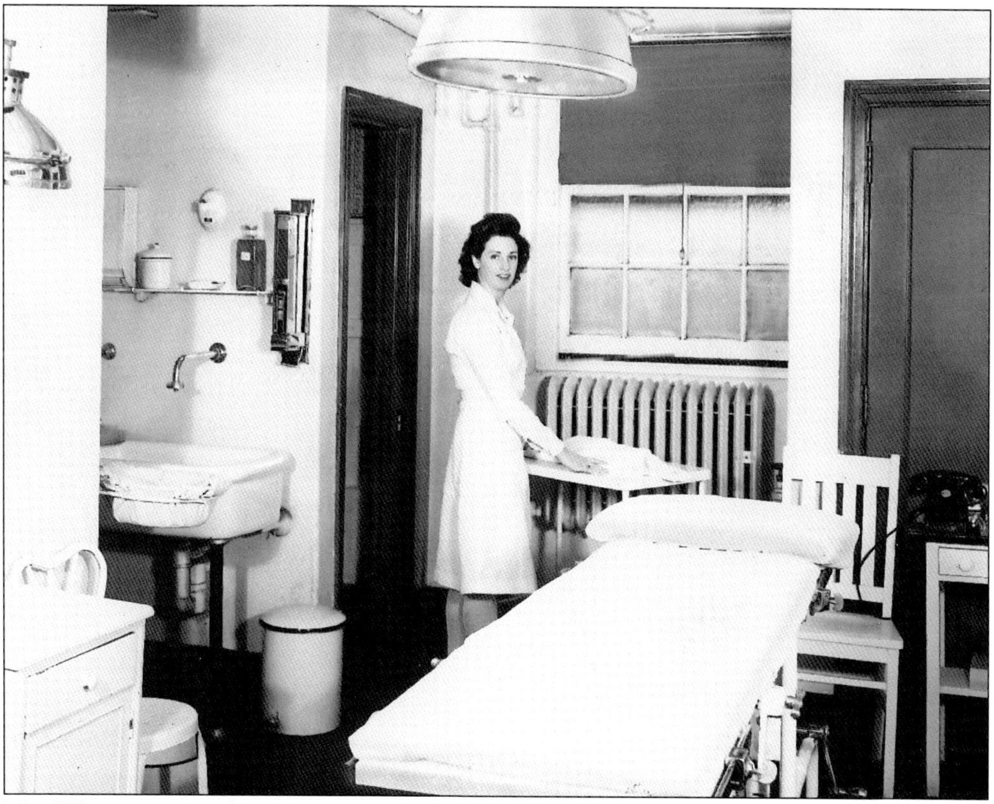

Miss Ella Patricia Dailey in the accident room at the Winchester Hospital in the fall of 1946.

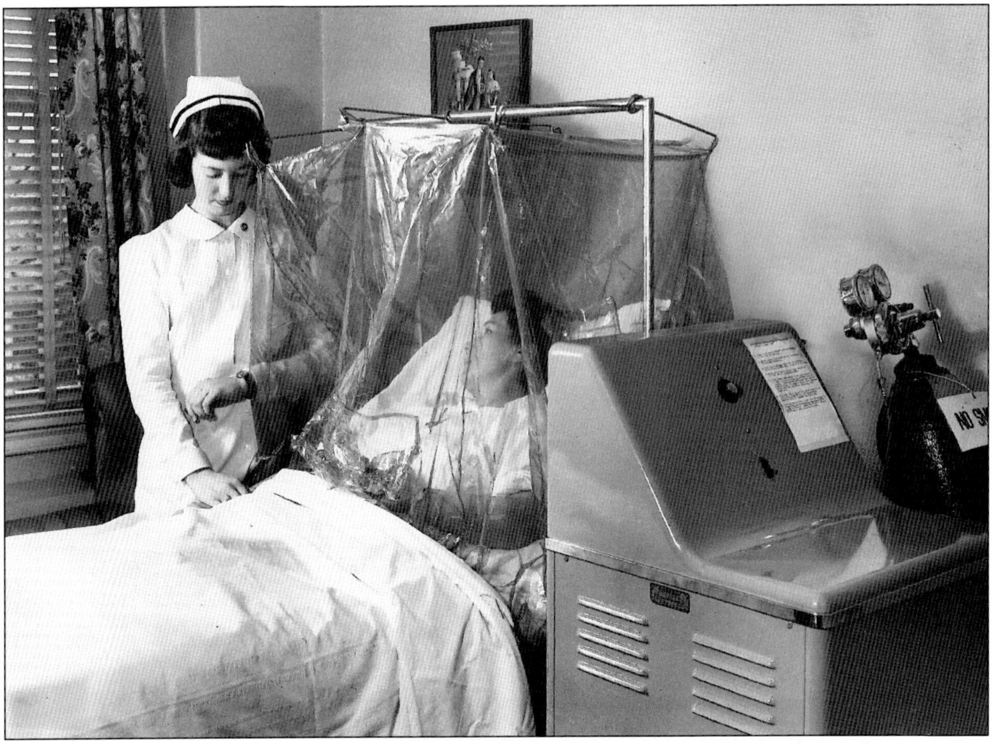

Miss Grace Foley is the nurse and Mrs. Arletta L. Sanderson is in the oxygen tent at the Winchester Hospital in the fall of 1946.

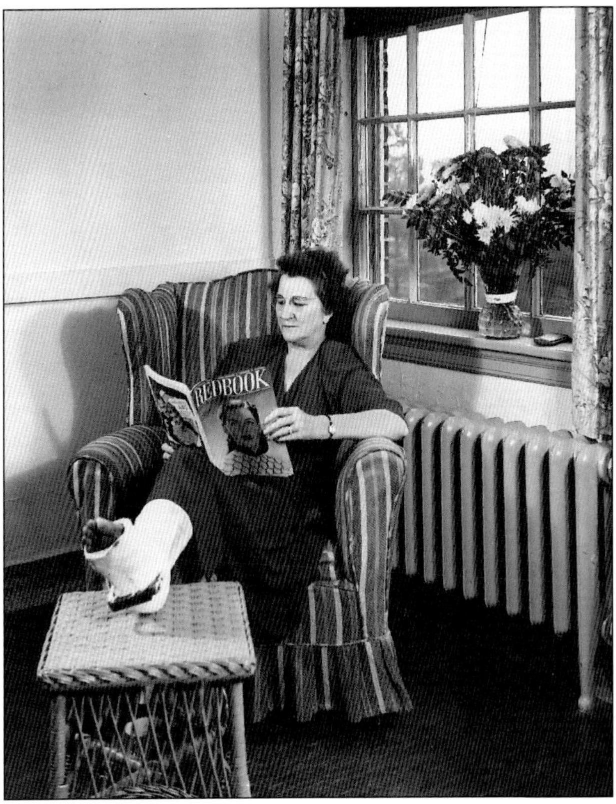

Mrs. Earl Richardson reads and rests her broken leg in the Winchester Hospital sun parlor during the fall of 1946.

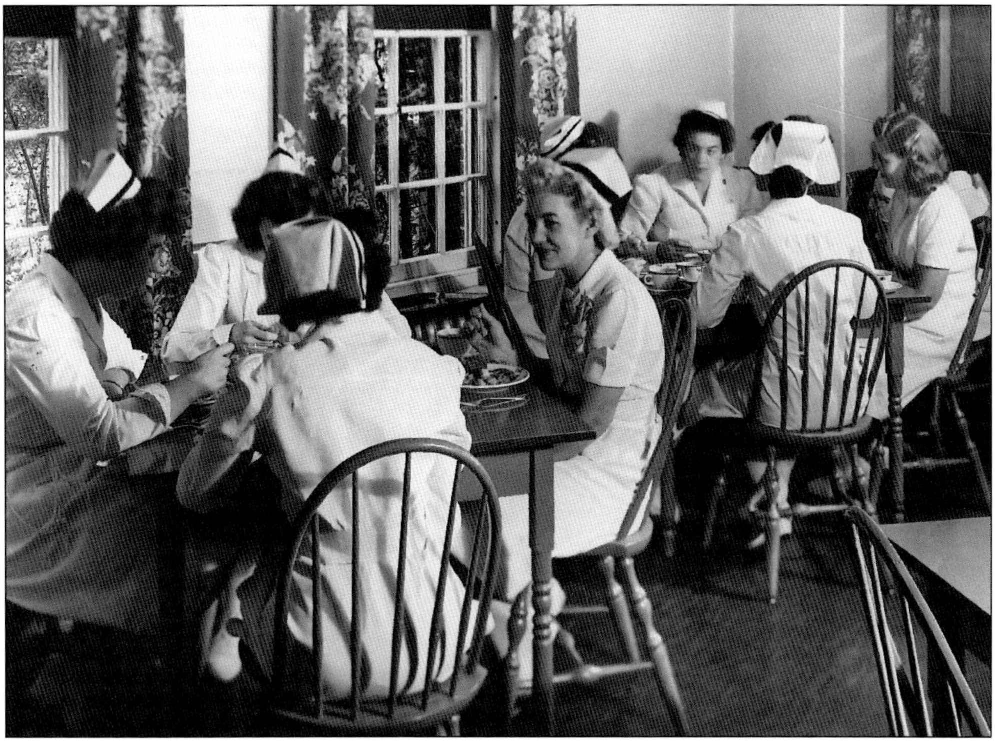

The nurses' dining room at the Winchester Hospital in November 1946.

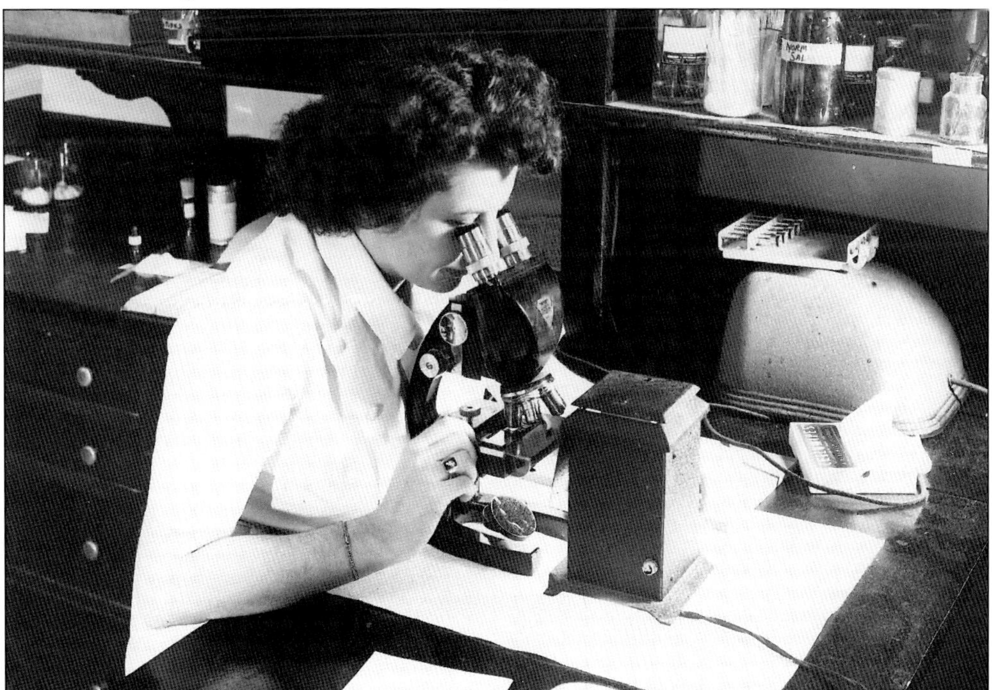

Miss Eleanore C. Nicgorska in the Winchester Hospital pathology laboratory in the fall of 1946.

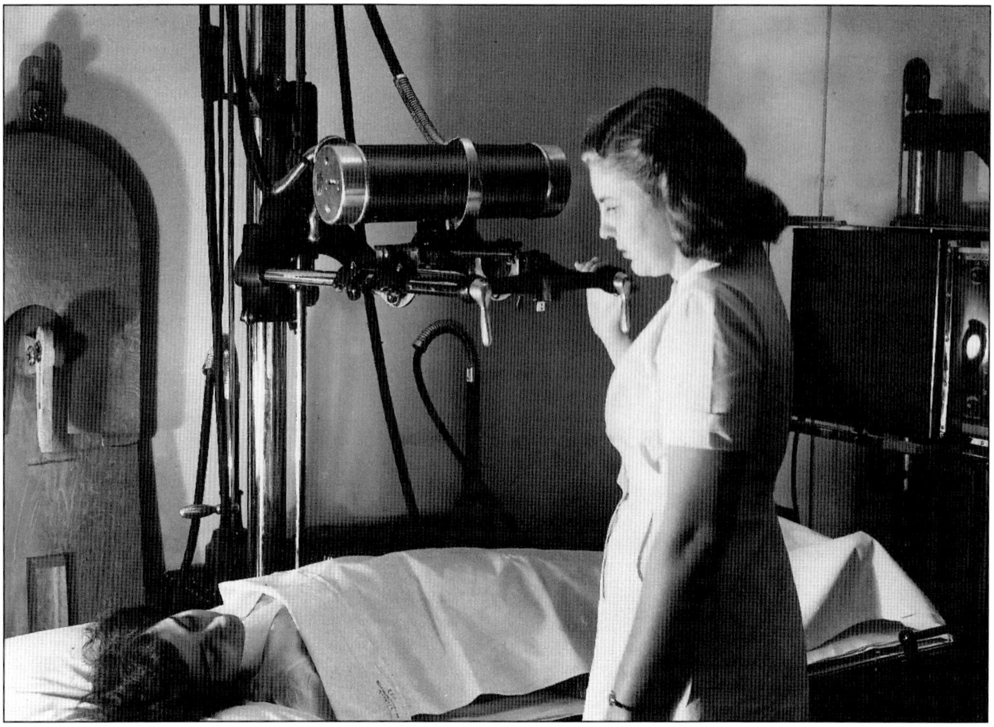

Mrs. Sybil Baxter and Miss Schipellite in the X-ray laboratory at the Winchester Hospital in the fall of 1946.

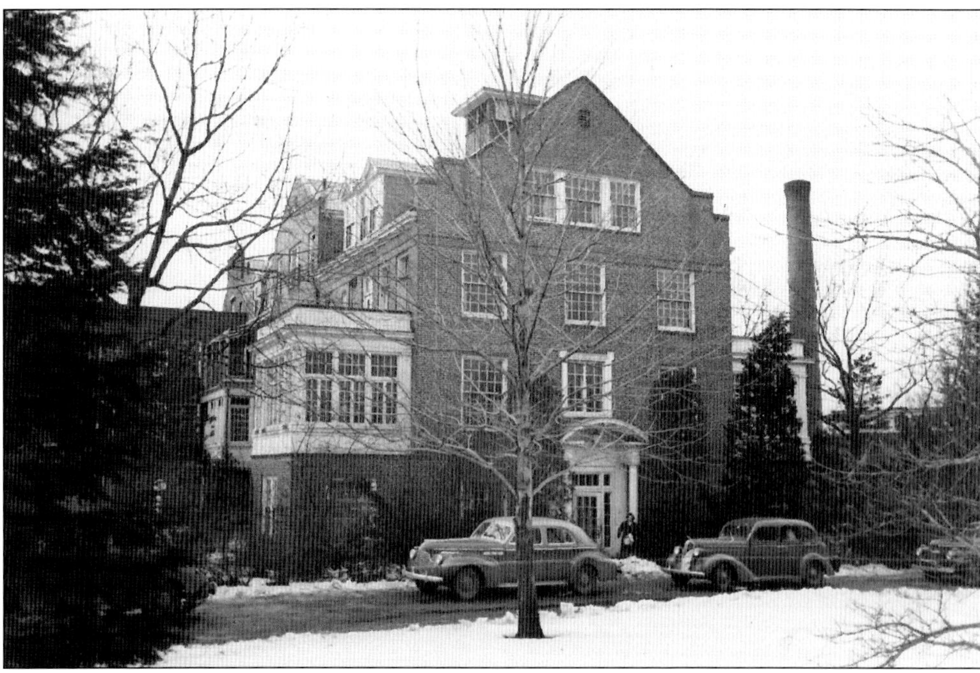

The Winchester Hospital in the late 1940s.

Edward Wright, engineer and rod man, works May 25, 1950, on the addition to the Winchester Hospital.

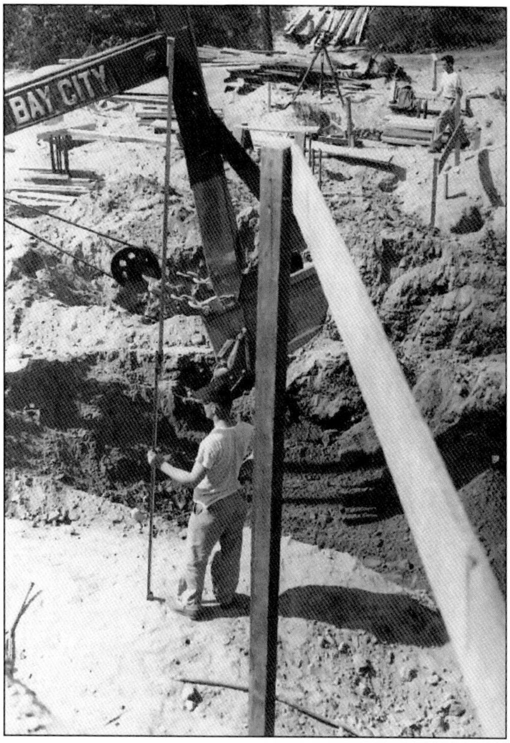

President Edward H. Kenerson (left), of the Winchester Hospital Board of Directors (he was also the president of Ginn & Co., the publishing firm), thanks the heads of the hospital building fund upon the completion of contributions totaling more than $500,000, May 12, 1950. From left to right from Kenerson are Mrs. Ernest Richmond (of Reading, Massachusetts), Frank E. Crawford, Mrs. George A. Marks, Ralph H. Bonnell, and Howard Bartlett.

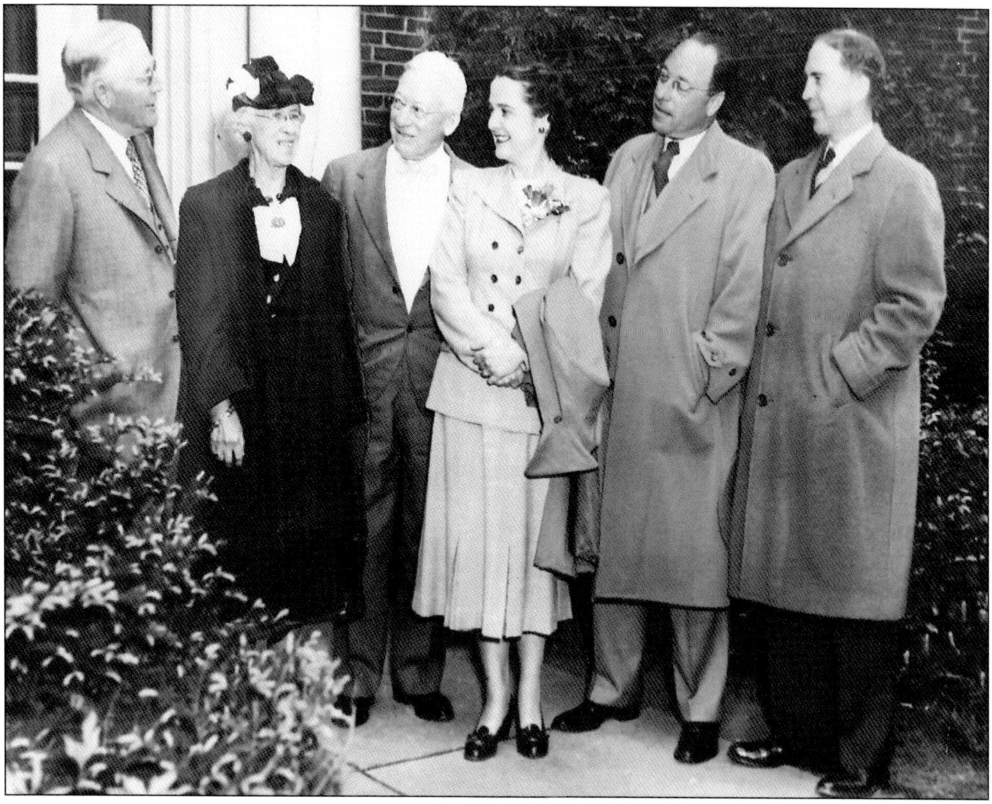

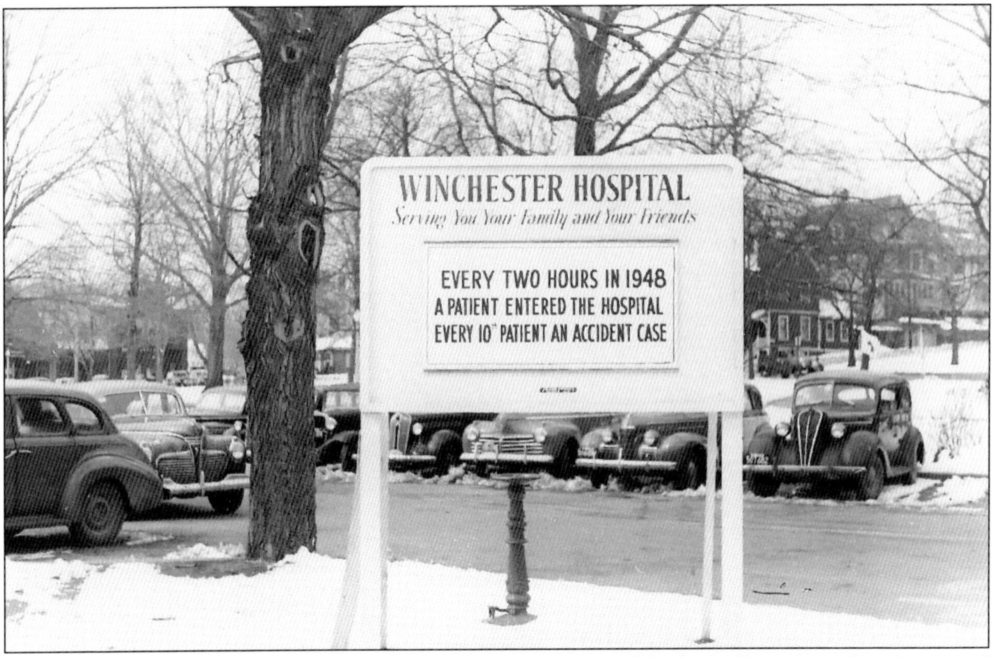

At a busy downtown corner in 1949, the Winchester Hospital had a bulletin board with a panel bringing a different message every two weeks.

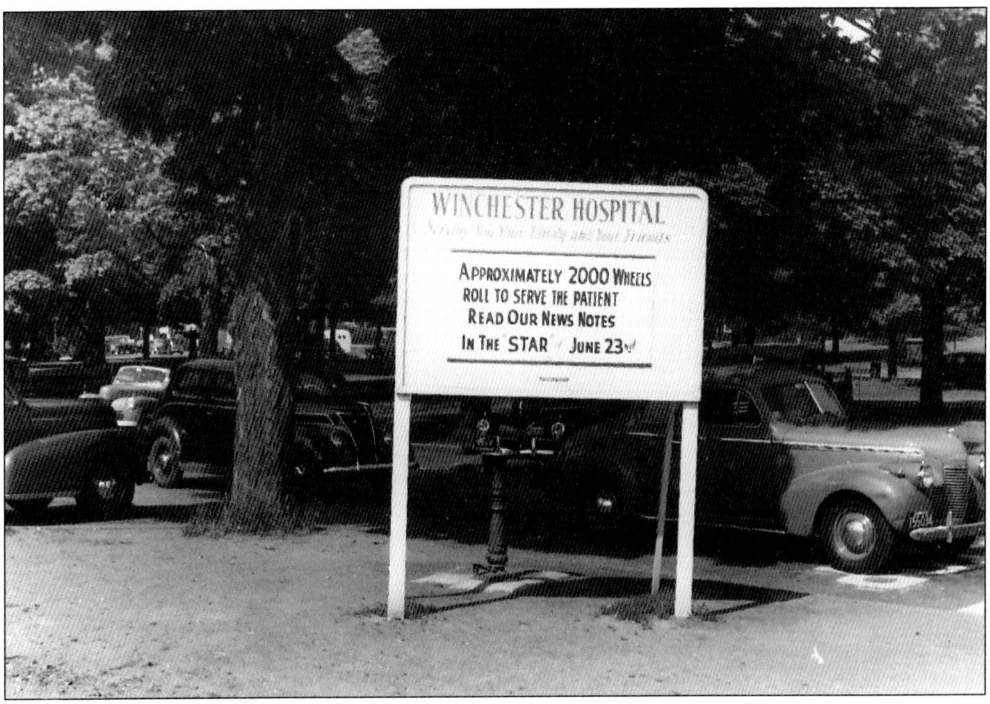

Another message on the 1949 panel.

Winchester Post 97, American Legion, gave the first donation for this refrigerator at the Winchester Hospital. The refrigerator keeps whole blood stored in it at a constant temperature, c. 1950.

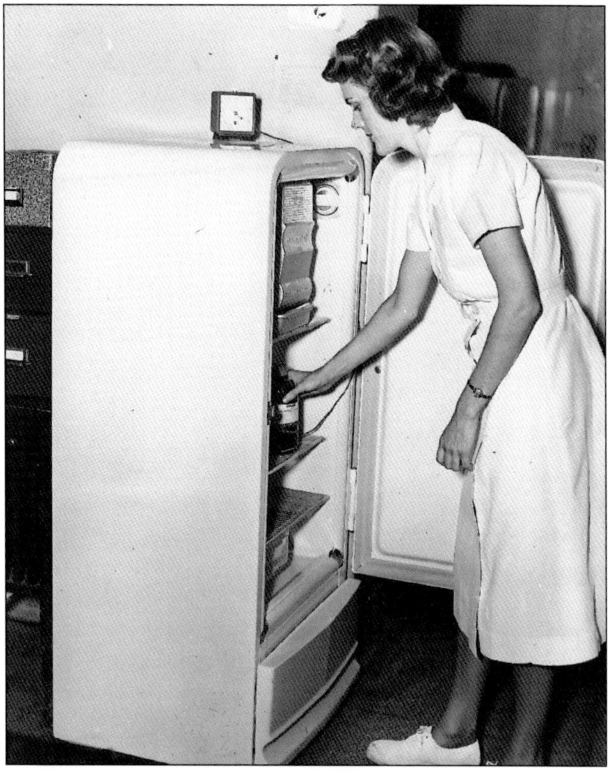

The Winchester Hospital Blood Bank gives its first donor registration card to Commander Robert F. Murphy of Winchester Post 97, American Legion. Nurse Dorothy Smith is at the desk.

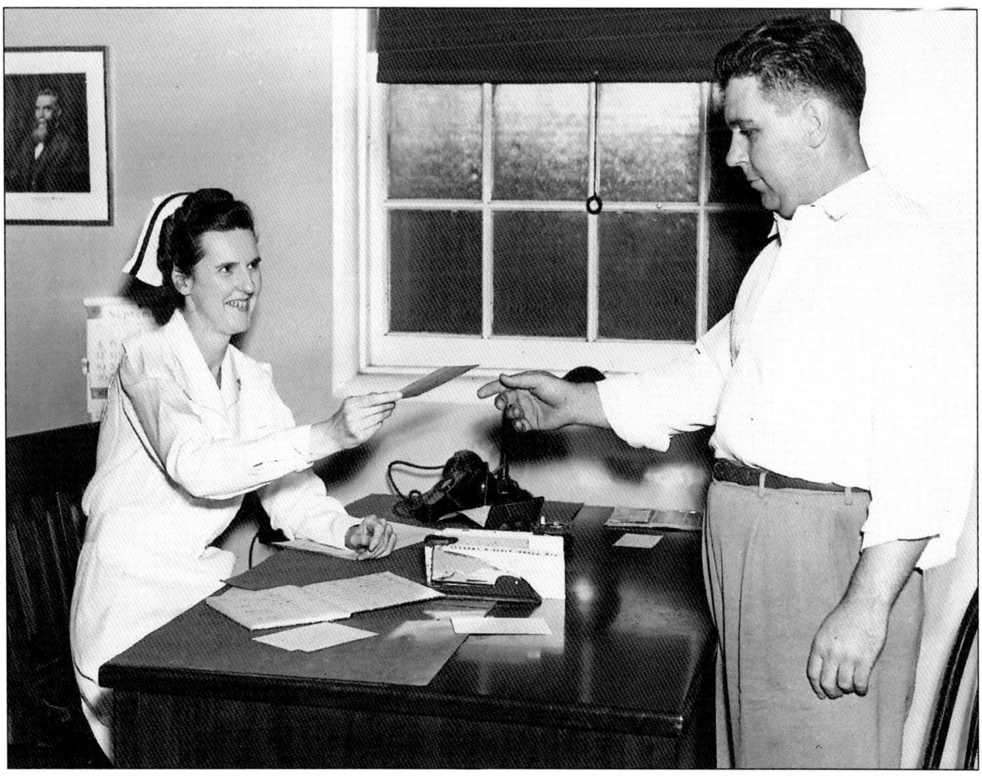

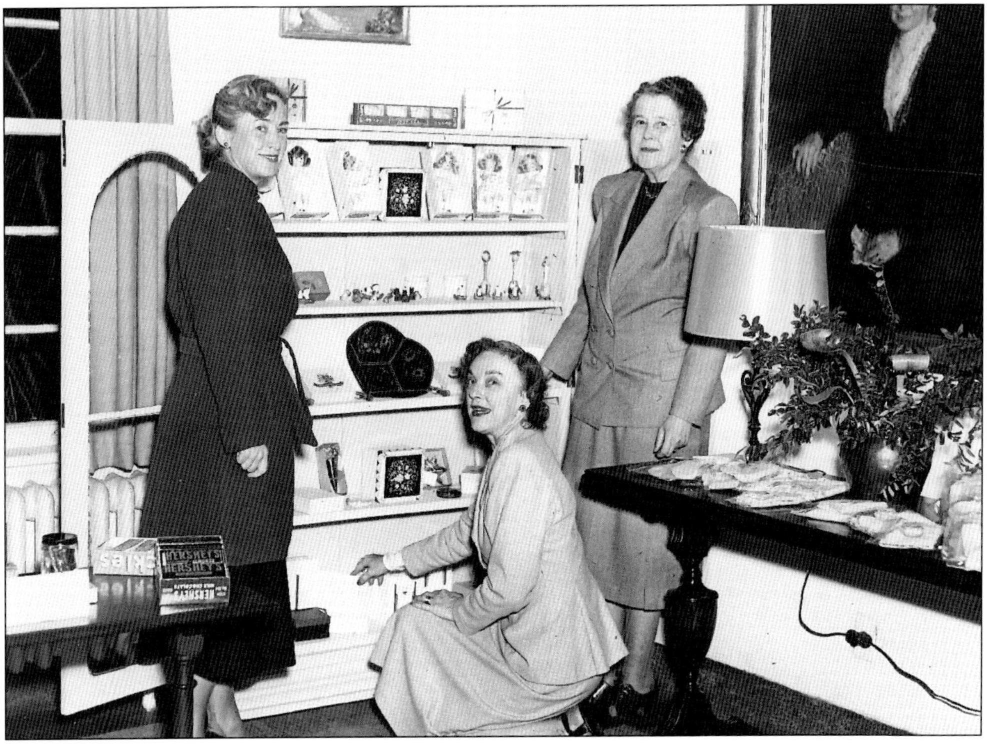

In charge on opening day of the Winton Club Gift Shop at the Winchester Hospital in 1949 are, from left to right, Mrs. Clarence McDavitt Jr., Mrs. Fulton Brown, and Mrs. Milton Grush (chairwoman). Receipts from sales were used for the club's hospital linen fund.

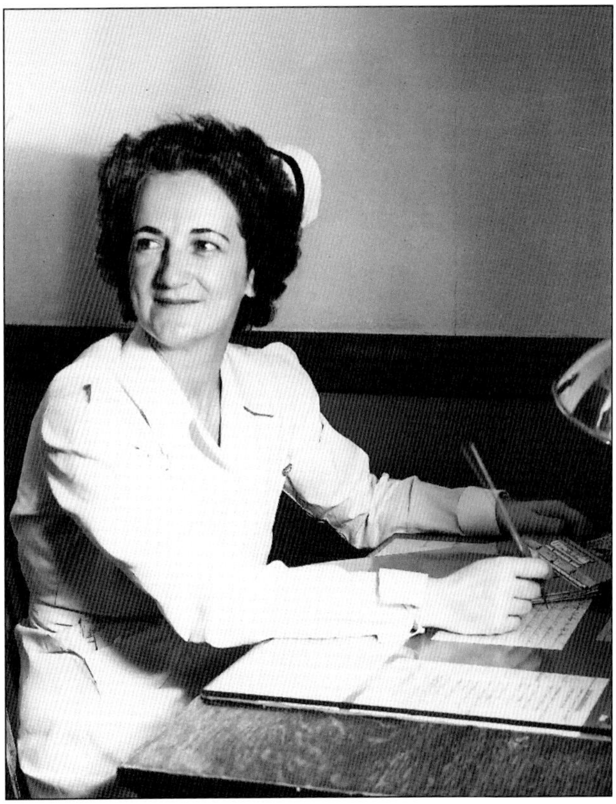

Miss Laura Rogers, R.N., was the superintendent of nurses in the Winchester Hospital, 1950.

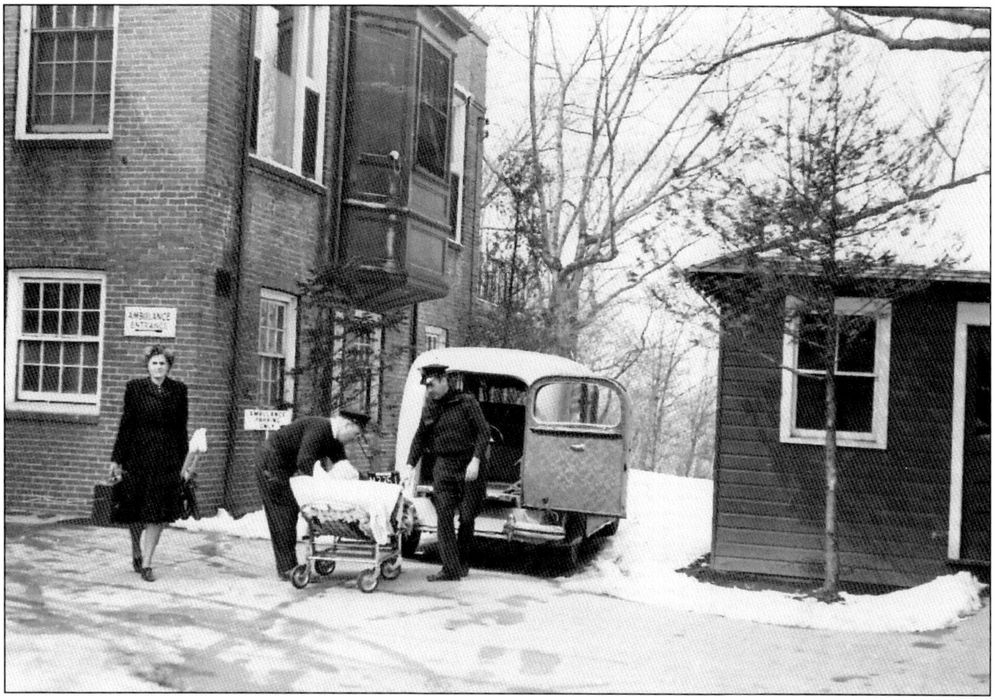

An ambulance arrives with a patient at the Winchester Hospital in the late 1940s.

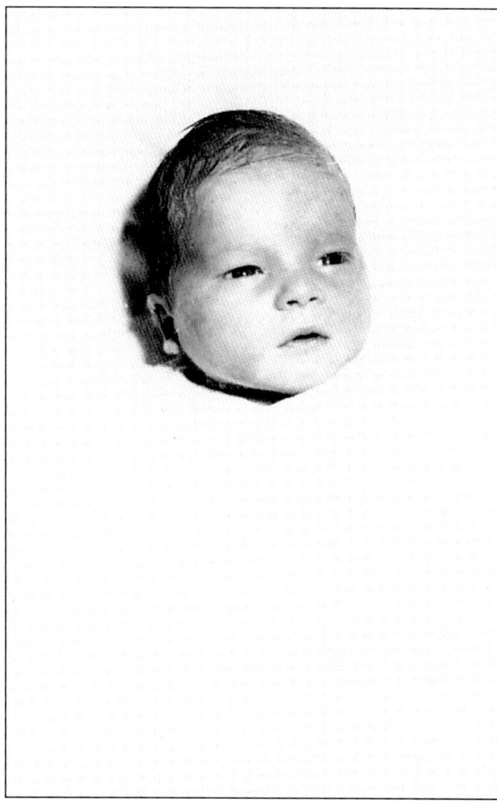

Thomas Jeffrey Howe, born February 5, 1950, was the first baby photographed at the Winchester Hospital under the En Ka Baby Photo Service. Every baby can be photographed in the hospital nursery by a special camera which takes a photograph of the baby in its bassinet. En Ka is a charitable organization which grew out of a banned girls' sorority at Winchester High School.

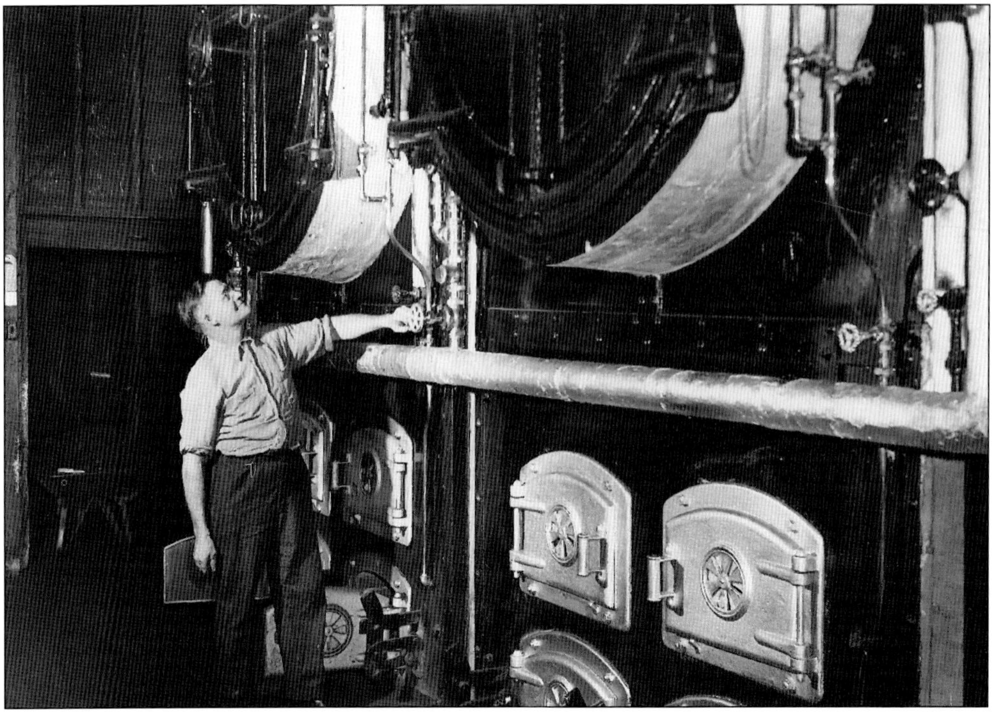

Mr. Thompson, engineer, in the Winchester Hospital boiler room, 1950.

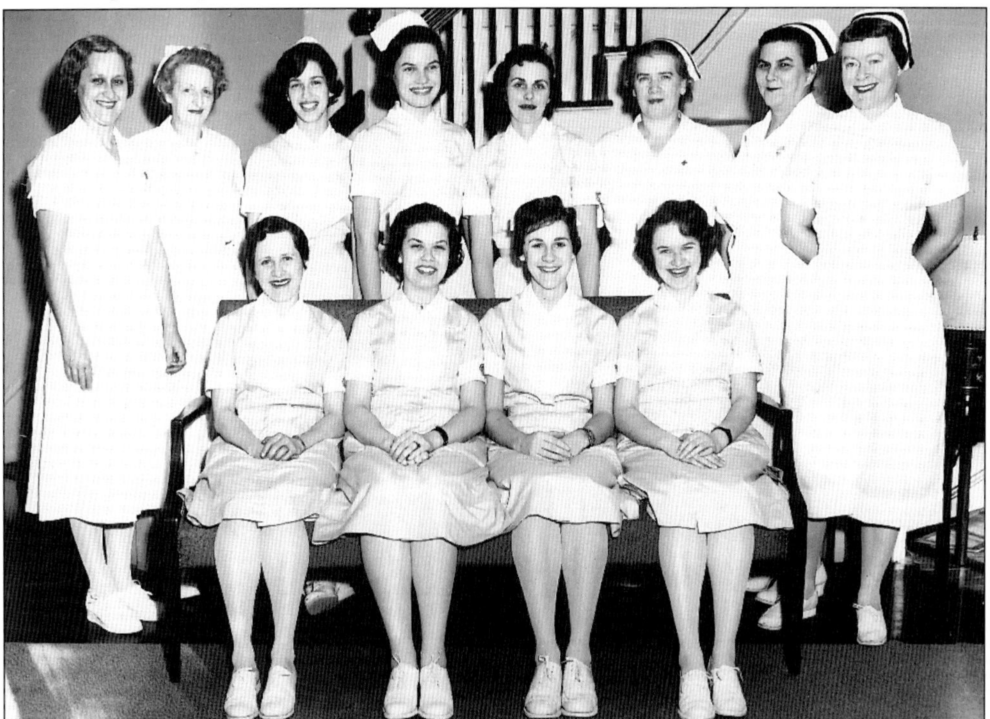

The first class of students from the Newton (Massachusetts) Junior College Regional School of Nursing to train at the Winchester Hospital, February 1960.

Four

A Sports-Loving Town

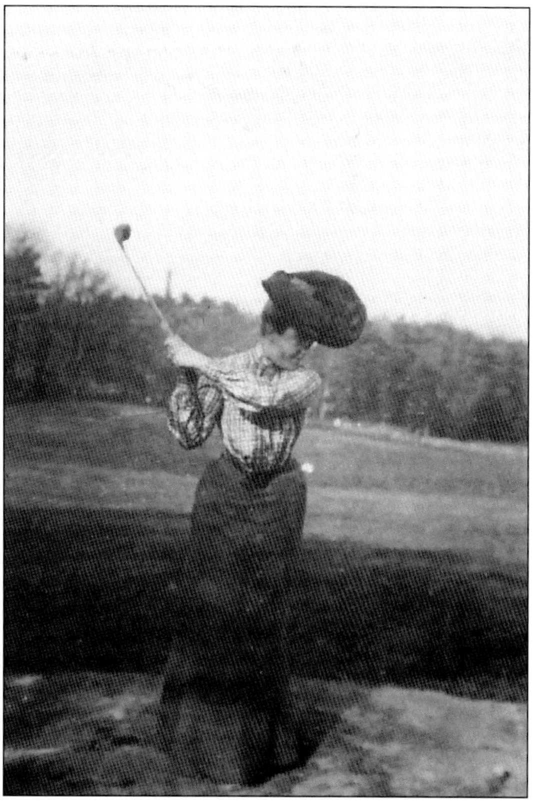

Mrs. Elmer Prescott Randlett readies for a golf shot at the Winchester Country Club in 1903, the year the club expanded its golf course to 18 holes. Her husband was one of the original members and financial backers of the club. He was president-treasurer of the E.F. Harding and New England Fish Companies of Fishermen's Wharf in Boston. The Randlett family moved to Winchester in 1903. Randlett was originally from Belmont, New Hampshire.

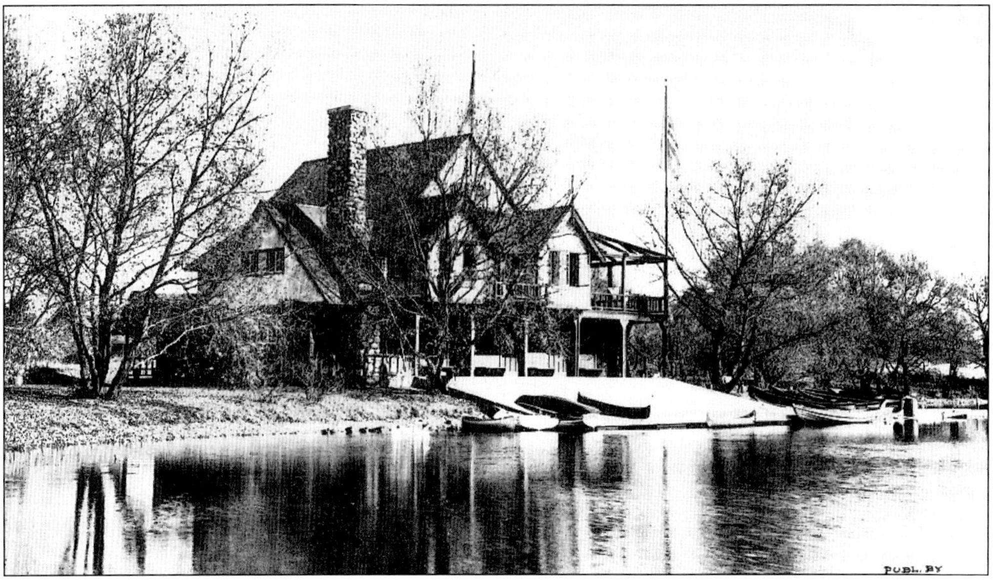

The Winchester Boat Club House, *c.* 1900. First famed for its championship canoeing, it later moved into sailing.

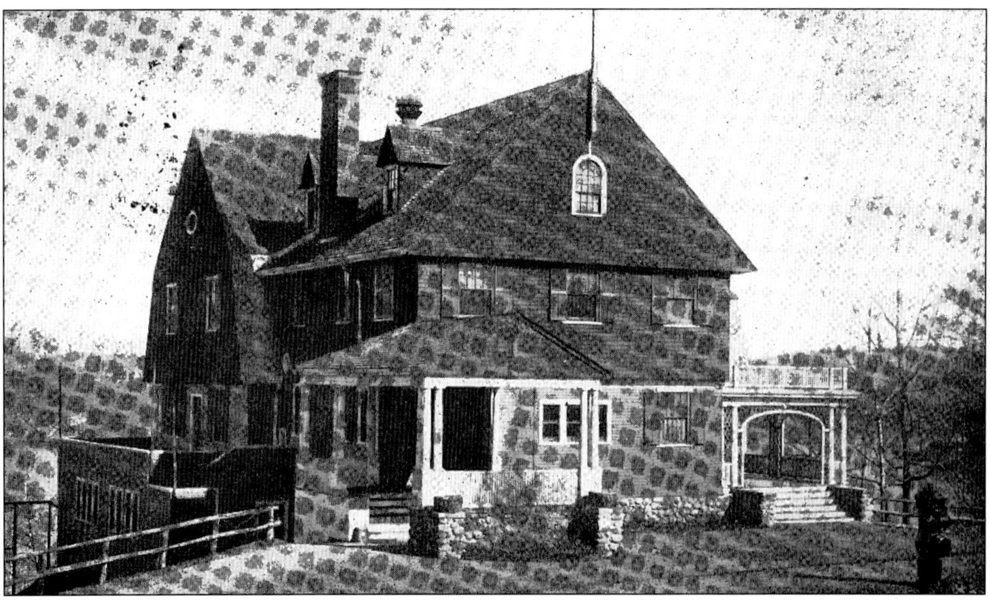

The Calumet Club, *c.* 1900. It was involved in various leisure time activities, but no longer exists.

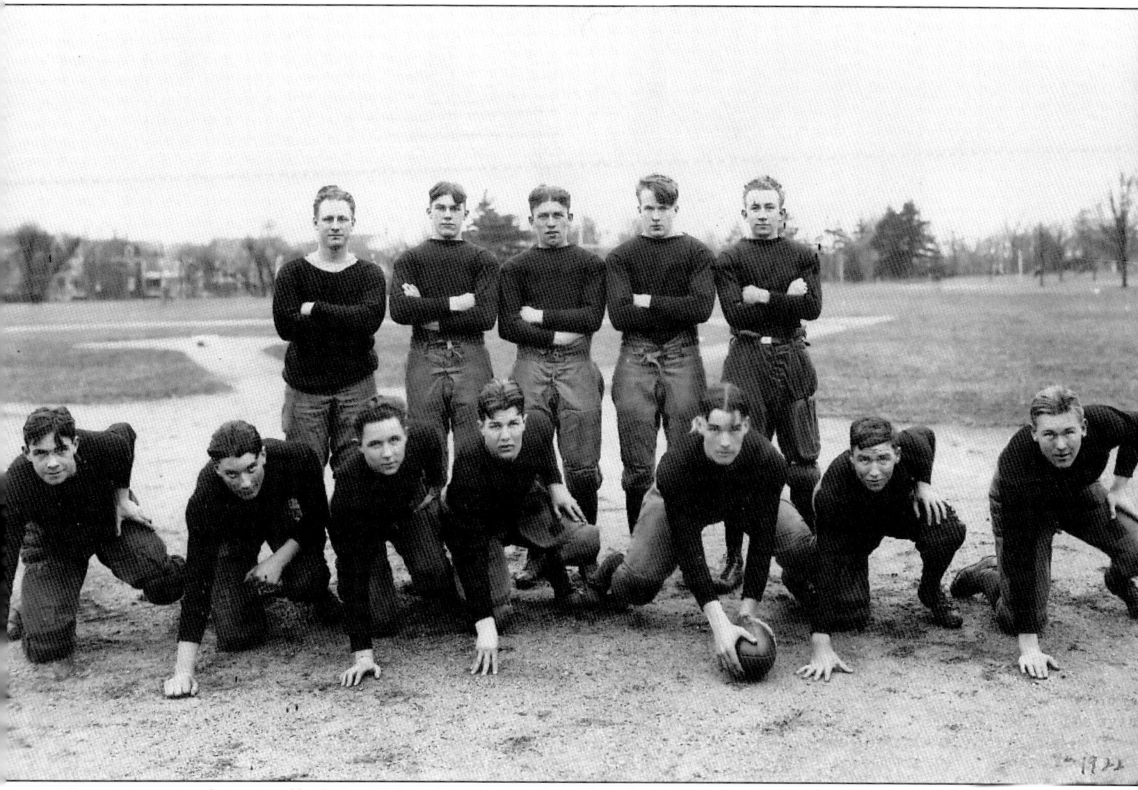

Some experts have called this Winchester High School's greatest football team ever. In 1922, it was the undefeated Class A champion, beating such teams as Everett and Malden. From left to right are: (front row) Stan McNeilly, James Fitzgerald, ? O'Connor, Prescott Randlett, Francis Melley, ? O'Connor, and Clint Mason; (back row) Rufus Bond (coach), Glen Kendrick, Abe Winer, Arthur French, and Dana Kelly.

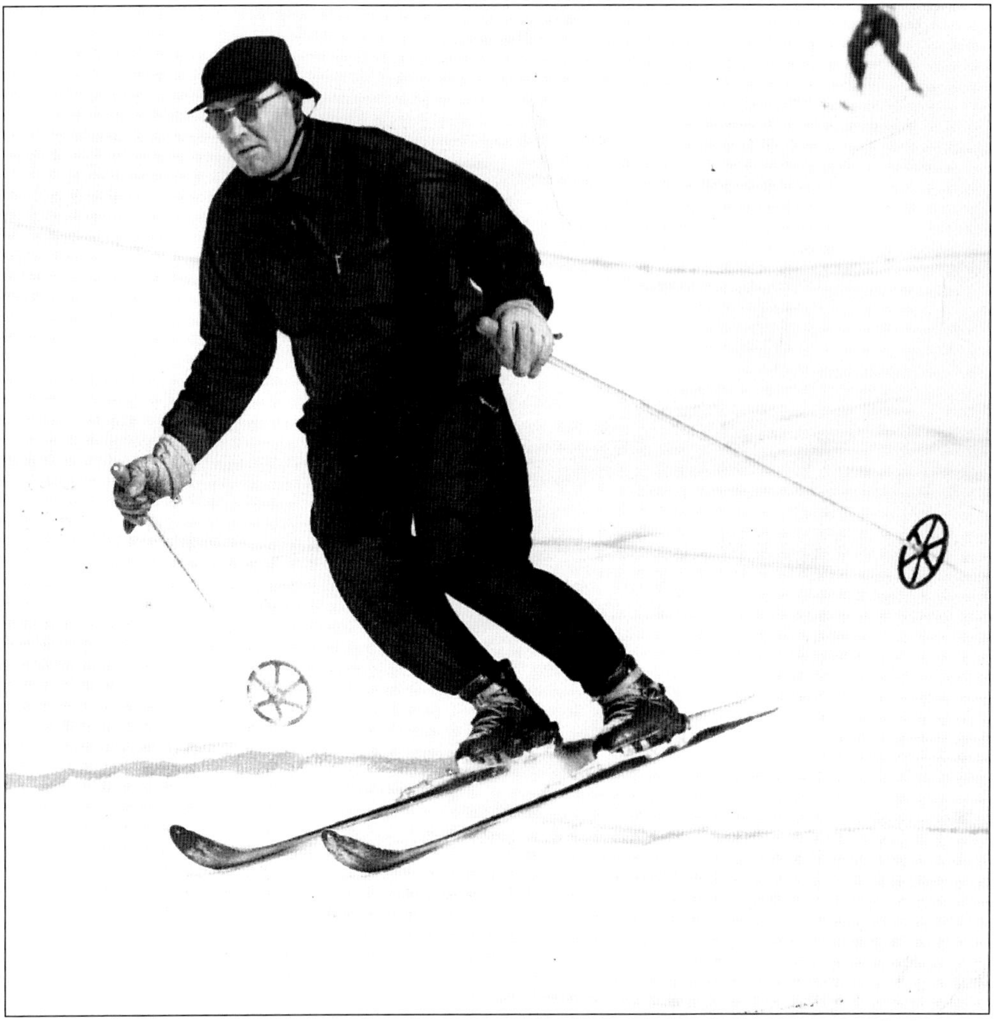

Harry Chefalo skiing at Cranmore Mountain, New Hampshire, *c.* 1960. Harry is still skiing at age eighty-eight, and is also an avid golfer. Participant sports loom large in Winchester.

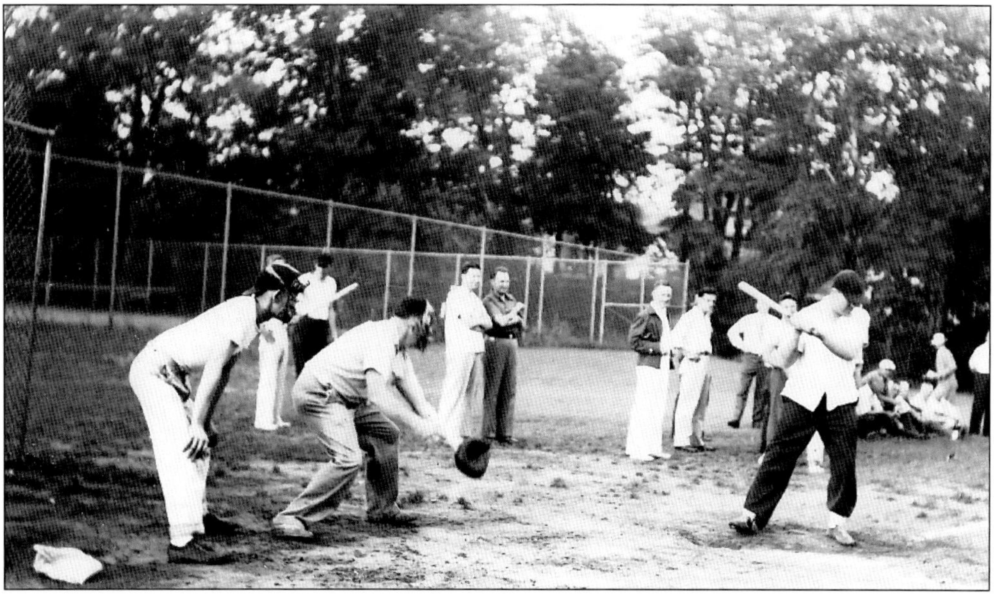

The Winchester auxiliary police playing softball in 1942 during World War II.

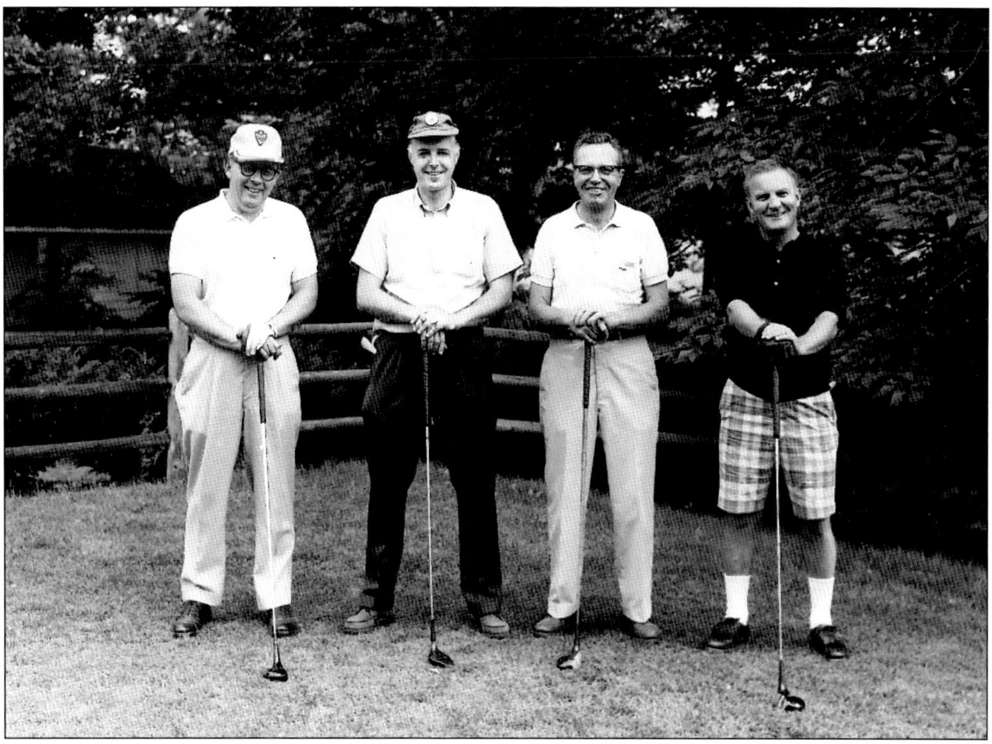

At the Winchester Country Club, *c.* 1950s, are, from left to right, Mike Shaughnessy, Sam Perkins, Harry Chefalo, and Bob Fitzgerald. It seemed quite hilly.

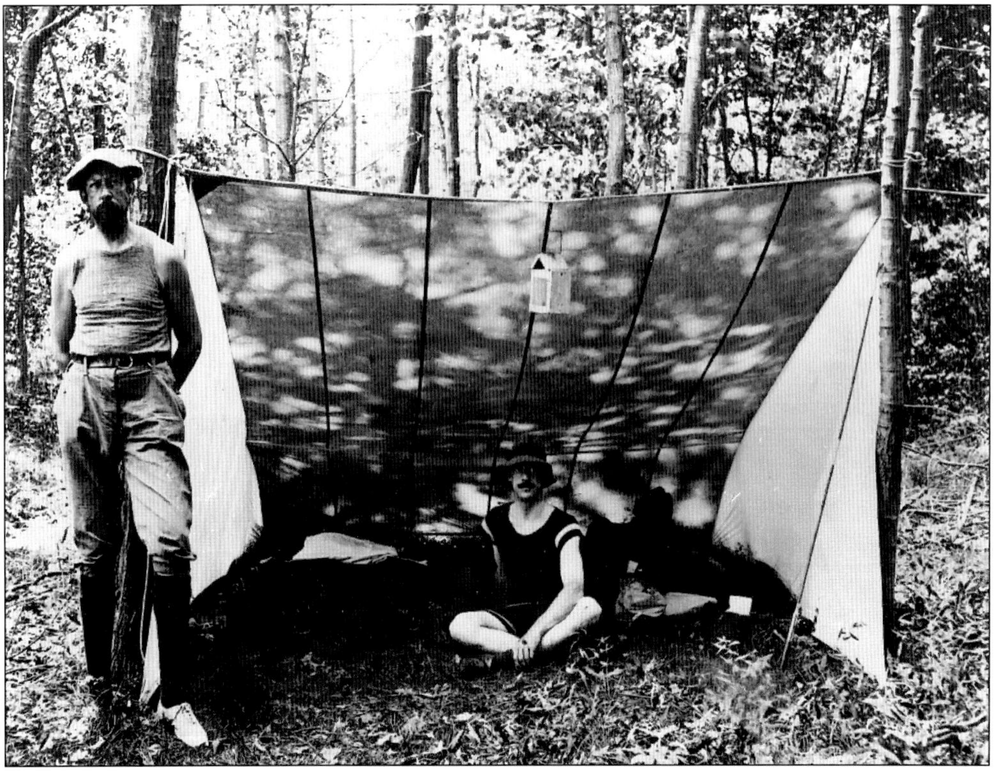

Winchester artist and world champion canoeist Herman Dudley Murphy (left) camps in New York State in the 1910s. He was one of the founders of the Winchester Boat Club, was on the faculty of the Harvard School of Architecture many years, and was even a skilled picture framer.

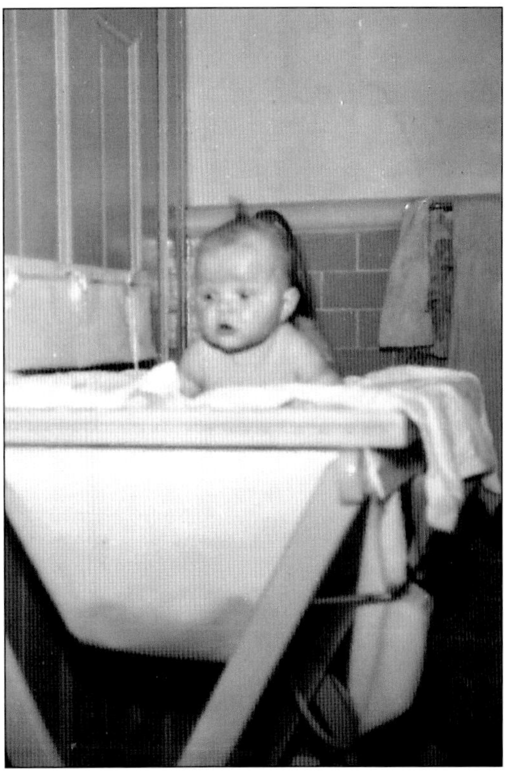

Alison Hersey Risch in her bassinet at the age of six months. She grew up to become a Winchester Sports Hall of Famer, for her international eminence in both field hockey and lacrosse.

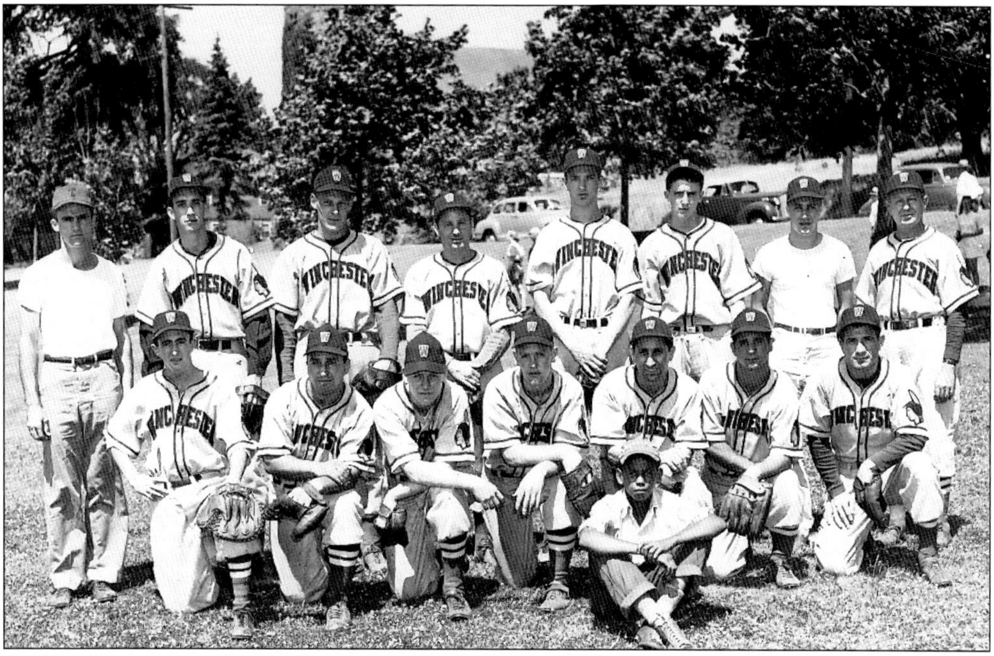

A Winchester town baseball team in the 1950s. From left to right are: (front row) ? Cogan (catcher), Sam Provinzano (left field), Jim Oliver (second base), unknown, Ted O'Rourke (first base), unknown, Sammy Bellino (outfield), and unknown; (back row) Dick Murphy (third base and infield), Dick Coon (pitcher), Sam Tompkins (pitcher), unknown, Verne Slack (pitcher), unknown, Shorty ?, and Lew Warsky (manager). The batboy is one of the Wests.

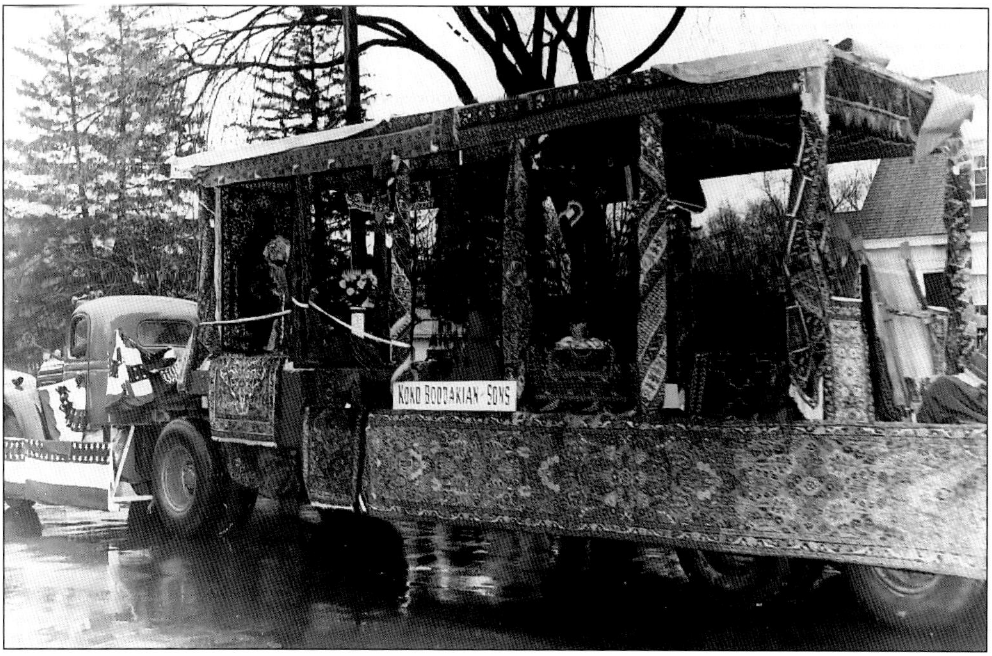

Leisure time wasn't all sports, of course. There were parades. Here's the Koko Boodakian & Sons float in the wet 100th anniversary parade in 1950. Plastic covered the oriental rugs atop the float and collected water which cascaded off when the float turned a corner.

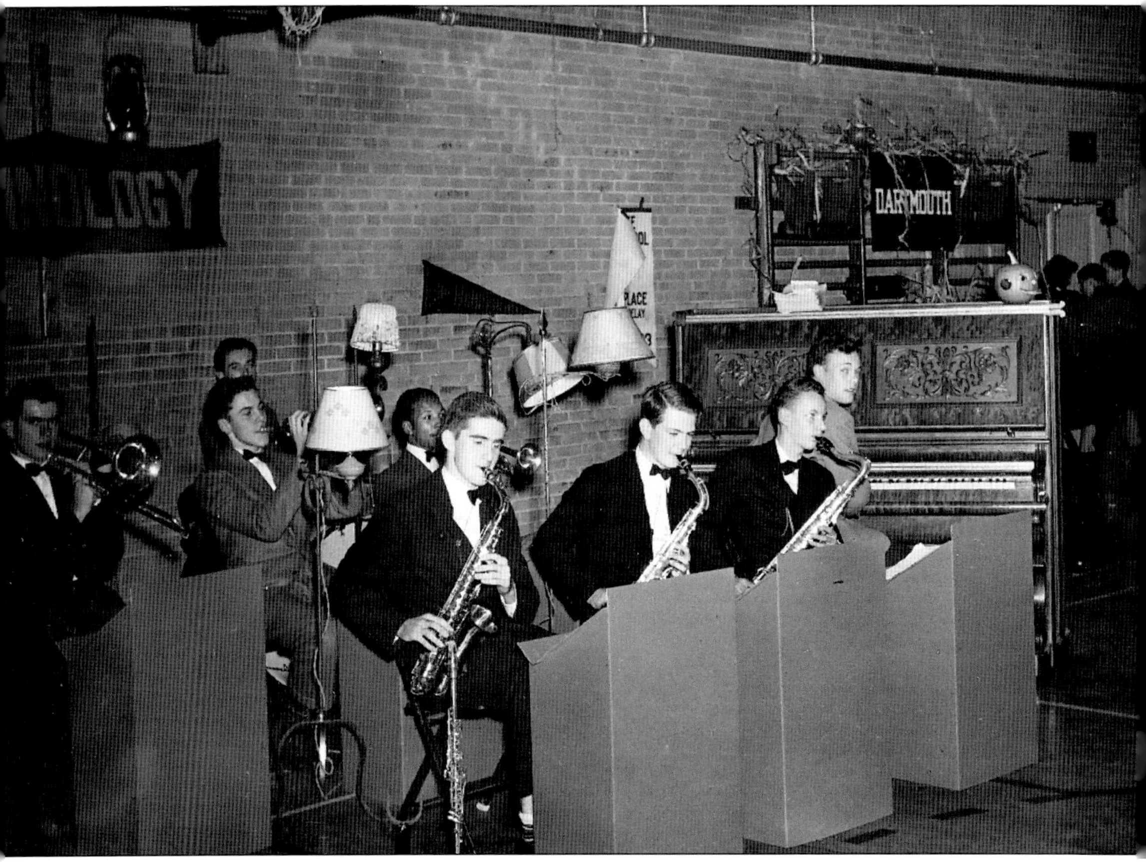

Another leisure time activity was dancing. Courtney Crandall's orchestra plays at the Fall Sports Dance at Winchester High in 1941. From left to right are: (front) on the saxophones, Dick Gallagher, Bill Dowden, and Bing Grindle (son of long-time Winchester High principal Wade Grindle), with leader Crandall at the piano; (back) Evan Ramsdell, Walt Howland, and Kermit Edmunds, with Ed McDevitt on the drums in the far rear. Crandall, who became one of the Boston area's best-known public relations men, still plays with his orchestra on occasion. His 1941 theme song, "Sophisticated Swing," was big for Courtney some time before the Les Brown Band made it more popular than ever.

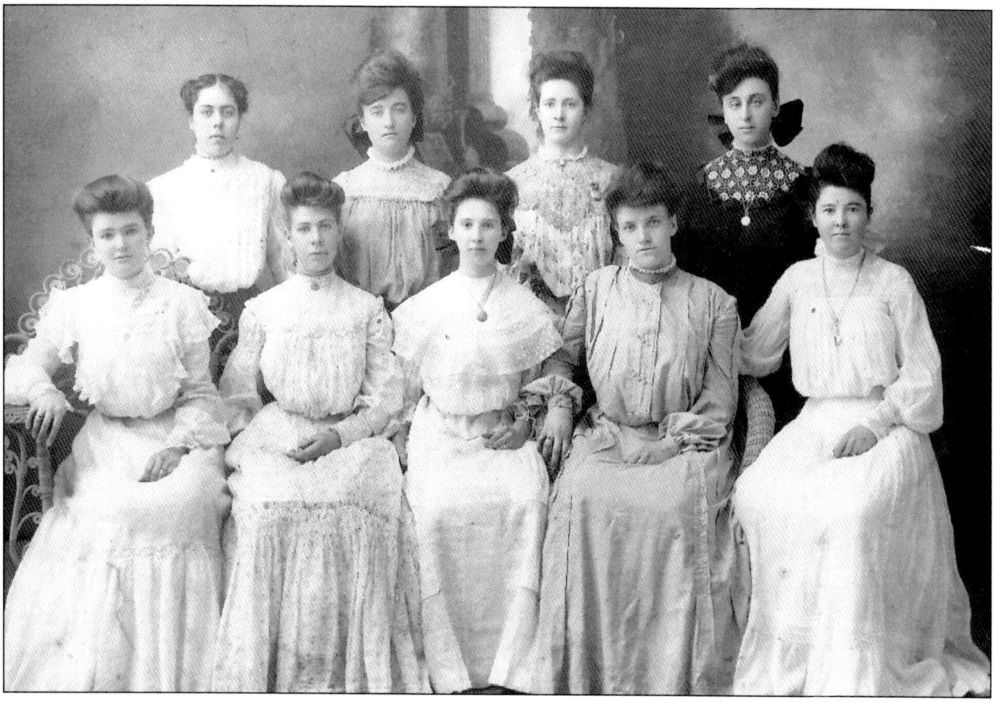

And there were many peaceful moments of leisure time activity. In this photograph the Wisteria Club sits for a portrait in the 1890s.

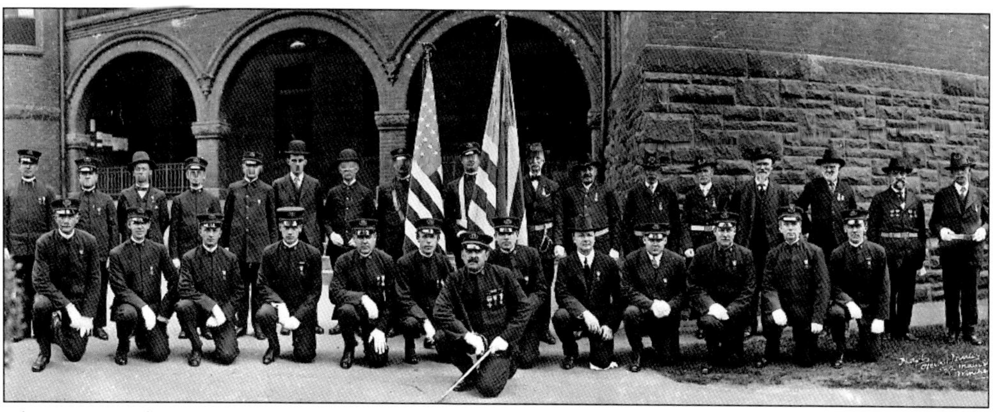

There were the veterans' activities in leisure time. Here are the Sons of Veterans and the Veterans of the Civil War are shown in Winchester probably in the 1900s. From left to right are: (front) Irving Johnson; (middle row) George Potter, unknown, H. Wadsworth Hight, Gordon Parker, unknown, George Morse, unknown, Reverend Joel H. Metcalf, ? Richburg, William J. Palmer, unknown, and Ollie Weld; (back row) ? Johnson, unknown, Augustus Coffin, Thomas Barrett, J.C. Adams, unknown, Henry Smalley, unknown, ? Johnson, ? Billings, ? Snow, unknown, unknown, Samuel Carr, unknown, unknown, and unknown.

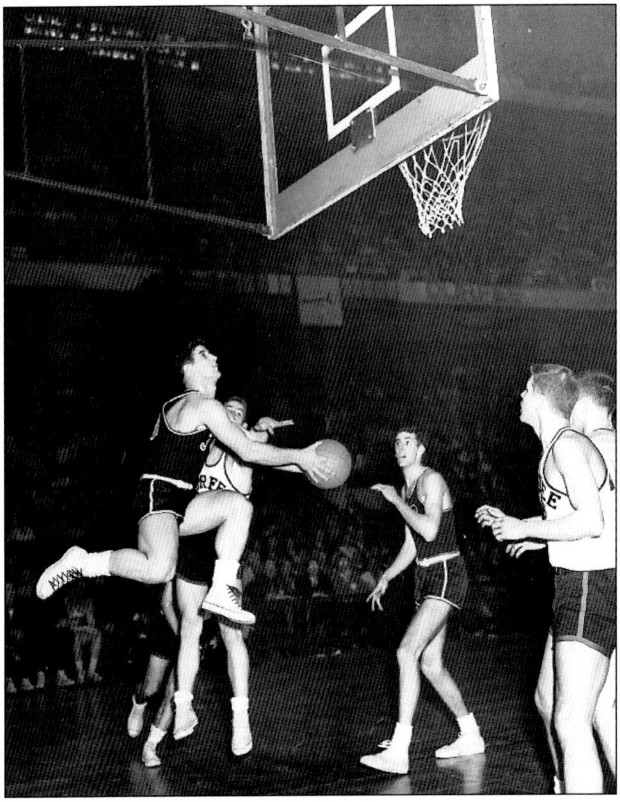

Joe Bellino, better known for his football playing (he won the Heisman Trophy in 1960 as this country's leading college football player while attending the U.S. Naval Academy) takes a shot during the 1956 Class A basketball state final against Durfee High of Fall River. Bellino starred in football, basketball, and baseball at Winchester High.

Joe Bellino stands between Mrs. Cynthia Laraway Barone and Dr. William D. Barone, co-collaborators on a book about the Heisman Trophy winner.

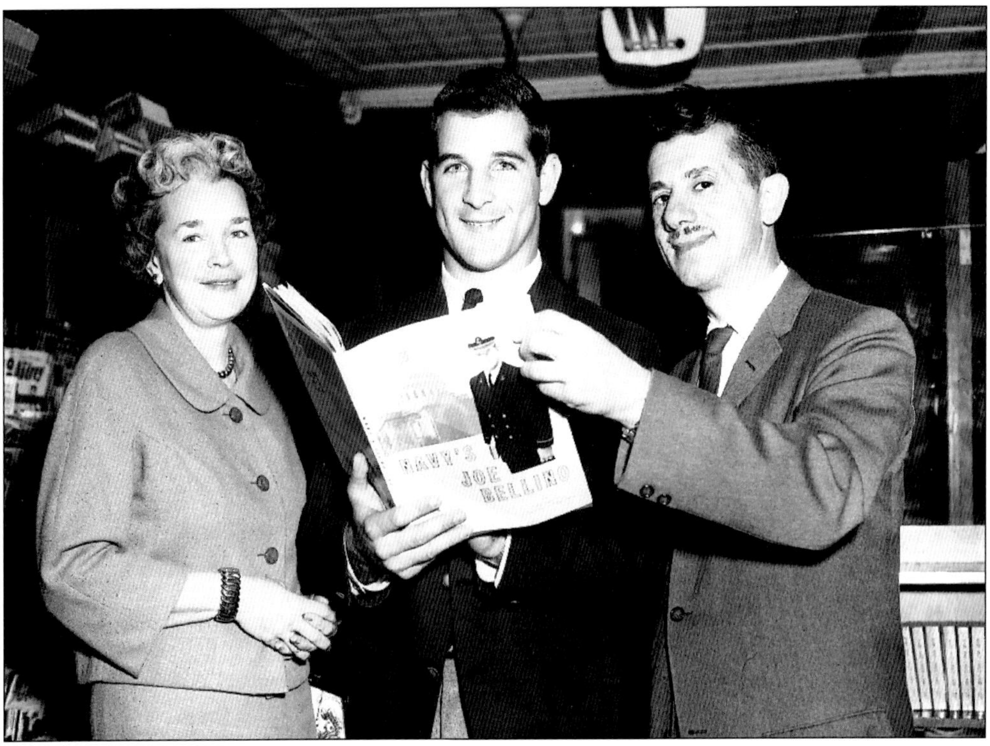

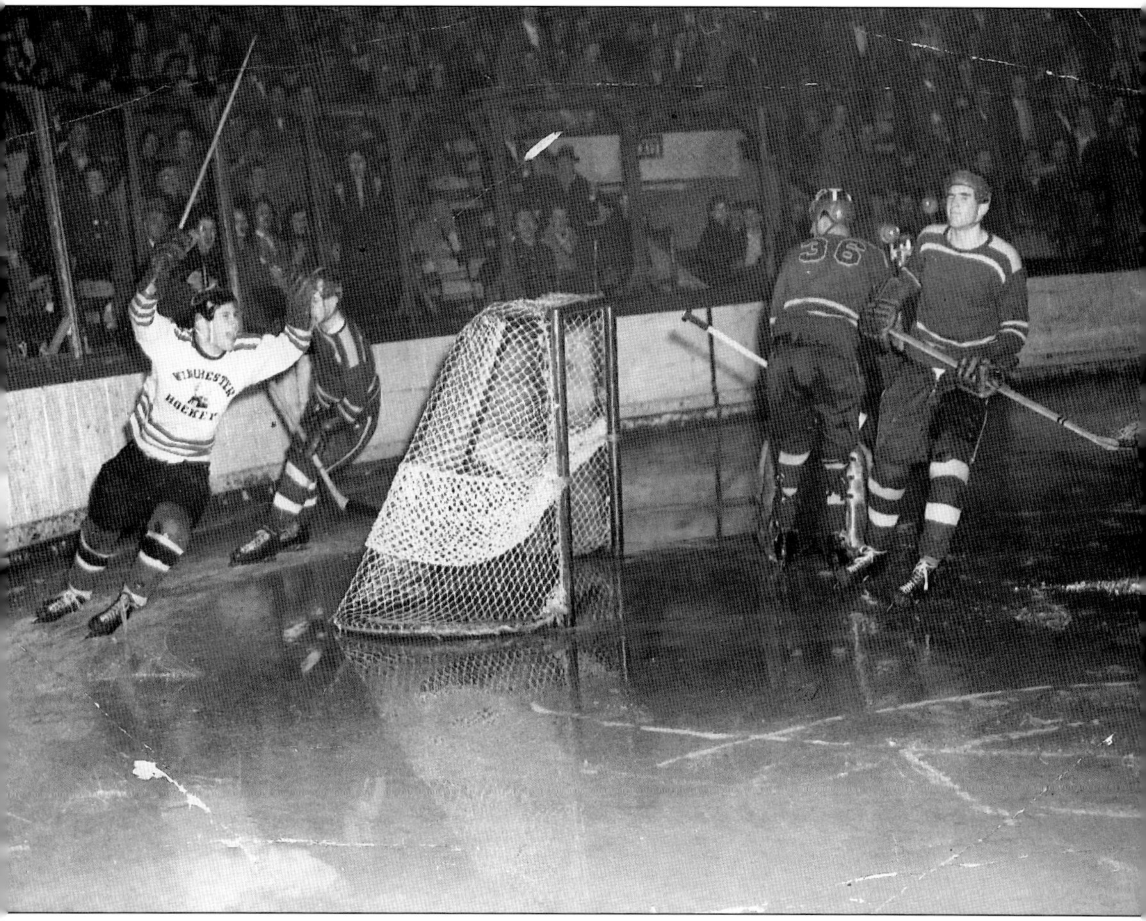

Wing Walter Cowles scores Winchester High's third goal, the winning goal, in the 5–2 victory over Belmont High School for the 1955 Class A state hockey title. Cowles was named the most valuable player in the state tourney. In the photograph for Belmont beside the goalie are George McLaughlin and George Higginbotham. The same night in March 1955, Winchester won the Class B basketball title. The two titles in one night are unprecedented in Massachusetts high school sports history.

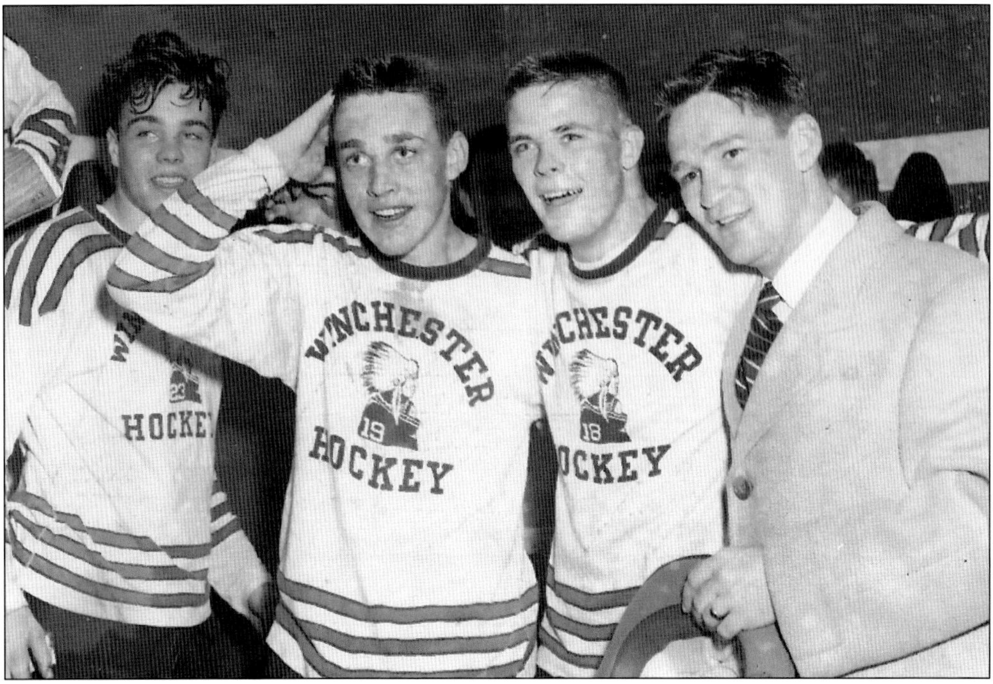

Winchester High's hockey team celebrates its 1955 state title with its coach. From left to right are Dana Sawyer, Leo Callahan, Walter Cowles, and Coach Francis X. Finigan.

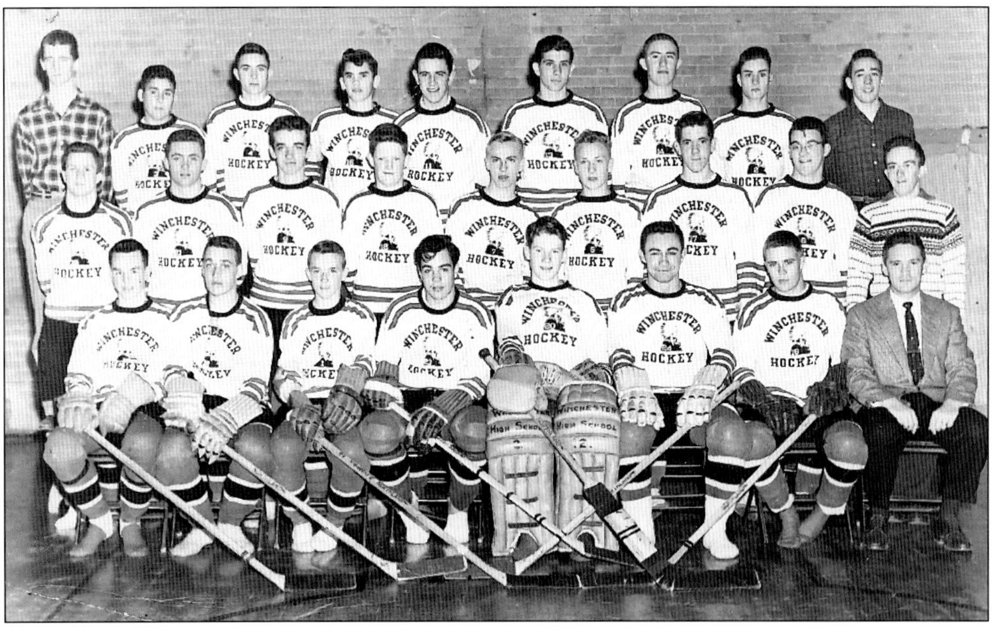

The 1955 Winchester High state champion ice hockey team. From left to right are: (front) Joe Cussen, Leo Callahan, Richie Johnson, George Denton, Mike Murphy, Wayne Cowles, and Francis X. Finigan (coach); (middle row) George Bodman, John Murphy, Dave Manning, John Sullivan, John Zirkel, Ron Parker, John Herzog, Jay Robertson, and Joe Keating (manager); (back row) Bob Page, John Urmson, Charley Urmon, Norman Farrar, Dick Gibbons, Neil Karrigan, David Howard, and Dan Doherty.

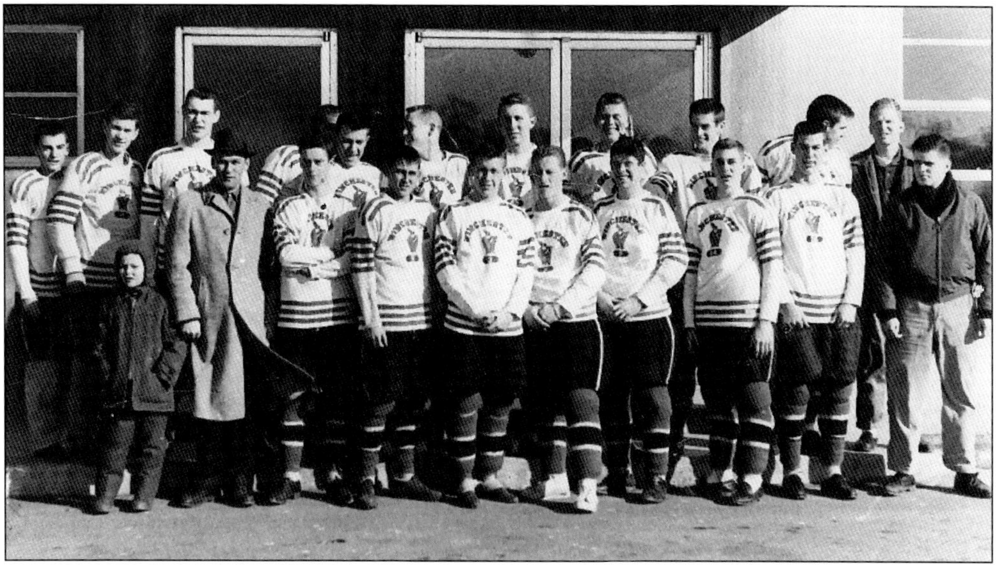

The 1960 Winchester High hockey team which went to the state semi-finals and won the Middlesex League championship. From left to right are: (front row) Frank Finigan Jr. (who was six years old and attended all games), his father Francis X. Finigan (coach), Richard Tierney, Tom Bell, Bill Lamarche, Whitey Allen, Roger Griffin, Doug Scott, Phil Davenport, and Bill Kirkpatrick; (back row) Frank Curtis, Bob Tierney, Bill Callahan, Bryan Cullen, John Hosmer, Dana Kelley, Peter Branch, Bob Eaton, unknown, and Bob Goway (manager).

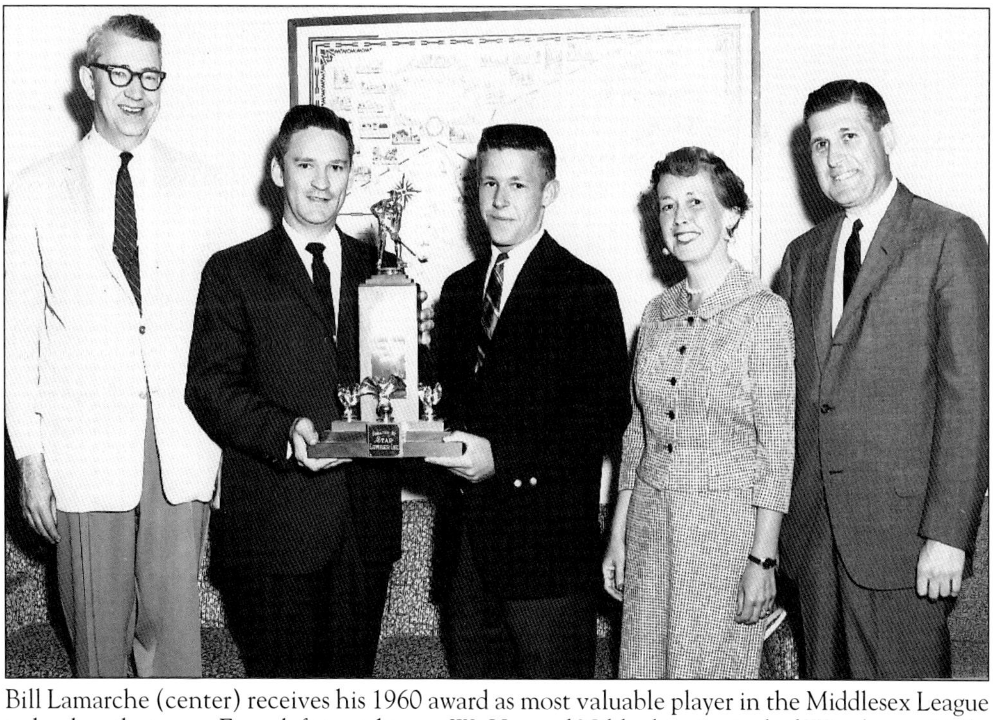

Bill Lamarche (center) receives his 1960 award as most valuable player in the Middlesex League in hockey that year. From left to right are: W. Howard Niblock, principal of Winchester High; WHS Hockey Coach Francis X. Finigan; Lamarche; and his mother and father, Mr. and Mrs. William Lamarche Jr.

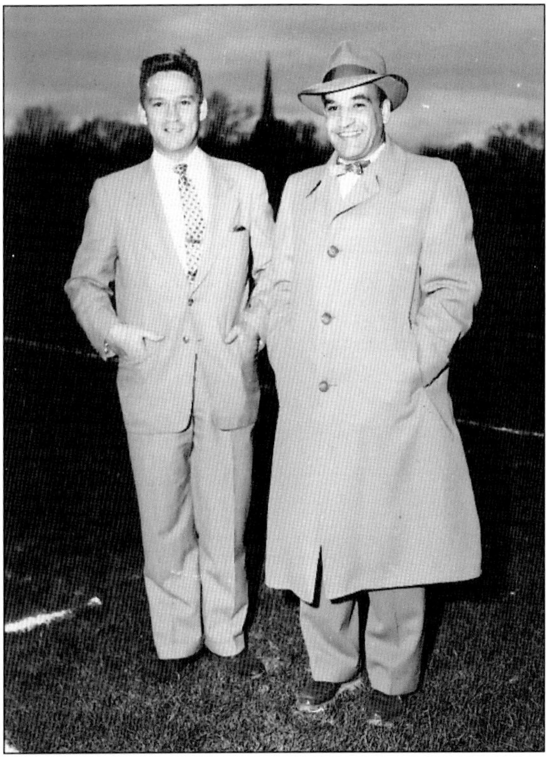

Two assistants to head coach Henry Knowlton of the Winchester High football team stand on Manchester Field in 1954: Francis X. Finigan (left), better known as the school's ice hockey head coach and science teacher, and Frank Provinzano, backfield coach and former WHS football great.

Three coaching greats at Winchester High School get together in 1956. From left to right are: Jim Phillips, basketball coach in the 1950s; Henry Knowlton, football coach from 1940 to 1967 and athletic director for a time after that; and Francis X. Finigan, ice hockey coach from 1952 to 1962.

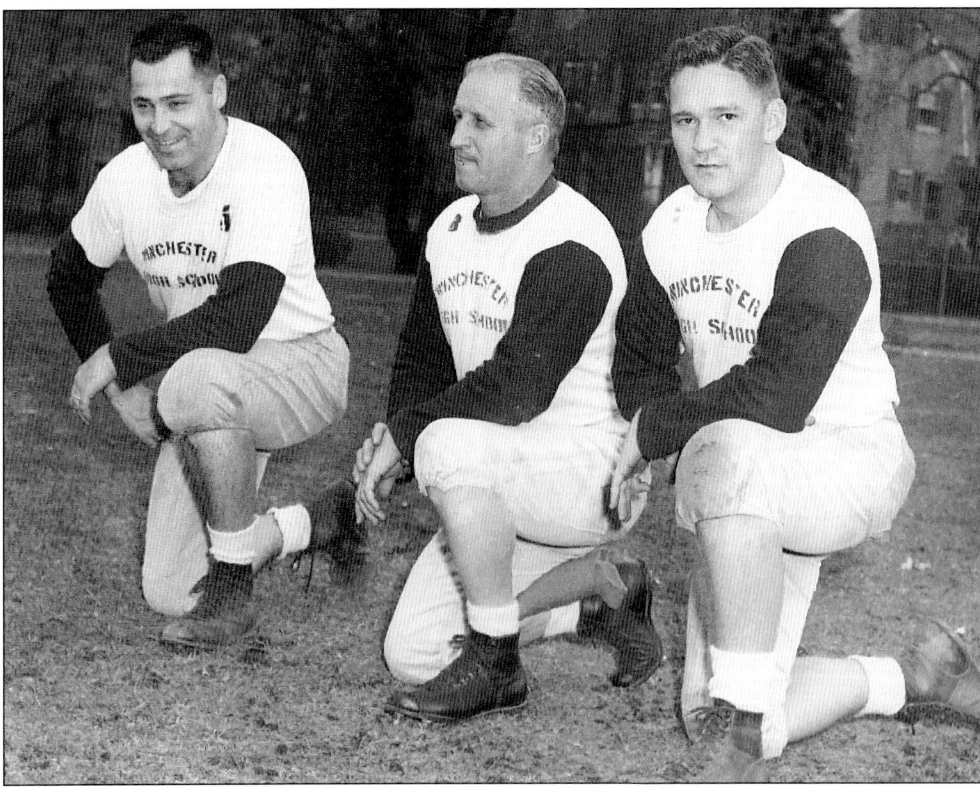

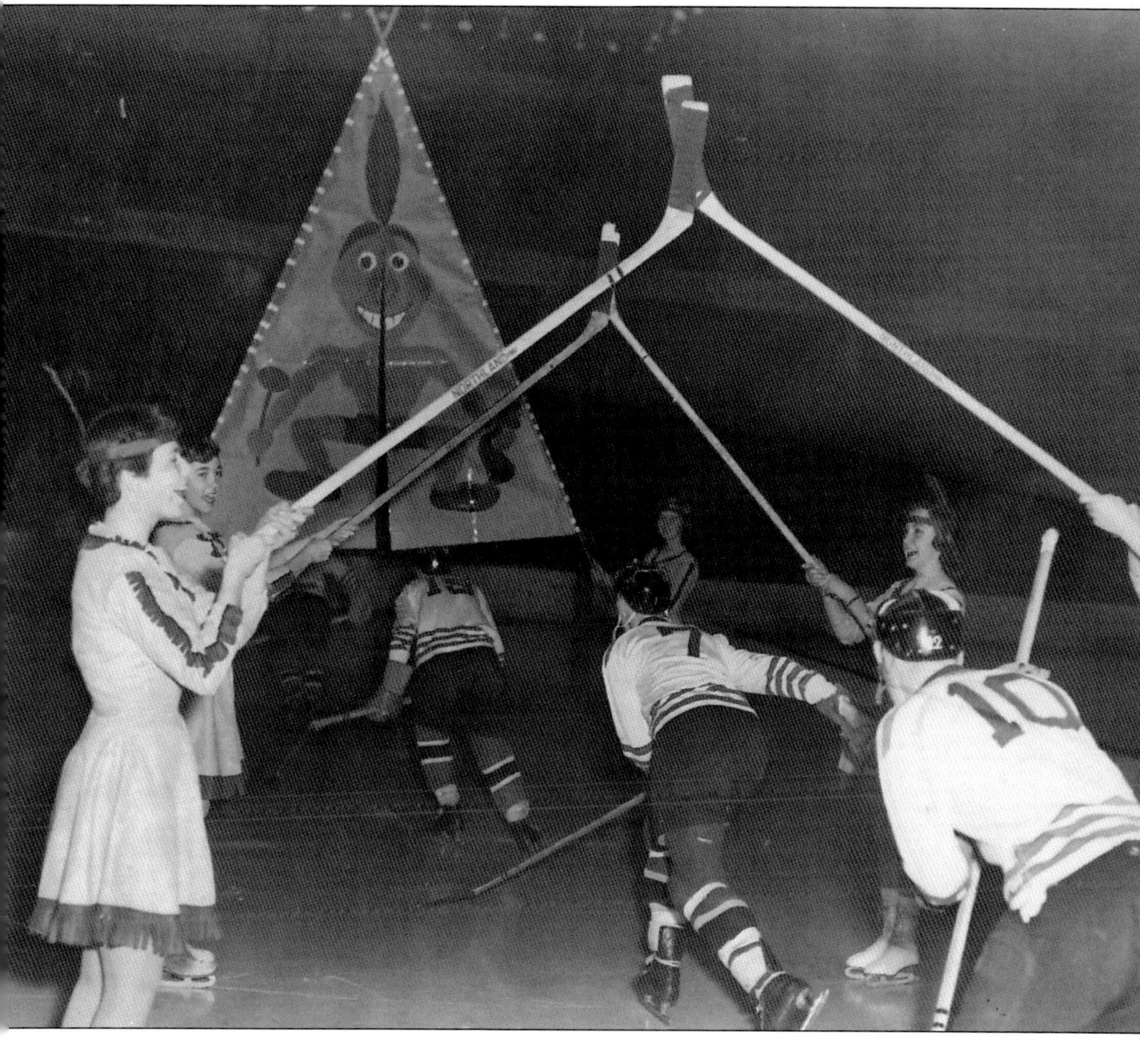

Winchester High School innovates. The first high school ice hockey cheerleaders on skates were introduced by WHS at the 1955 state championship game versus Belmont High. They were made formal in 1956 but eventually were ended because of opponent crowd comments. The Indian costumes, of course, fit in with the Sachem team nickname. Margie Thompson is on the right. Lines were sent out under the crossed hockey sticks. This line was made up of Joey Cussen, John Zirkel, and Leo Callahan.

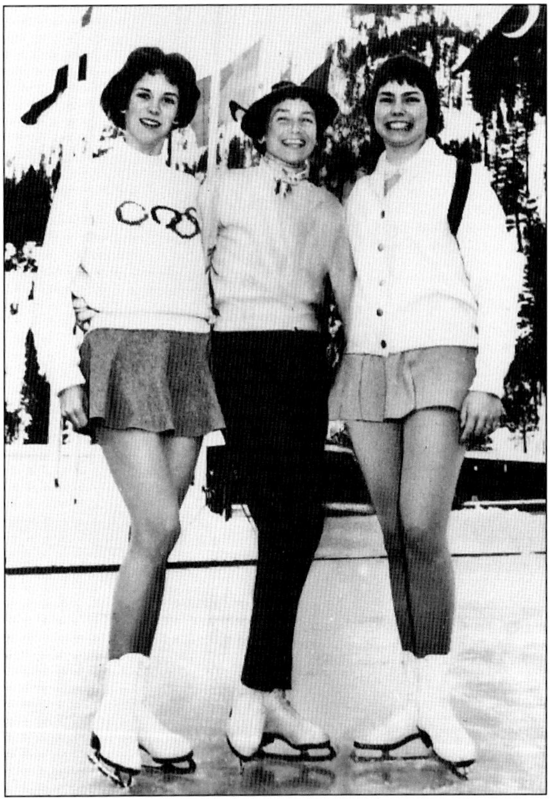

The figure-skating Vinson-Owens family. Maribel Vinson-Owen (center) won nine national women's figure skating championships and was on three U.S. Olympic skating teams. With her are her daughters: Maribel (a national junior and, later, a national pairs figure skating champ) and Laurence (a senior North American singles champion). A Brussels plane crash killed all three in 1961 on their way to the World Skating Championships in Prague. The Vinson-Owen School in Winchester is named after them.

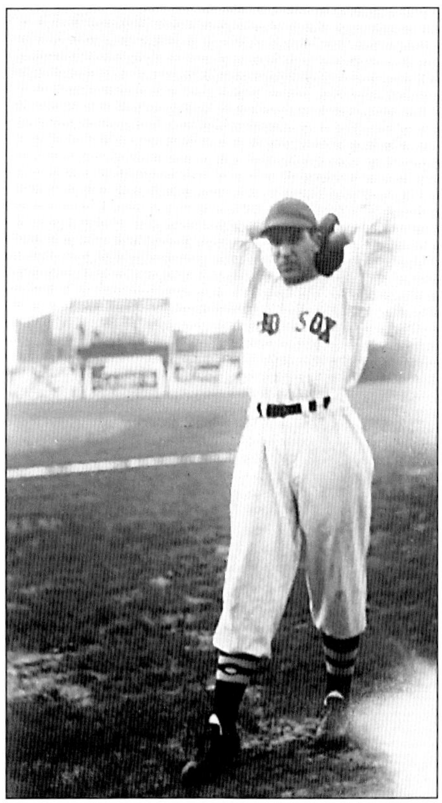

Pete Provinzano winds up on the mound for Scranton, an Eastern League farm club of the Boston Red Sox in 1943. Provinzano pitched a five-hit shutout against Wilkes-Barre on opening day, had a 7–2 record when called into the service. After World War II, he was in the Red Sox and Chicago White Sox farm systems from 1946 to 1951. His former football coach, Henry Knowlton (whose brother Hal worked in the Harvard athletic department), was helpful in getting Pete his trainer's job at Harvard.

Benjamin Franklin Blank (left), one of three brothers who owned Blank Brothers Tannery which burned in 1910 in Winchester and much real estate in the town, stands at the beach in the early 1900s with Barbara Blank (Sherburne). Busy people still had leisure time fun.

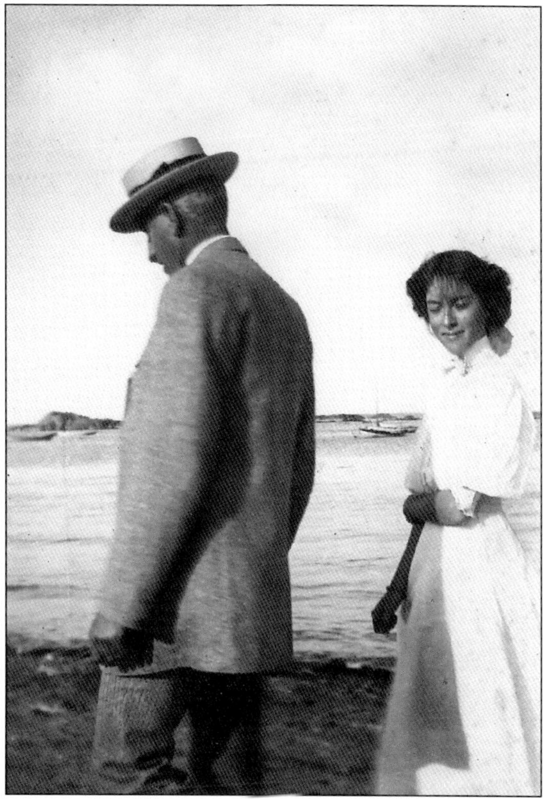

Willard Hudson of Winchester had his own motorcycle from the age of fourteen. During World War I as a sergeant, he was a motorcycle dispatcher and rode all along the front lines. This was taken shortly before the United States entered World War I.

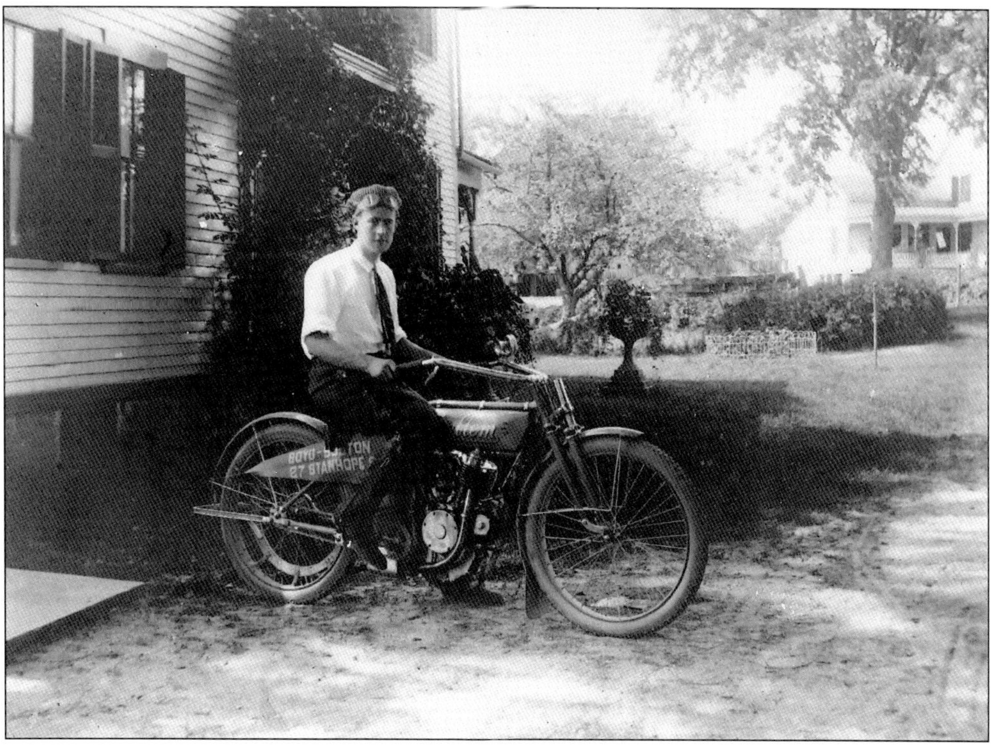

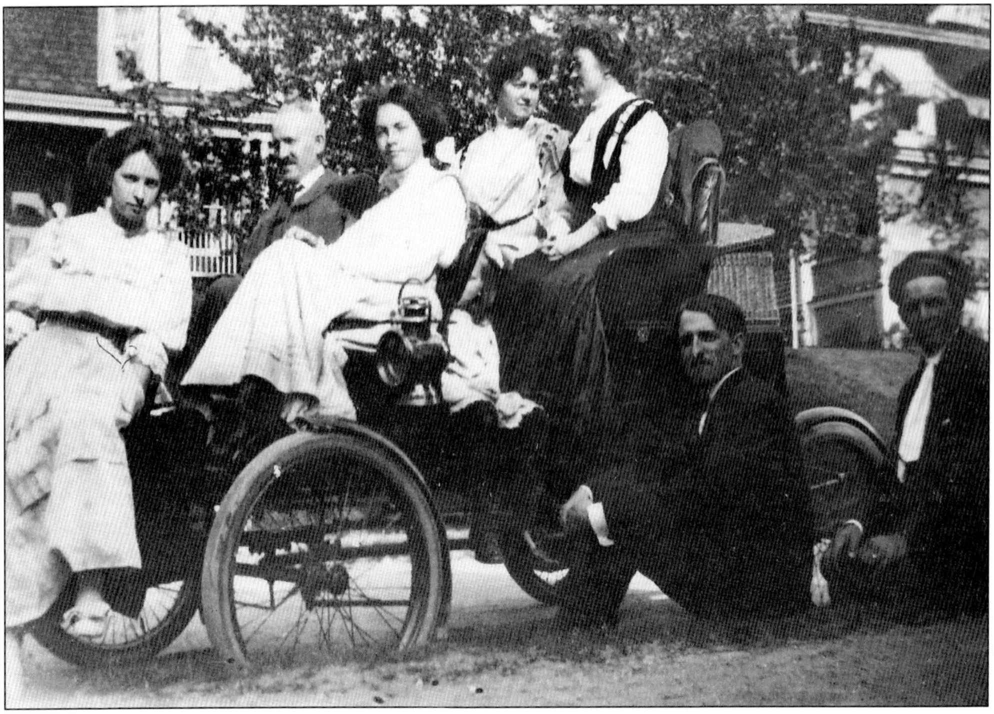

In the 1910s having fun with an early car are, from left to right, Pauline Blank, Benjamin Franklin Blank, Barbara Blank, unknown, and Grace Belle Manning Blank, with two other unknown young men.

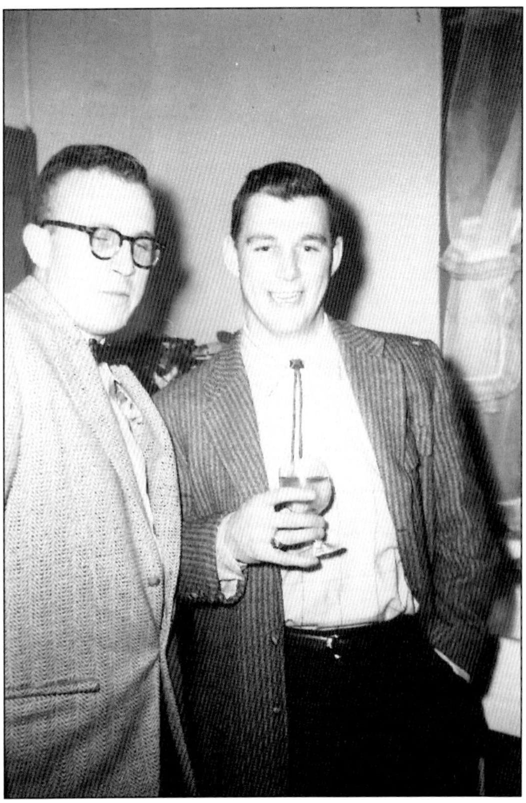

Charles D. (Chucker) Roche (left) and Charles (Sarto) Walsh in the 1950s. Both played football and baseball at Harvard after graduating from Winchester High.

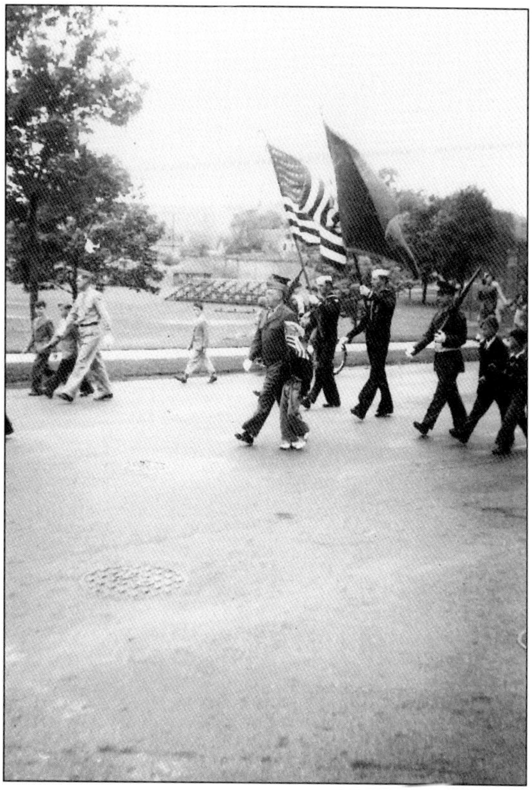

An American Legion parade passes Leonard Field on Washington Street in Winchester, c. 1946–47. In general, Winchester has an excellent playground system.

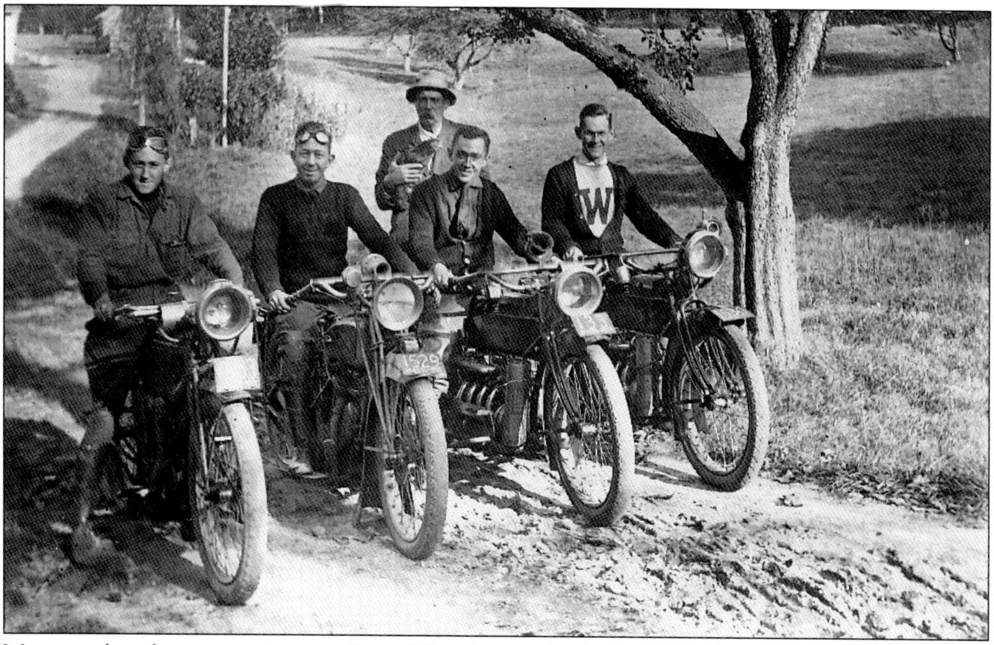

Motorcycle riding was quite popular in Winchester. In this c. 1913 photograph are, from left to right, Lloyd Goddu, Louis Goddu (the famed inventor of the staple), Paul and Warren Goddu, and Charles Merrifield (in the back, the uncle of the last two).

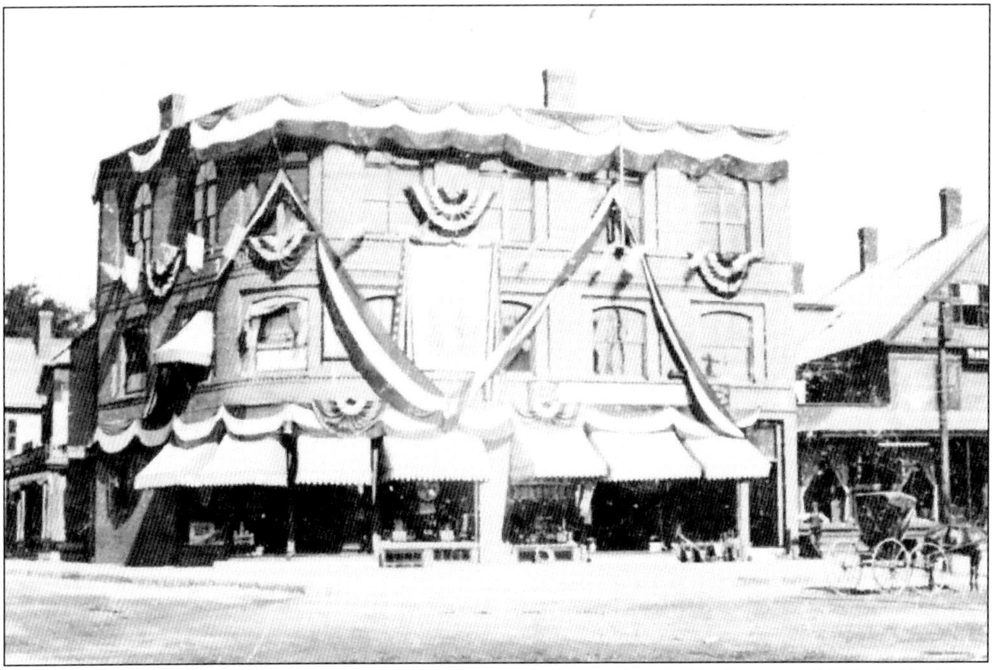

They knew how to dress up for celebrations in Winchester. This is the decorated White Building at the corner of Main and Church Streets ready for the 250th anniversary blowout in 1890.

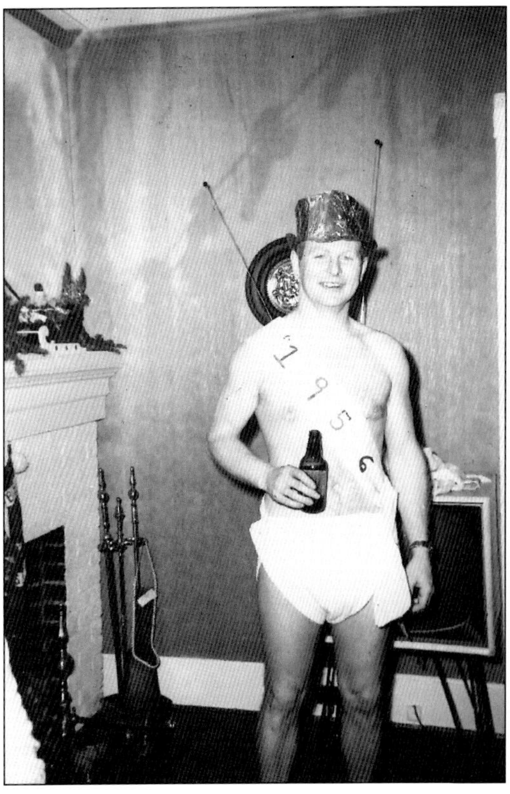

To wind up sports and leisure time matters, we show Bob Quine winding up 1955 and ushering in 1956 at his Webster Street, Winchester, apartment.

Five

A Scenic Town

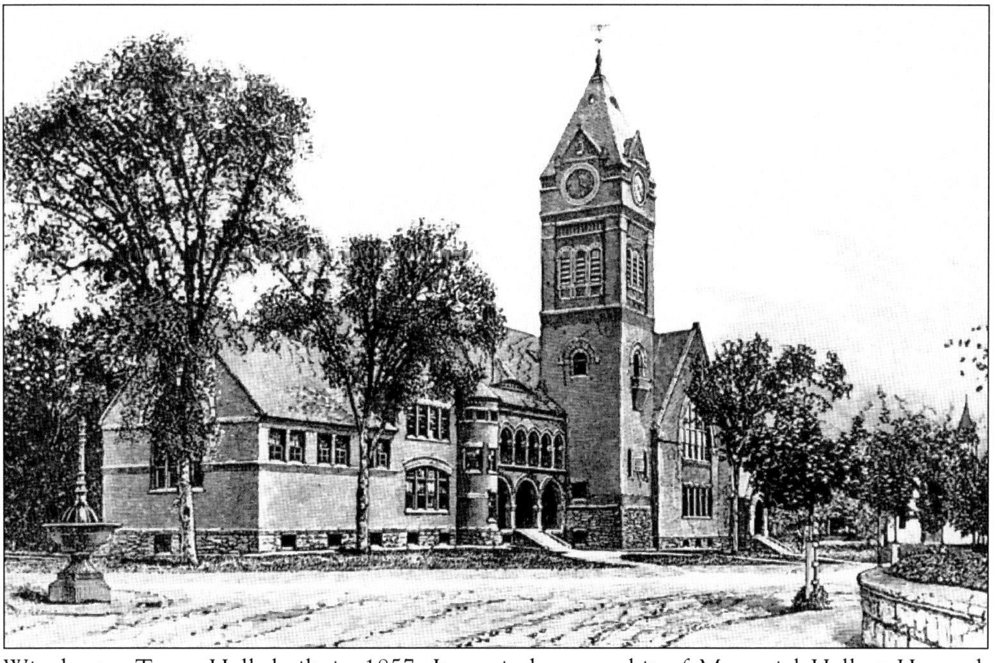

Winchester Town Hall, built in 1857. It reminds one a bit of Memorial Hall at Harvard. Obviously, it was built to last—and it has. Some consider it a bit of an eyesore but many more are struck by its imposing posture. The town would not be the same without it.

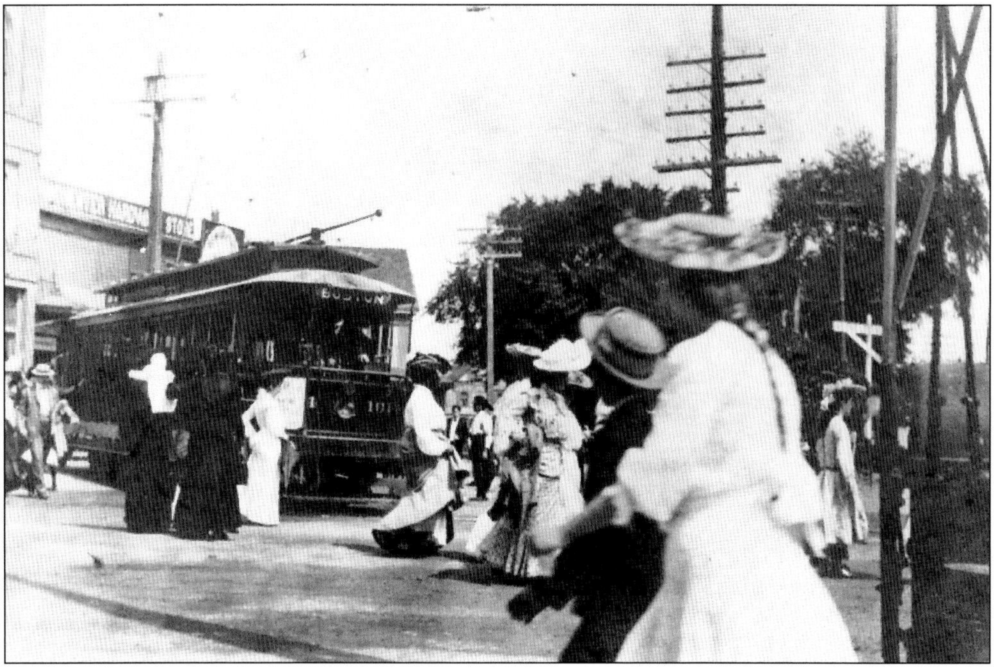

A trolley from Winchester to Boston, *c.* 1910.

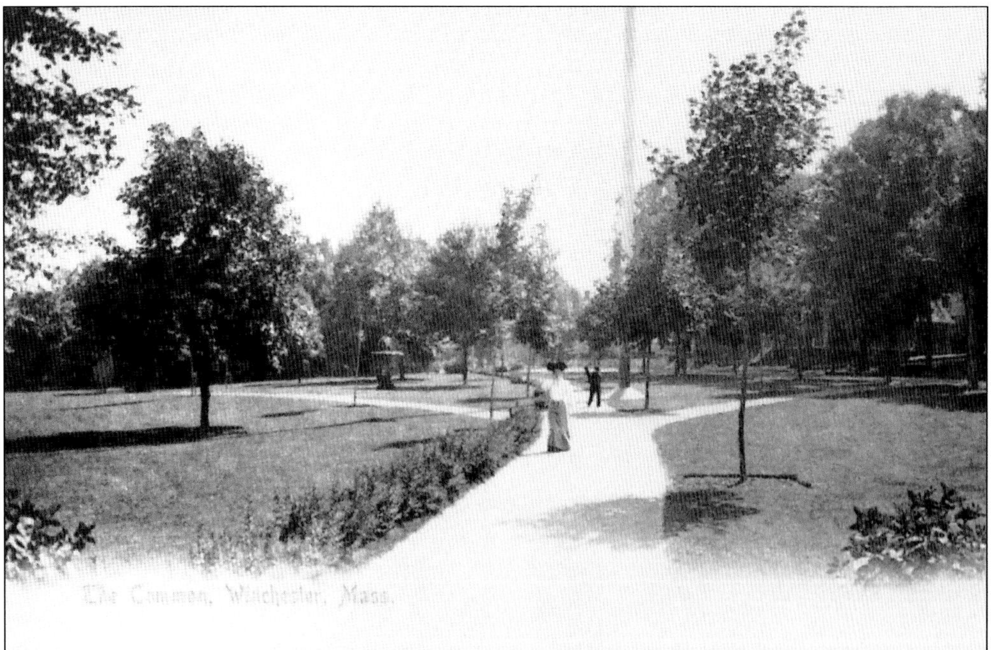

The common, Winchester, *c.* 1910. Winchester has one of the most beautiful town centers around.

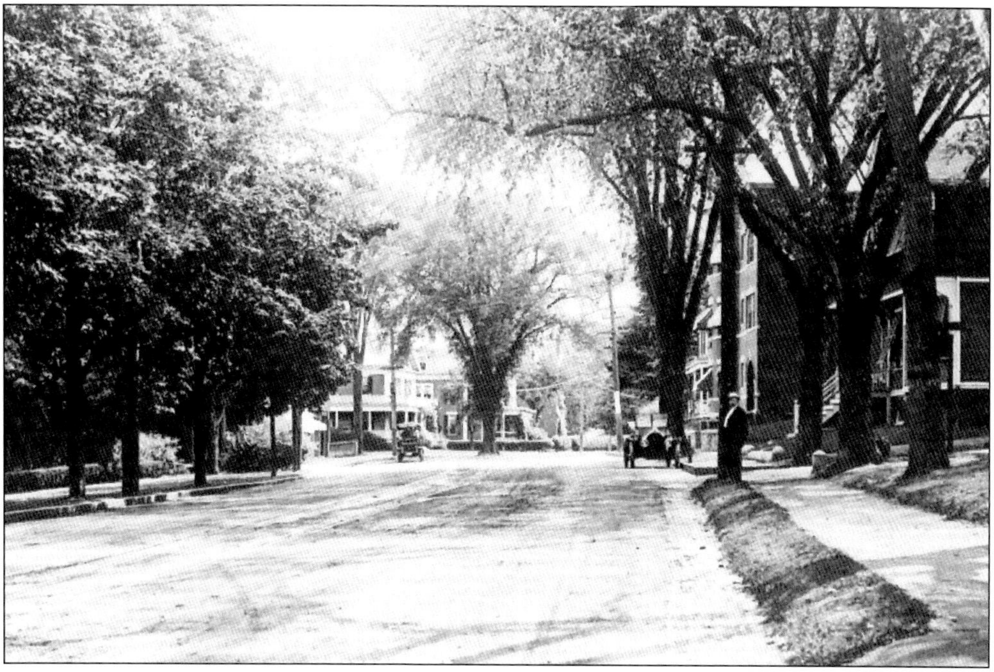

Church Street, Winchester, with elm trees, looking toward Waterfield Road, *c.* 1910.

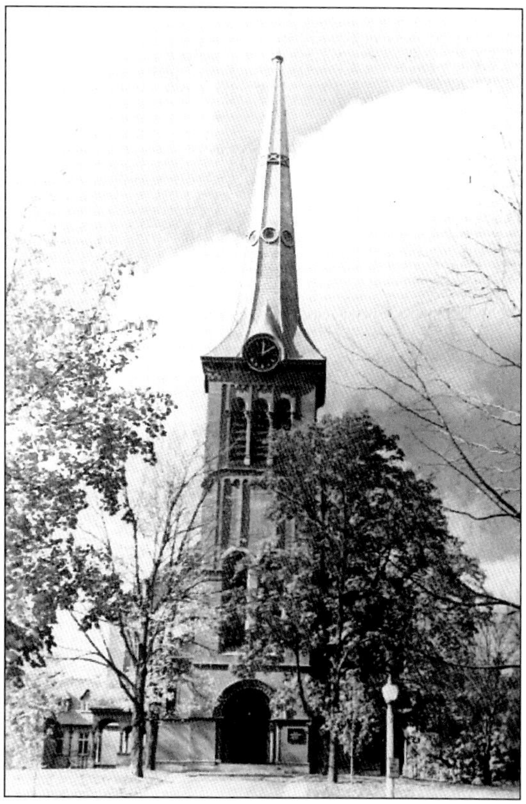

The First Congregational Church in Winchester. It is the oldest religious body in the town, formed in 1840.

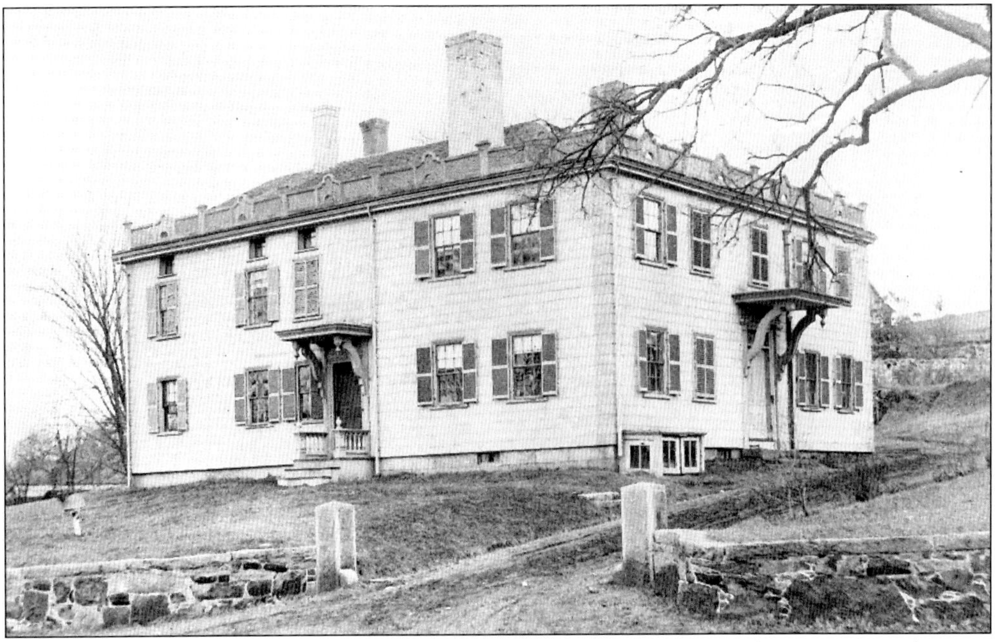

Black Horse Tavern in 1886. It was built about 1724 and was torn down in 1892 because it began to deteriorate. This was the location of meetings at the start of the Revolutionary War and Shay's Rebellion. It was on the main stage line from Boston to Portland, Maine. Built by William Richardson, it later passed into ownership (for a time) of the Wyman and Symmes families.

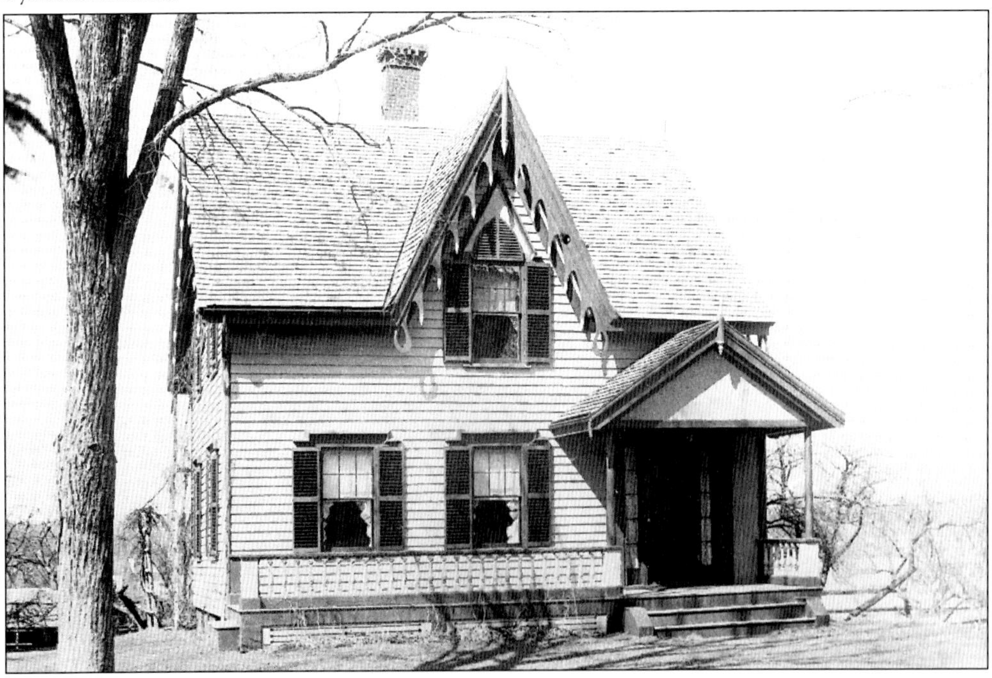

The S.B. White house at 8 Stevens Street, later owned by George Cooke. Samuel B. White, one of the earliest shopkeepers in what became Winchester, was active in the move to leave Woburn and was town treasurer for a time.

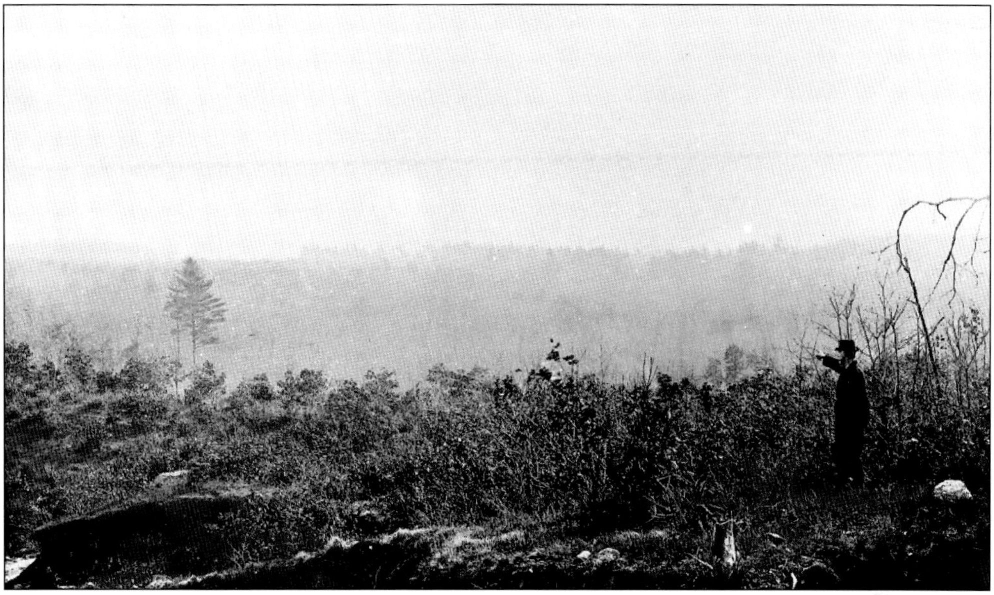

The Middlesex Fells in Winchester, November 23, 1893. Much of the beautiful wooded area was taken over by the Metropolitan Park Commission, assuring its preservation. It also included areas in neighboring communities, sharing its beauties.

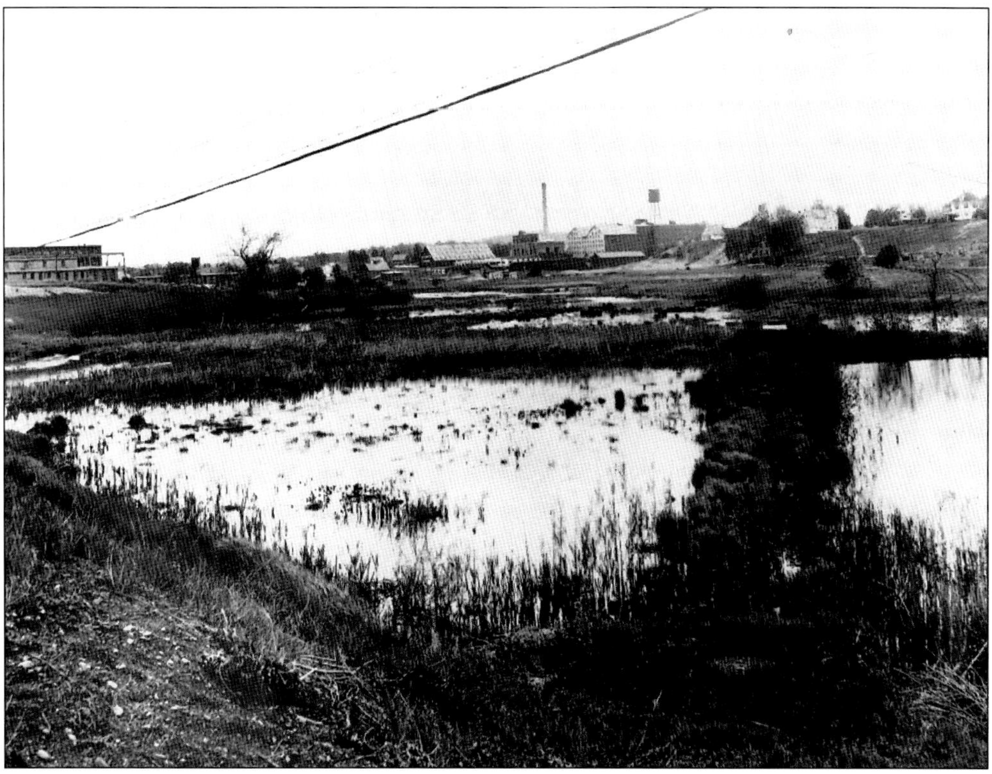

The Beggs and Cobb Tannery in Winchester closed in 1957 and burned in Winchester's largest fire ever in September 1959. That fire could have symbolized Winchester's shift away from industries like tanneries in the mid-twentieth century.

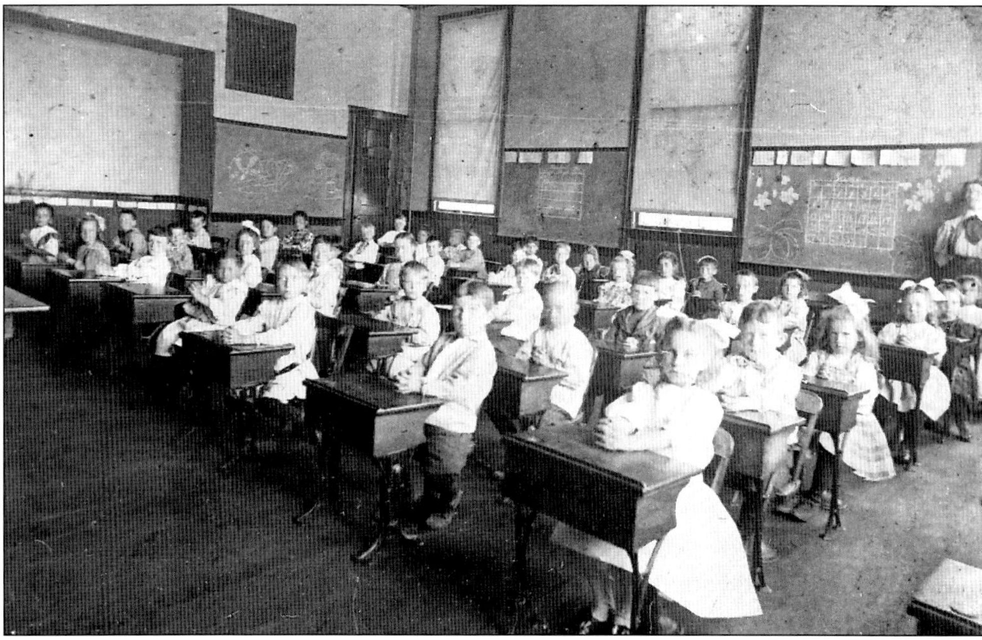

A Chapin School class in the 1900s. The quality of the town's educational system teaching, among other things, an appreciation of beauty, helps explain how the town has been able to preserve a good deal of green space.

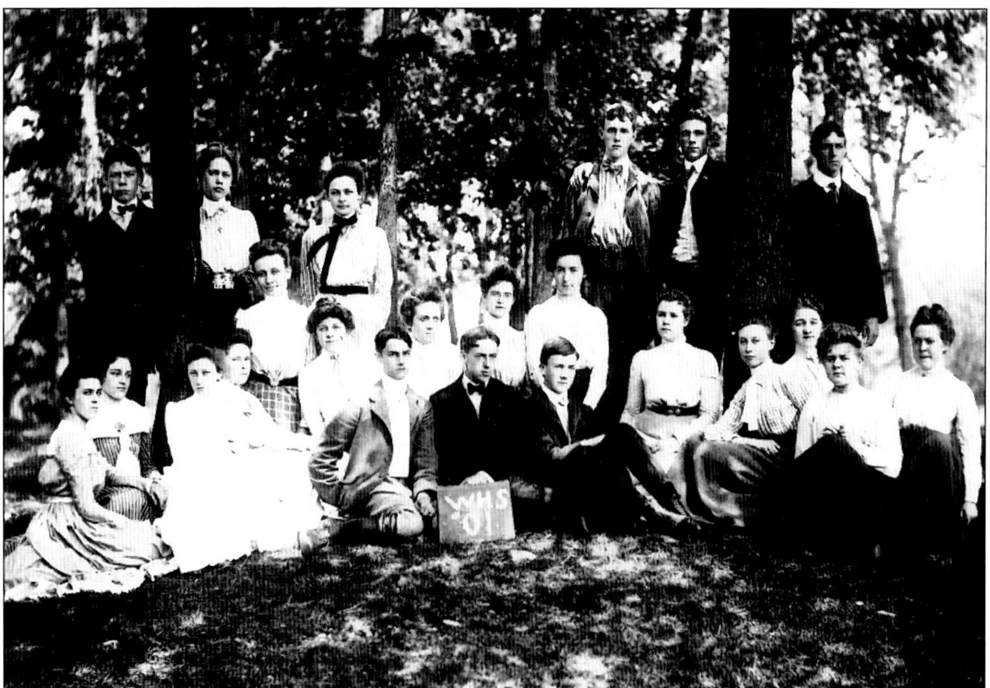

The Winchester High Class of 1901 at its 10th reunion held June 26, 1911, at the home of Edna Howes.

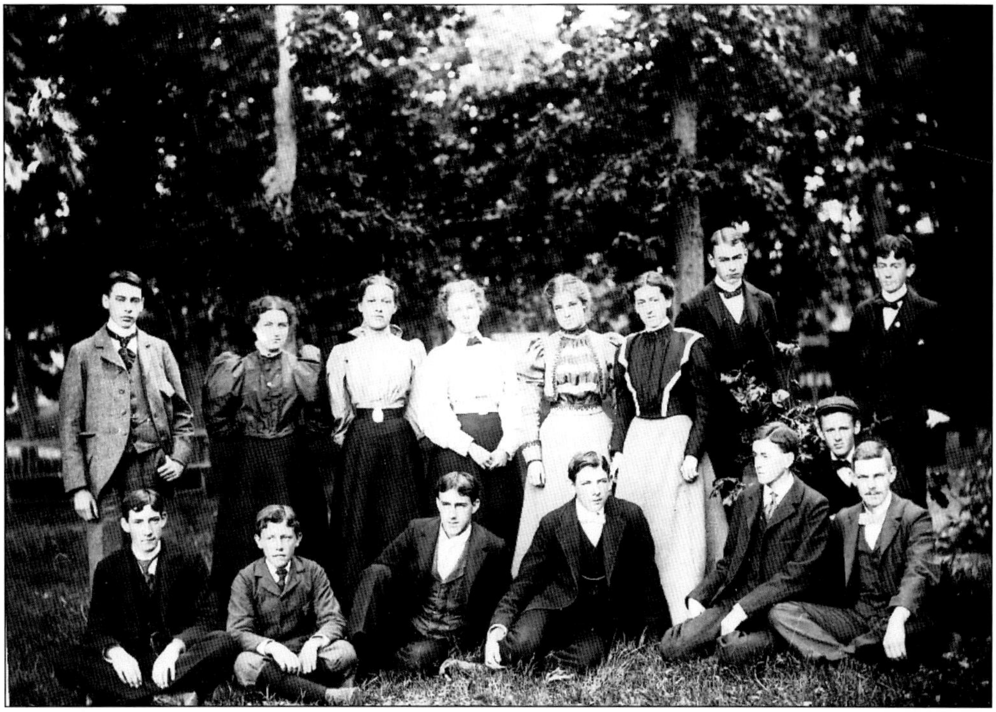

The Winchester High Class of 1897. Beautiful classes full of beautiful people were the rule.

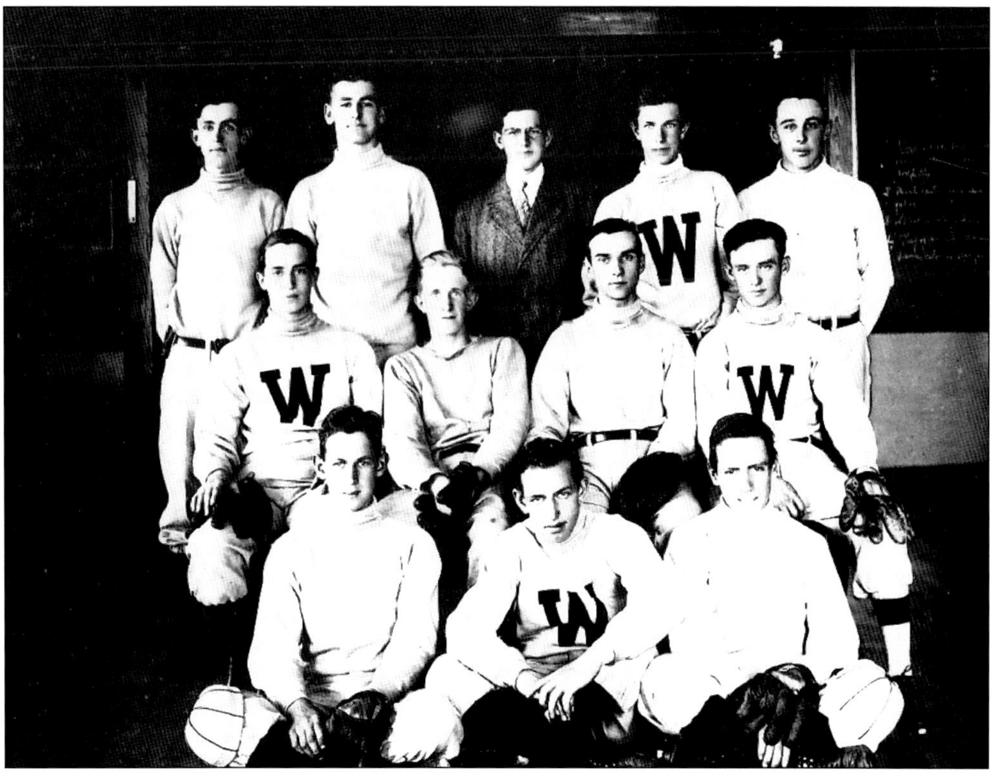

The 1910 Winchester High baseball team.

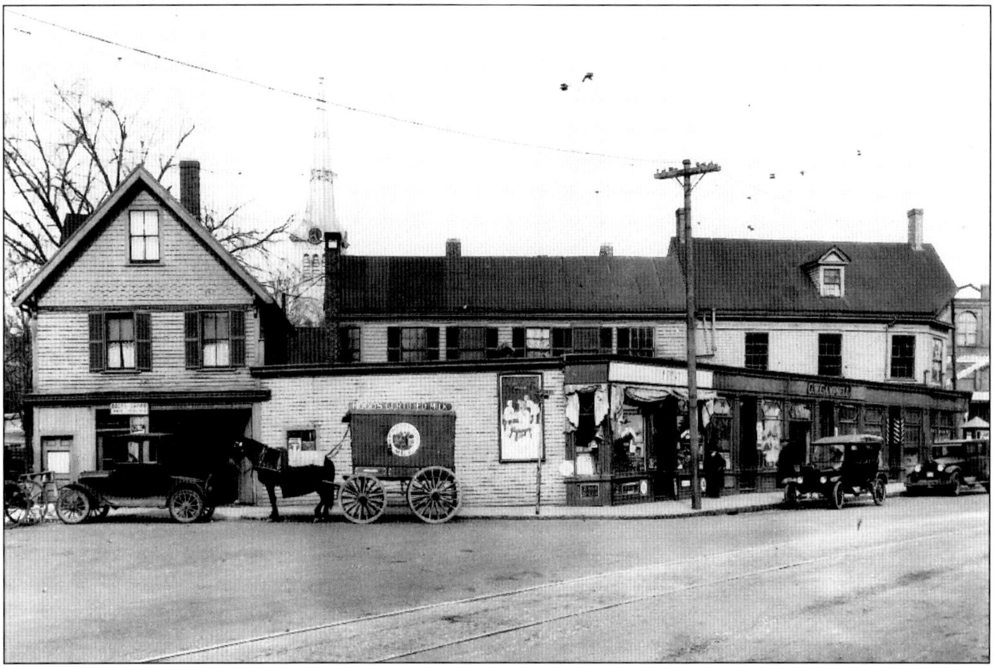

A block of stores at the corner of Main and Thompson Streets in the 1910s. G.W. Campbell and a Hood's milk wagon are in the scene.

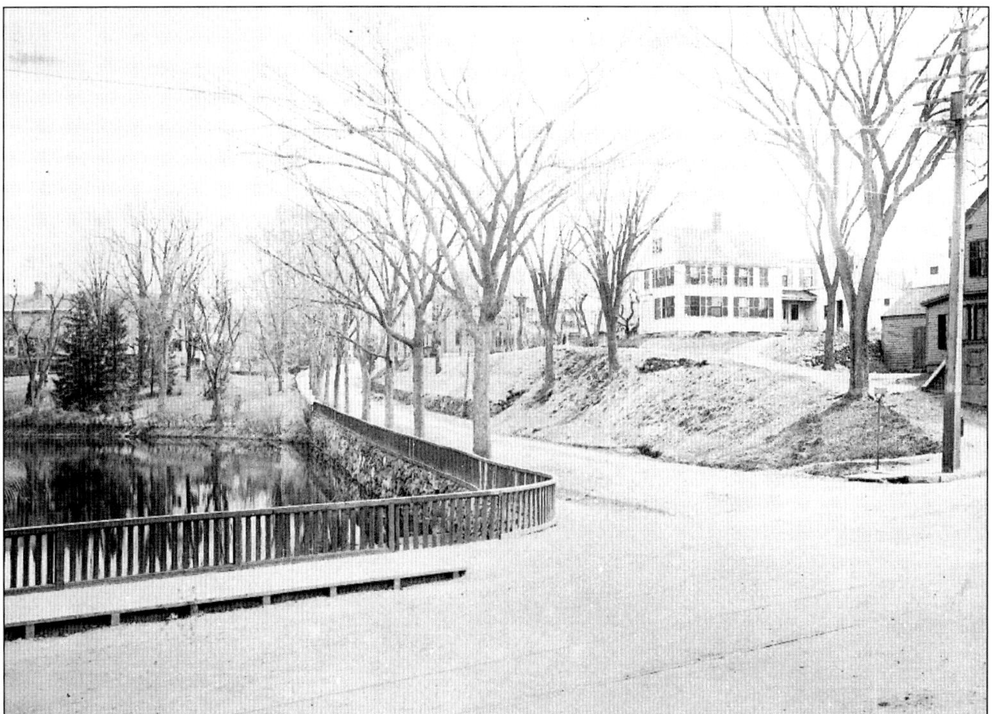

Walnut Street (Mystic Valley Parkway), site of the present Lincoln School, the former Winchester High School.

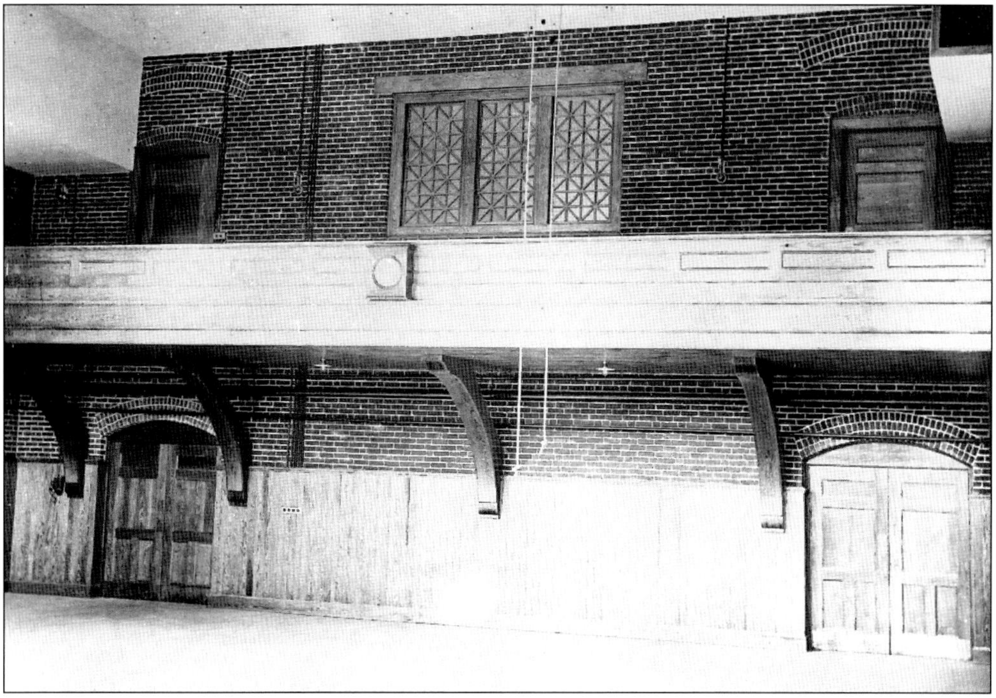

The Winchester High School gym in 1904.

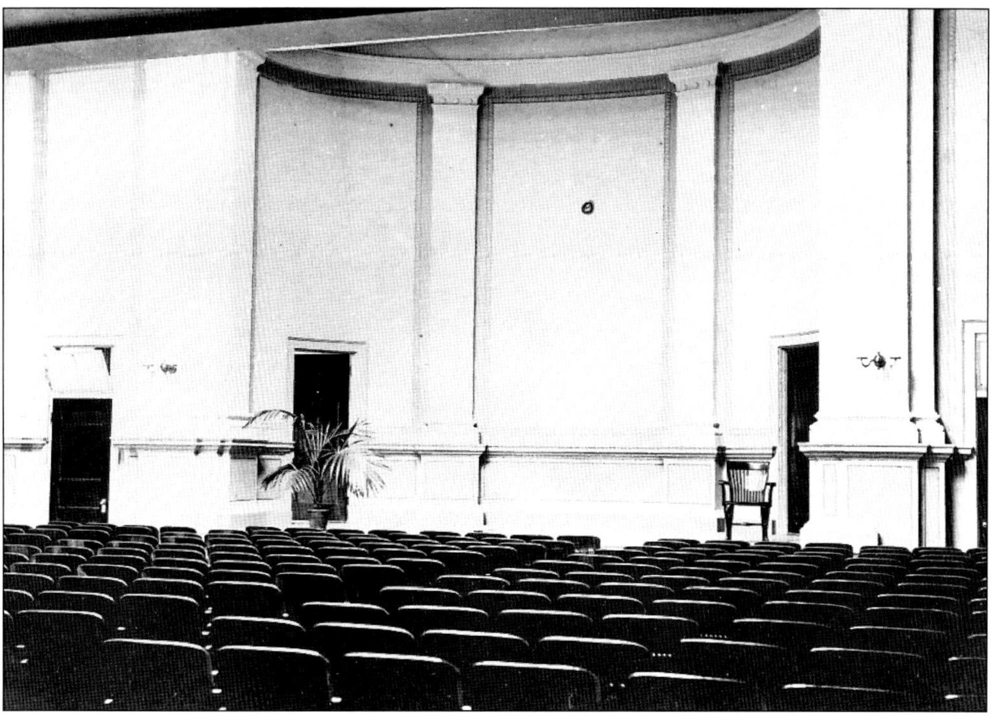

The Winchester High assembly hall, 1904.

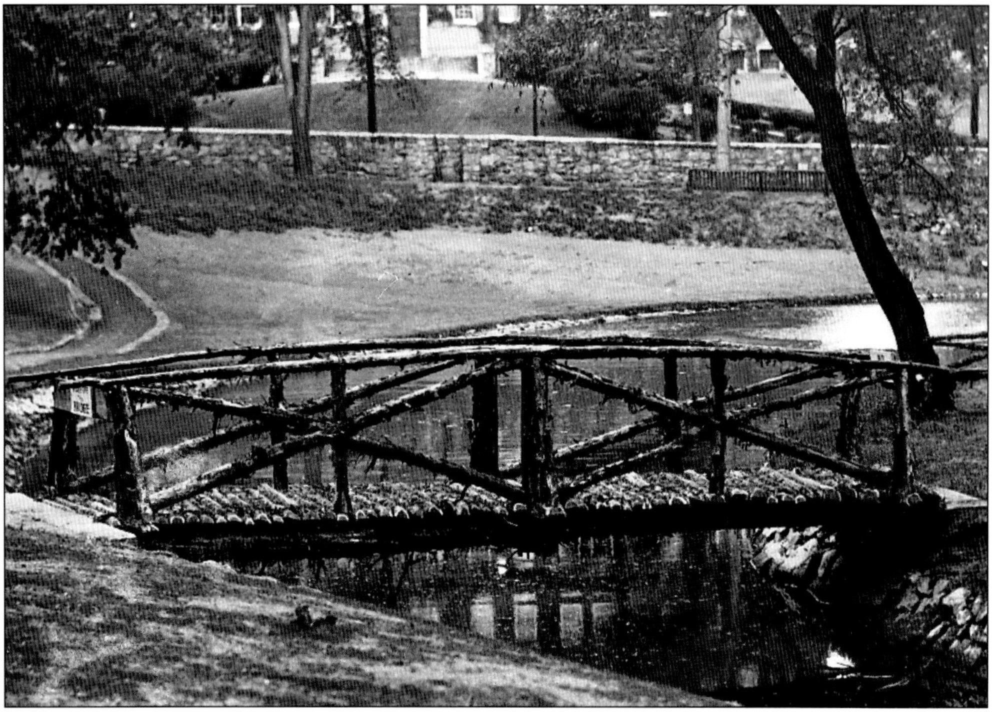

The old bridge over the Aberjona River. The area is better looking now.

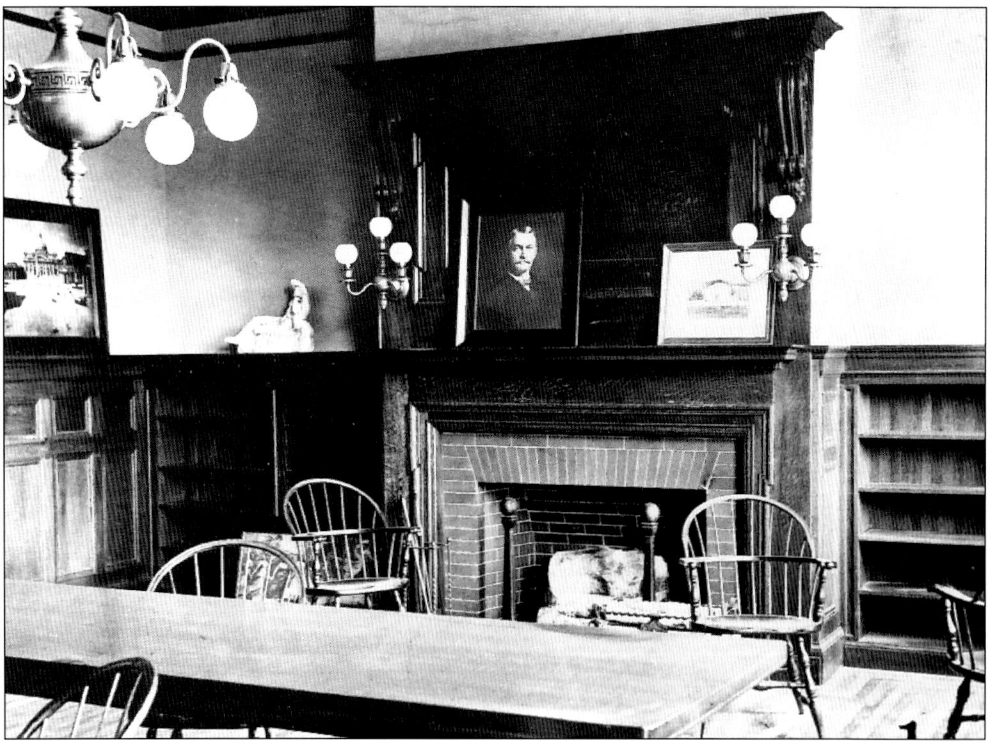

The Winchester High library in 1924 with a portrait of Lewis Parkhurst, who gave much money to that library.

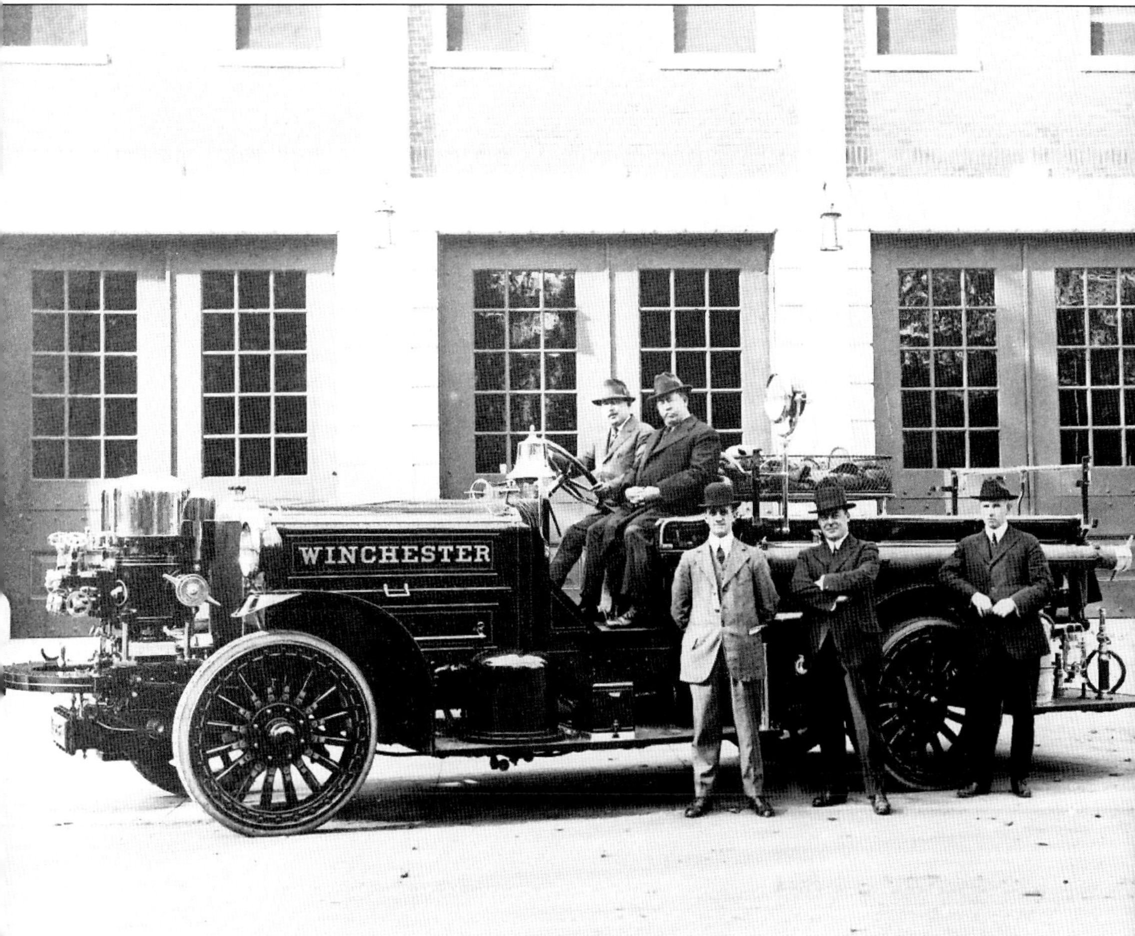

A 1915 Andrews Fox pumper, the first pumper the Winchester Fire Department ever had. From left to right are: (seated) Frederick Kerr (the driver) and Charles E. Kendall; (standing) George T. Davidson, Maurice E. Brown, and Harry C. Sanborn.

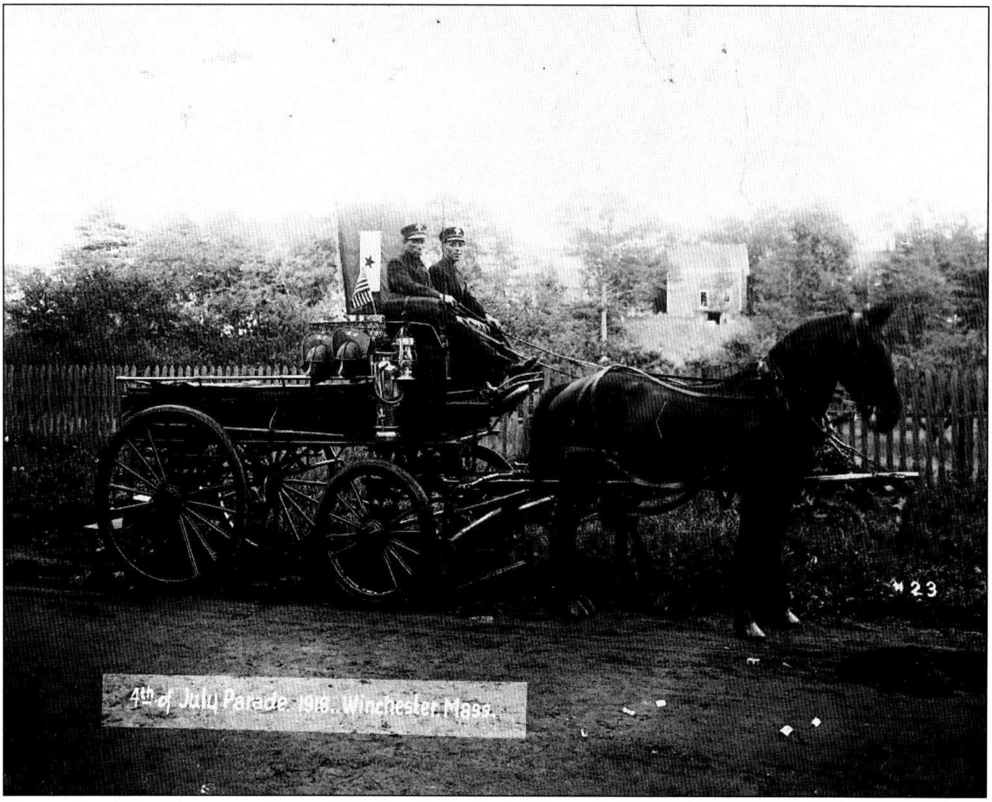

Hose #3, of the Swanton Street Fire Station, in the Winchester Fourth of July parade in 1918.

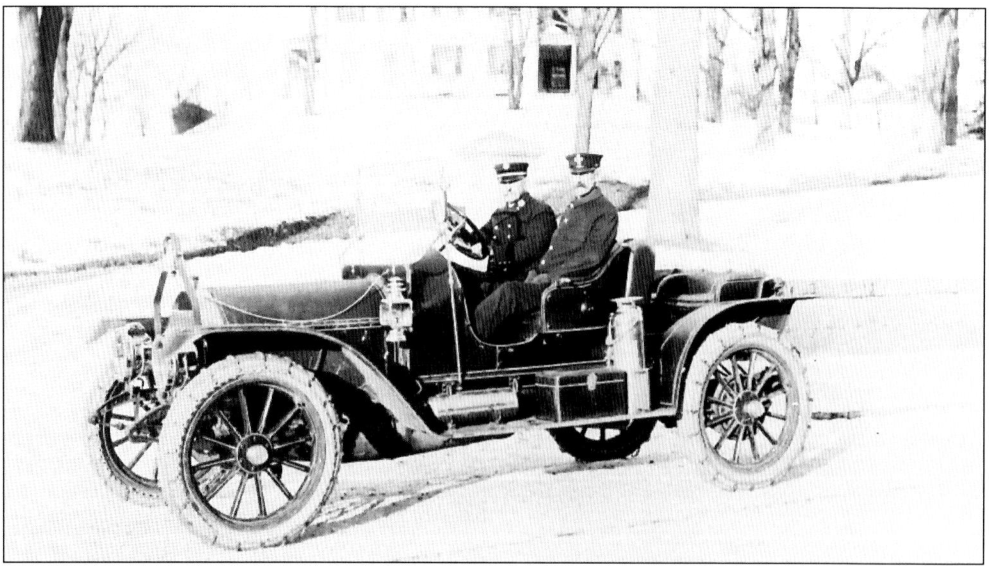
Fire Chief David H. DeCourcy (left) and Assistant Chief John McCarthy in the first chief's car in front of 9 Oak Street, the Skillings' Estate, during the early 1920s.

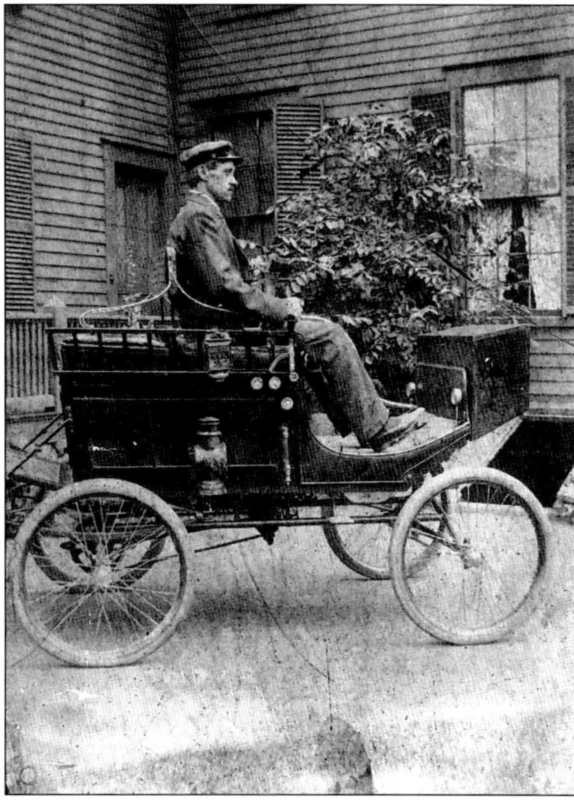

One of the first cars in Winchester, 1903.

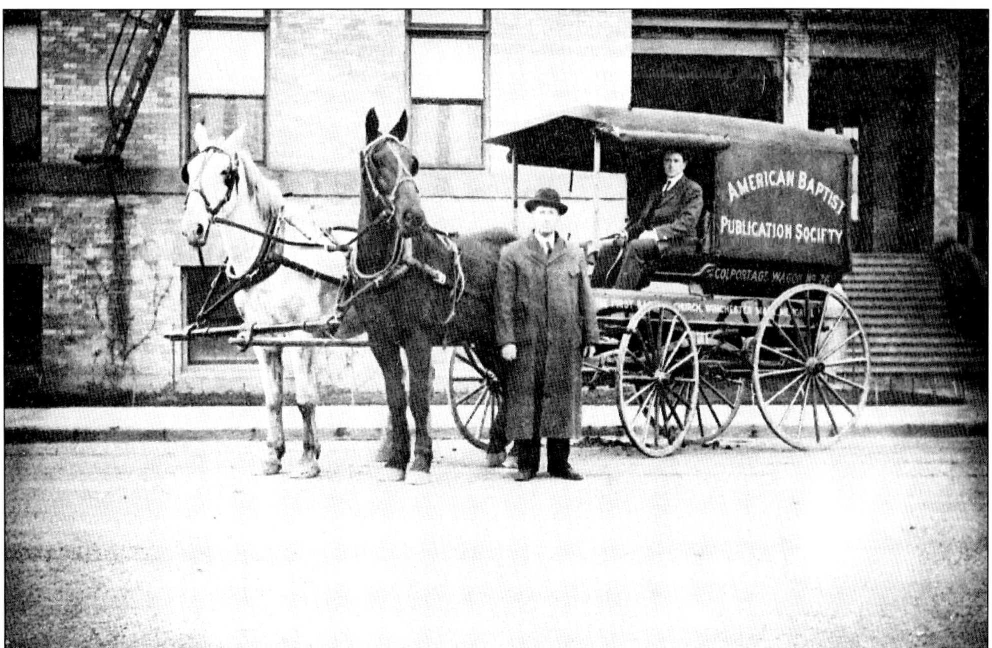

Colportage Wagon #76 in the 1900s. It was from the American Baptist Publication Society and was sponsored by the First Baptist Church in Winchester.

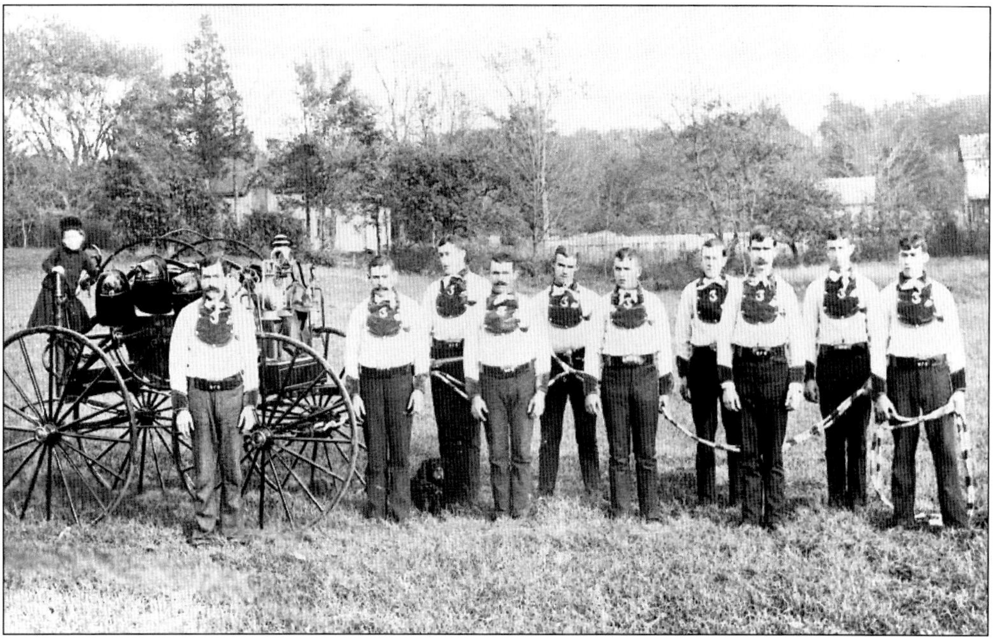

Excelsior Hose #3 of the Swanton Street Fire Station in 1889, taken on Washington Street between Park Avenue and Park Road. The Sanborn Estate (Chase and Sanborn Coffee) is in the left background.

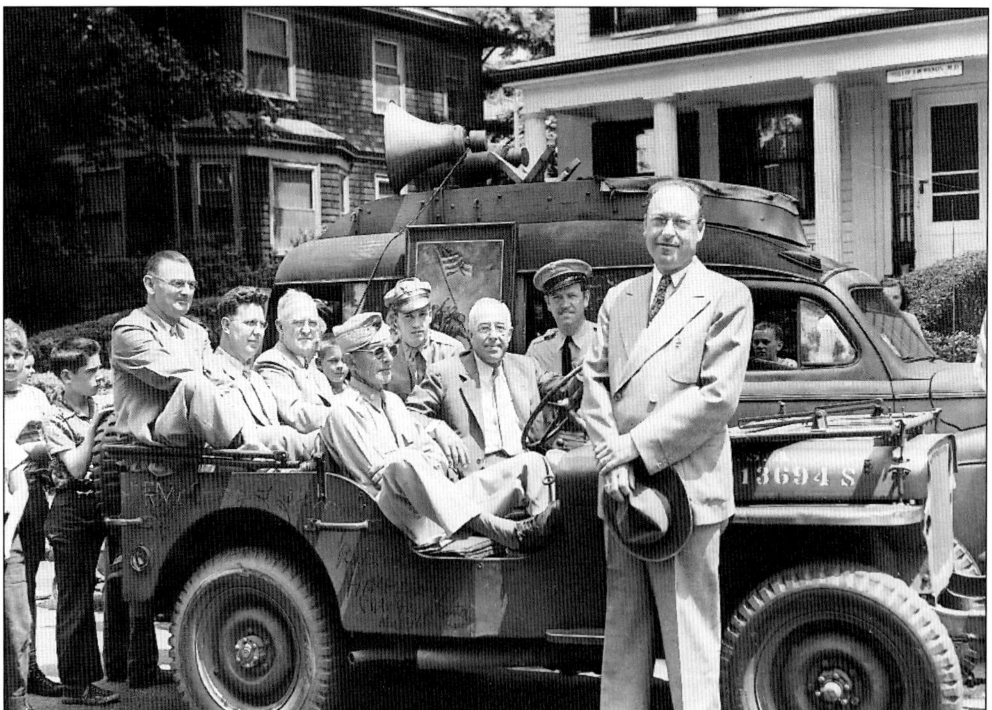

World War II was on as was a War Bond drive. Among the people shown here are Ralph Bonnell Sr. (standing at right), Pat Foley (left, seated in the back of the Jeep), and Maurice Bird (a town official).

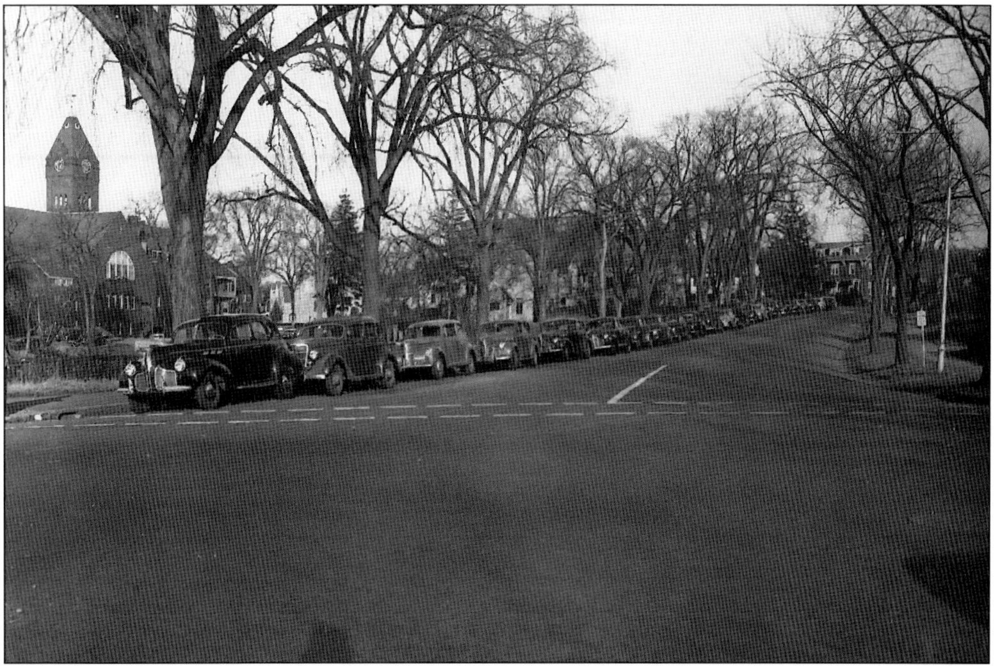

November 16, 1946, was a day when Winchester's police department took pictures of parking in the town. This is parallel parking next to the mill pond behind town hall.

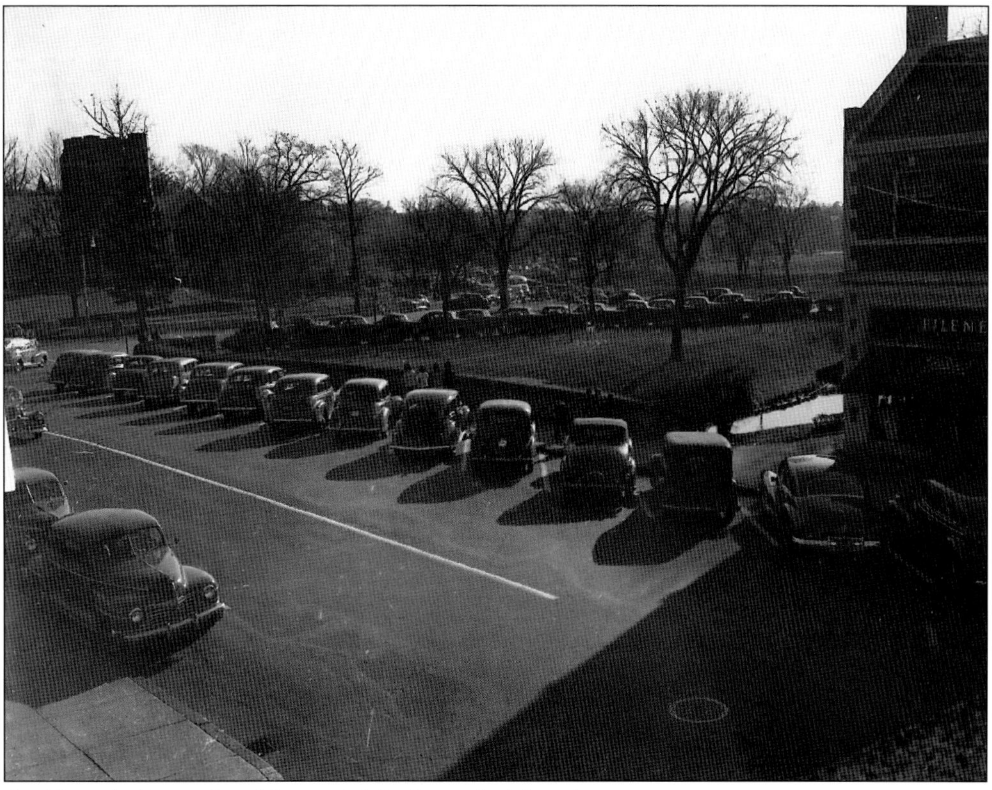

And here is diagonal parking on Main Street by Filene's.

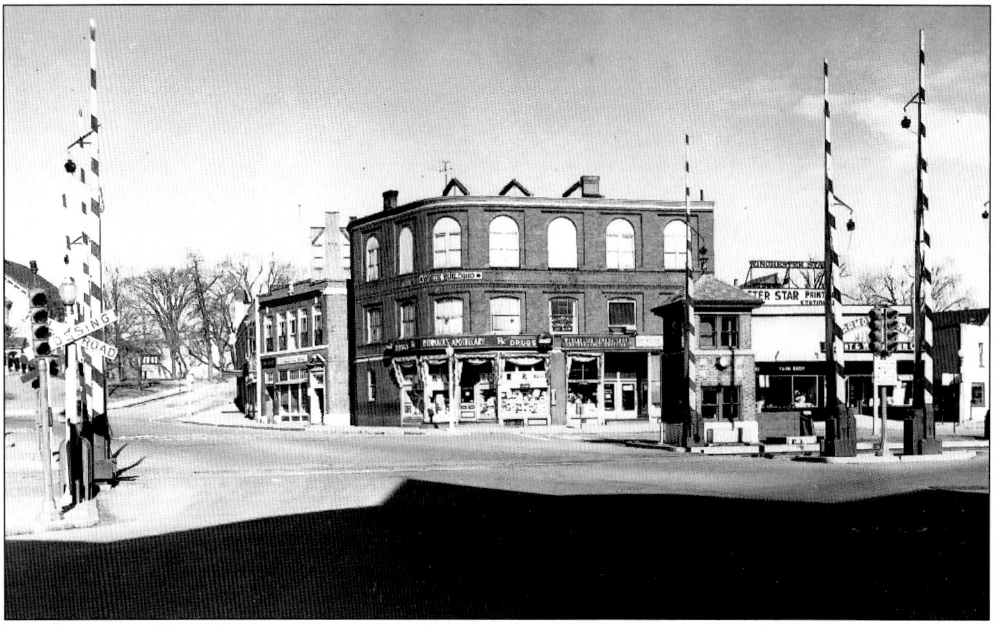

Winchester Center in the 1940s with the famous and controversial railroad crossing. The White Building behind the crossing had three stories then; it now has two.

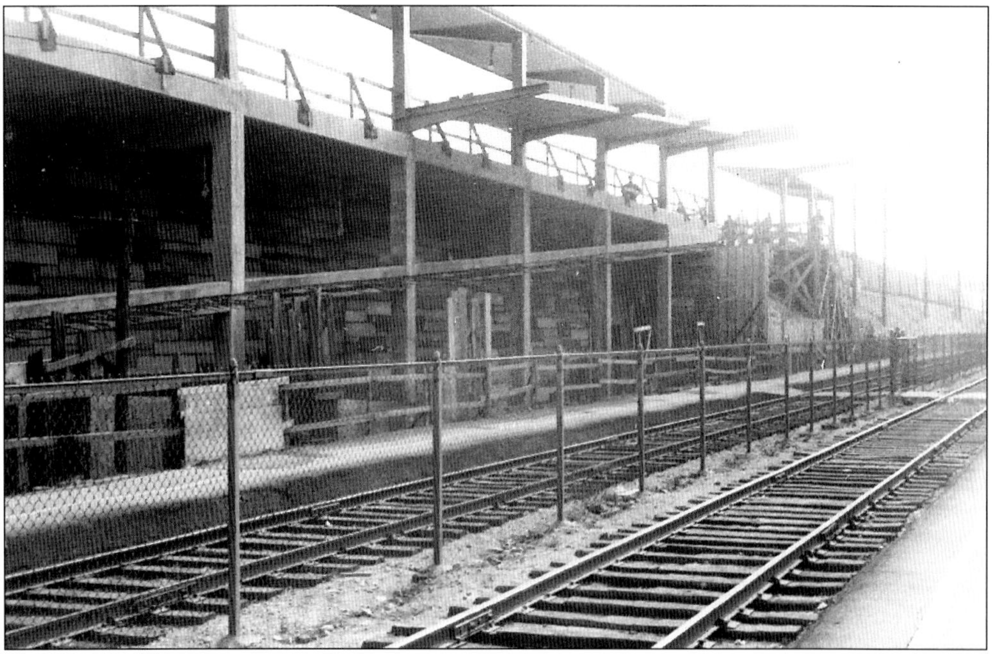

The temporary tracks (later torn up) and the new tracks (in the rear), *c.* 1956, when the new overpass was dedicated and the railroad crossing eliminated. Harry Chefalo, a selectman at the time, says selectmen made a deal with the Massachusetts commissioner of public works. The commissioner had a $500 million bond issue he wanted passed by the legislature. Harris Richardson of Winchester was the president of the senate. The commissioner said he'd include $5 million for the overpass in the bond issue if selectmen would help in getting Richardson to support the entire issue. That's the way it worked out.

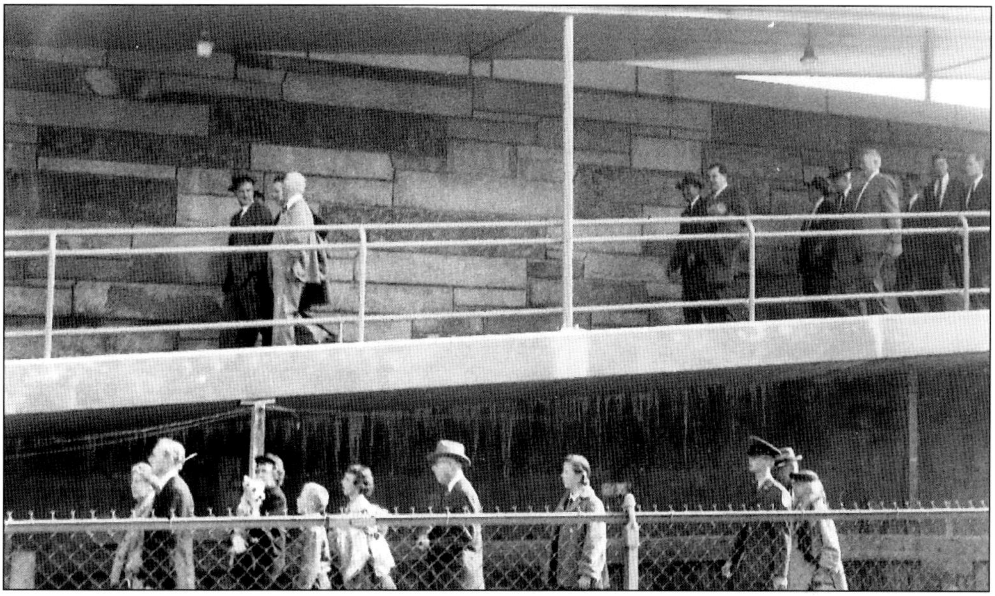

People walking to the dedication of the new railroad overpass in 1956. Winchester Center has become much safer as a result of the overpass and also looks better.

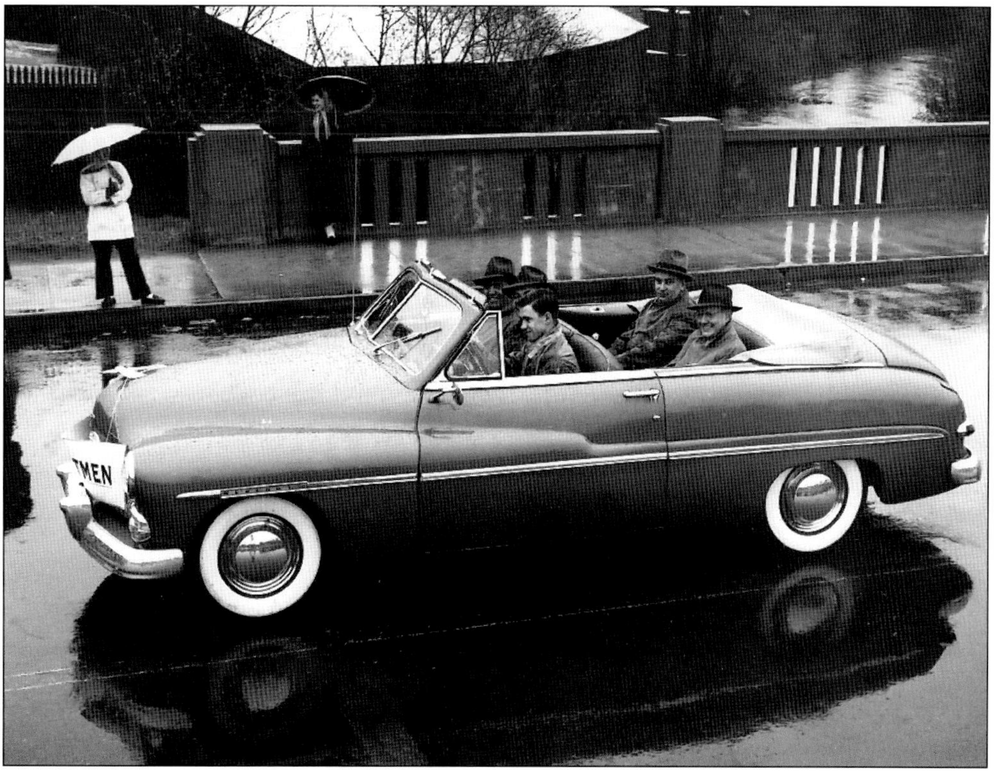

Four Winchester selectmen and their driver during the 1950 centennial parade, the largest parade in Winchester history, with buckets of rain. From left to right are: (front) Harry Chefalo, Harrison Lyman, and Ralph (Bunny) Bonnell Jr. (driver); (back) Nick Fitzgerald and Richard Cunningham.

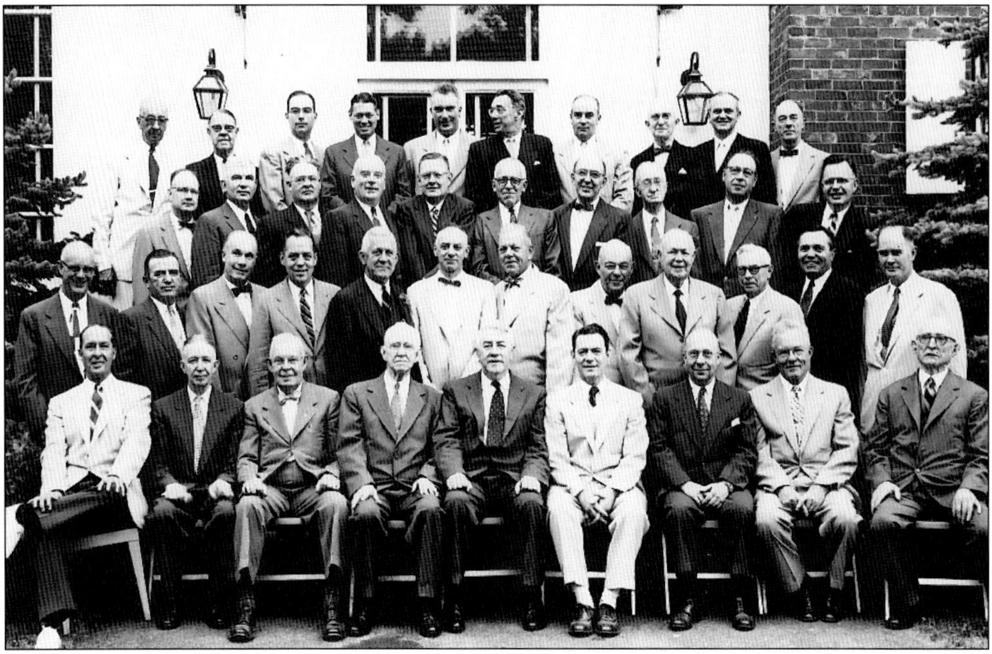

Most of Winchester's living selectmen, past and present, in May 1955. Among those in this photograph are: (front row, sixth from left) James Scott; (middle row, left to right) Ernest Dade, John Cullen, unknown, Bill Spears, unknown, Franklin Lane, Allan Wilde, Harry Chefalo, and Vincent Farnsworth; (third row, fourth from left) William Cusack; (back row, fourth from left) Jim Dwinell.

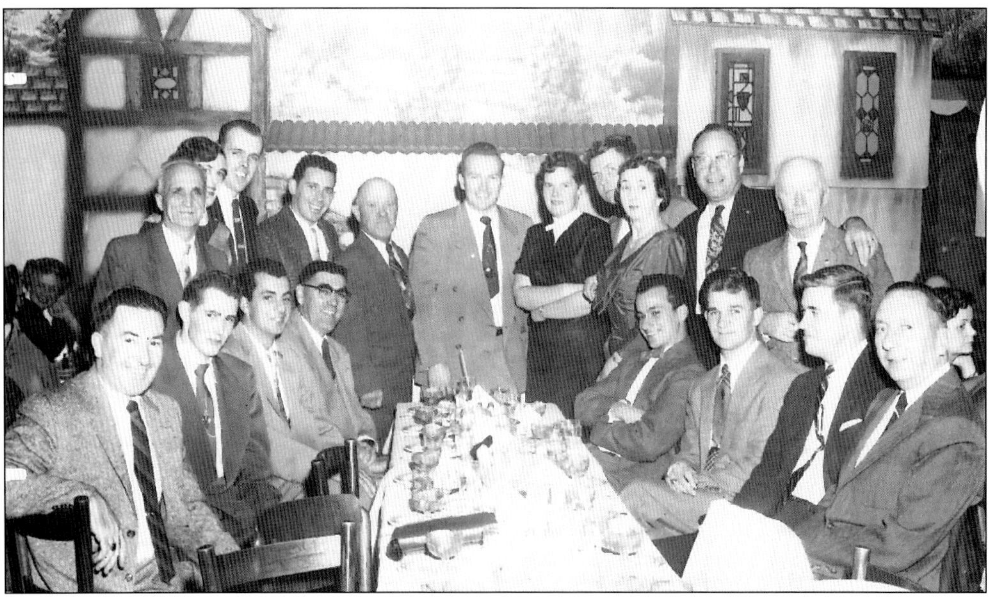

At a Christmas party for Bonnell Ford at Blinstrub's in Boston in the 1950s are, from left to right: (front) Ken Donaghy, Billy Reynolds, Frank Gillotti, Dan White, John Gillotti, Bob Hietz, and Ralph Bonnell Jr.; (back) Ellery McKall, Barbara Callahan, Gil Reynolds, Ronnie Purcell, Walter Reardon, John McCallum, Barbara Ficicello, Ivan ?, Gertrude Vallely, Ralph Bonnell Sr., and Pete Ryerson.

Yes, it was possible to get new cars during World War II. A shipment of station wagons arrives at Bonnell Motors in Winchester.

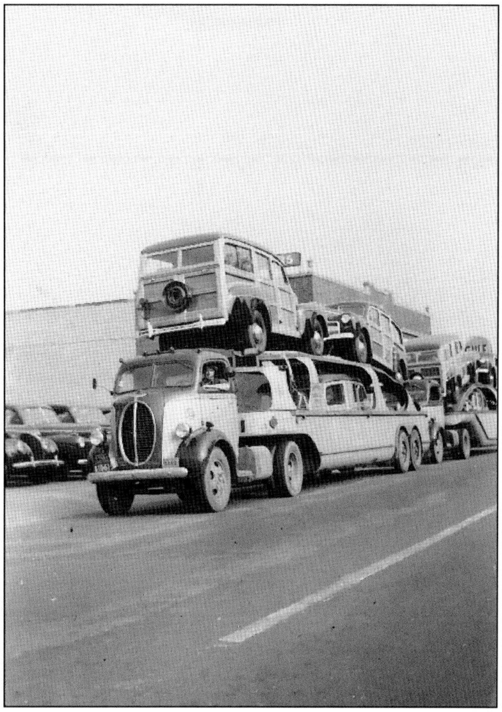

The staff of Bonnell Ford, Winchester, c. 1937. From left to right are Ralph Bonnell Sr., Mary McGurn, Ed McDonald, Charles Bonnell, Jack Stokes, Vincent Carroll, Ellery McKiel, Pete Ryerson, and Cecil Porter, with nine unknown people and William Richardson on the right end.

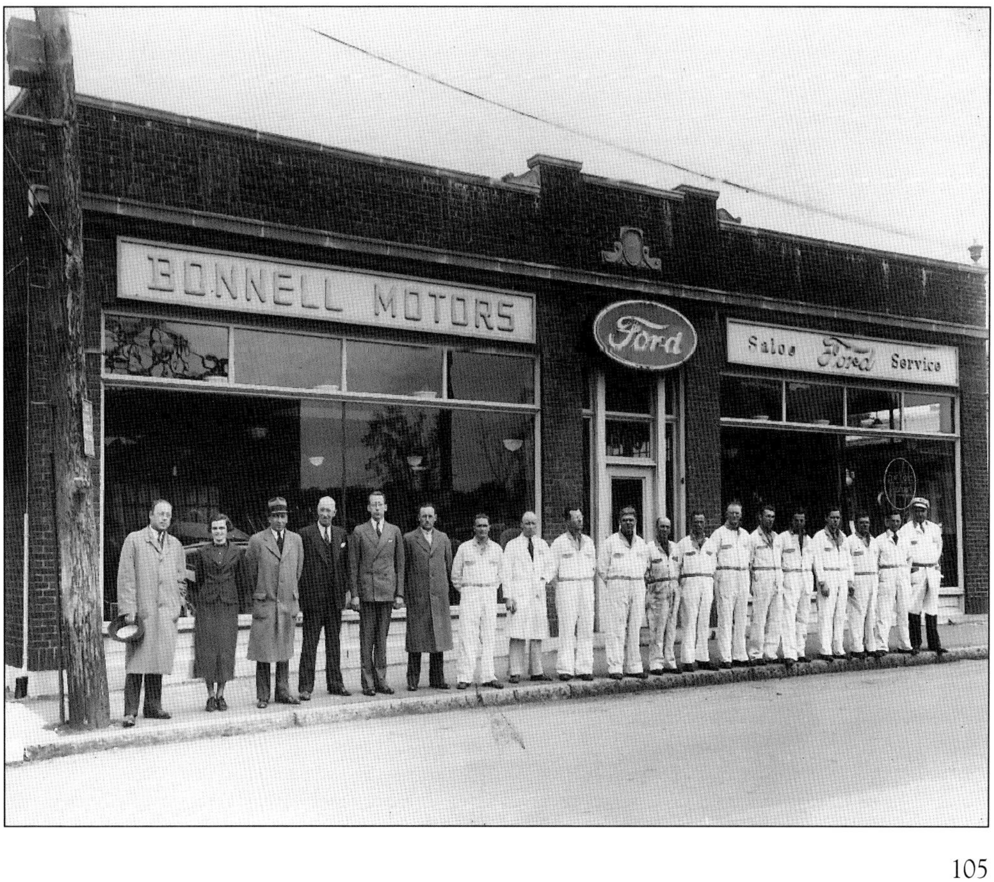

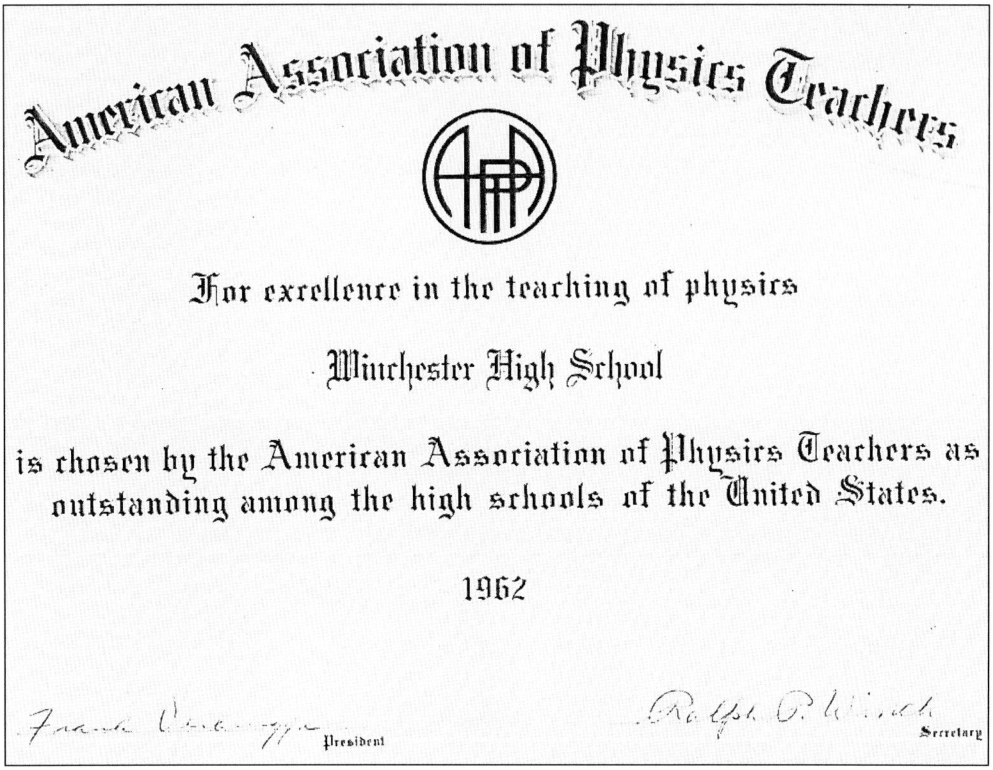

American Association of Physics Teachers

For excellence in the teaching of physics

Winchester High School

is chosen by the American Association of Physics Teachers as outstanding among the high schools of the United States.

1962

President

Secretary

The strong educational system of Winchester does get honors. This is a physics award received by Winchester High School in 1962. Francis X. Finigan was the teacher involved.

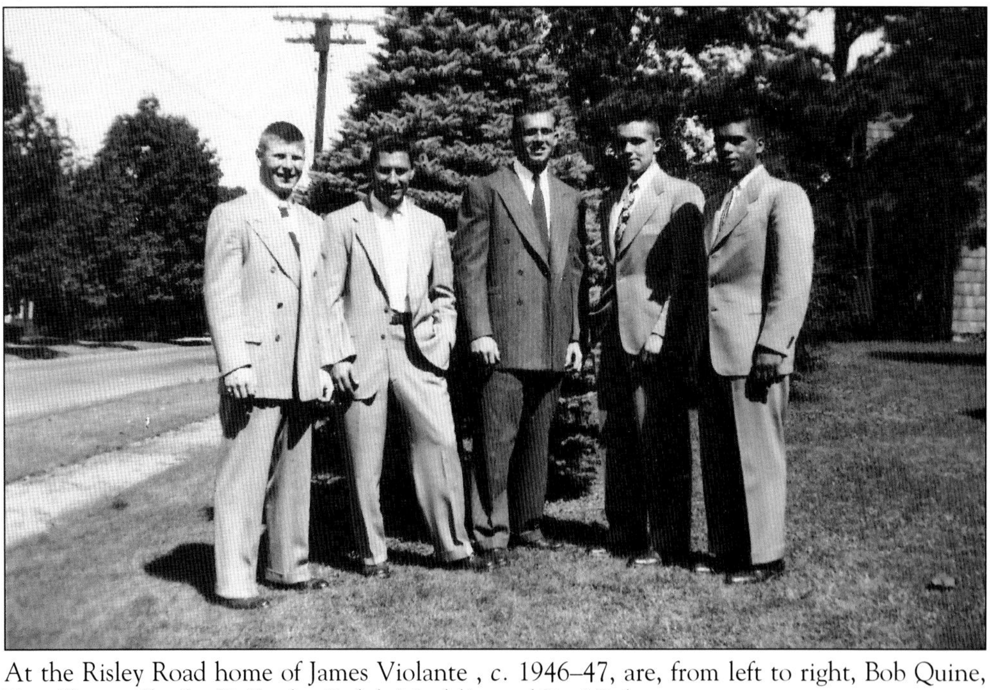

At the Risley Road home of James Violante , c. 1946–47, are, from left to right, Bob Quine, Tom Derro, Charles D. Roche, Ralph Meuhlig, and Jim Violante.

Six

Doers and Shakers

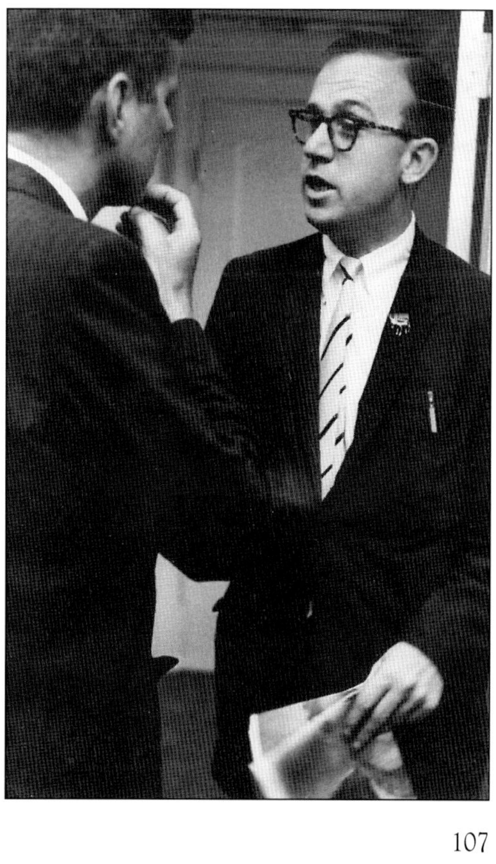

Charles D. (Chucker) Roche, right, of Winchester, makes a point with John F. Kennedy during the 1960 presidential campaign won by Kennedy. Roche became deputy chairman of the Democratic National Committee in 1961, the highest ranking national Democratic position ever reached by someone from Winchester. He later became a legislative aide to President Lyndon B. Johnson, president of the Freight Forwarders Institute in Washington, and a full-time political consultant.

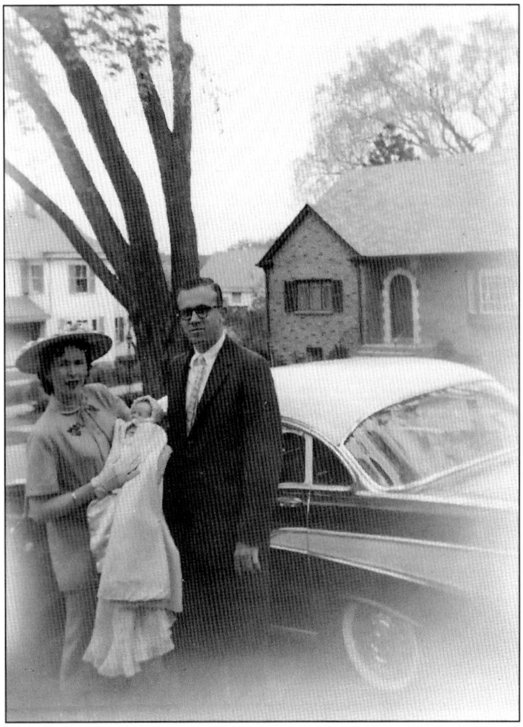

Charles D. Roche with his wife Kathy and their first born child. The couple eventually had nine children.

Bob Quine (right) and his father Francis (Frank) Quine in the mid-1950s. Bob was a top General Motors official in New England. His father was national sales manager for the E.L. Lebaron Foundry Co., Inc., of Brockton, Massachusetts, from 1932 to 1964.

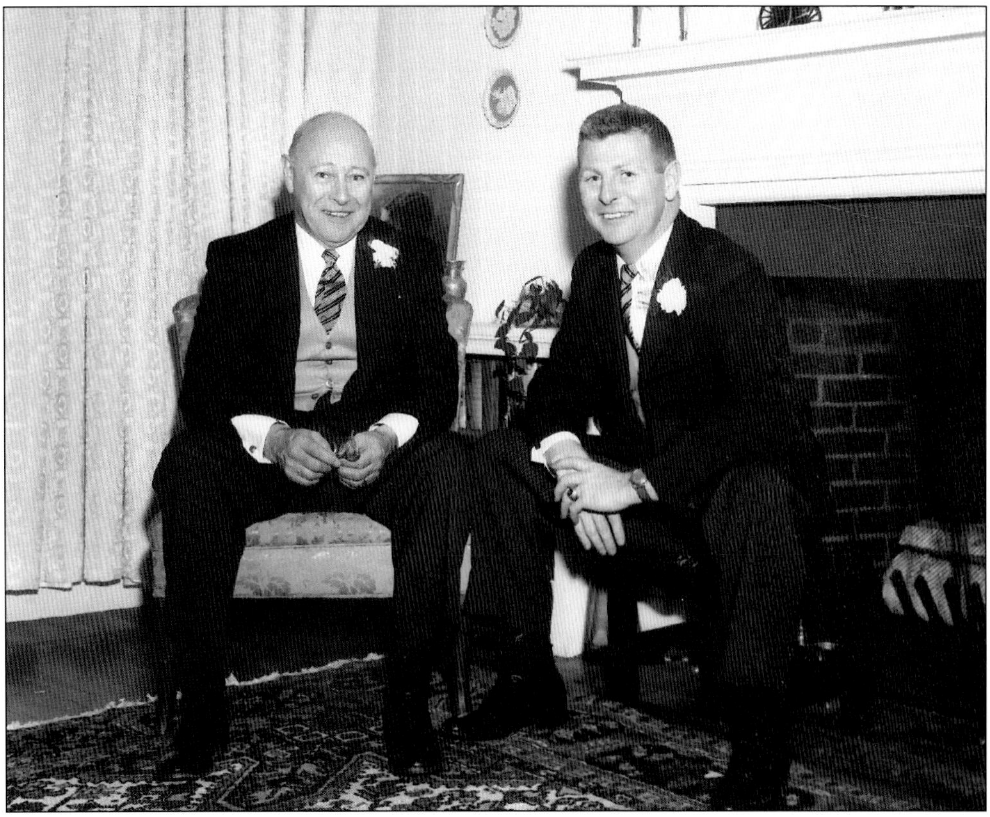

Louis Goddu, born October 1, 1837, probably in the province of Quebec in Canada but possibly in France. Goddu, who came to Winchester from St. Cesaire, Quebec, eventually patented about three hundred inventions, one of them the staple. He died June 18, 1917, in Winchester and lived most of his life there at 13 Madison Avenue.

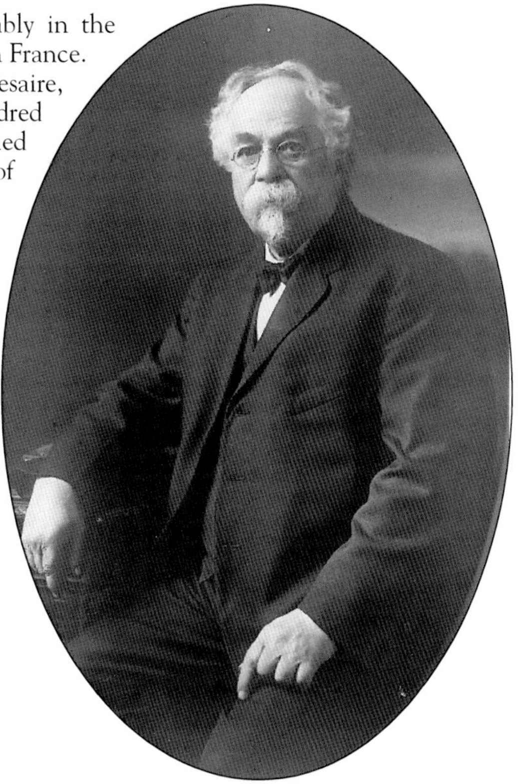

The Louis Goddu Shop at 13 Madison Avenue, Winchester, behind his home. On the left side is A. Van Wagener, one of his people, and on the other side are William, Louis, Elwar, and George Goddu. Many of Goddu's inventions involved the shoe industry.

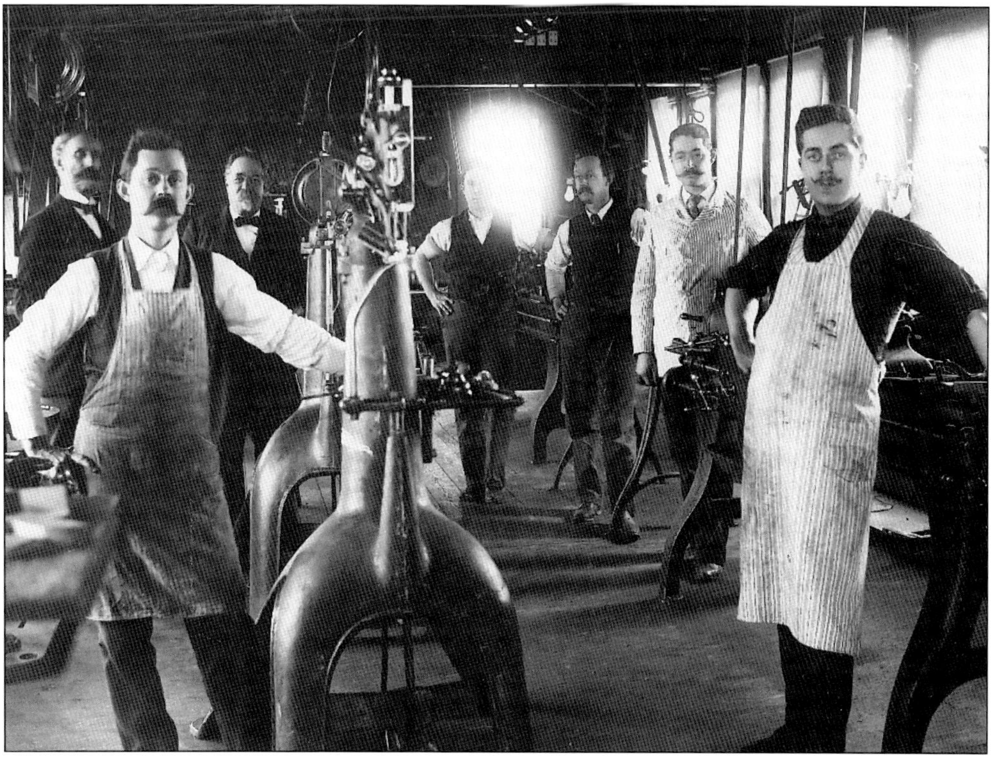

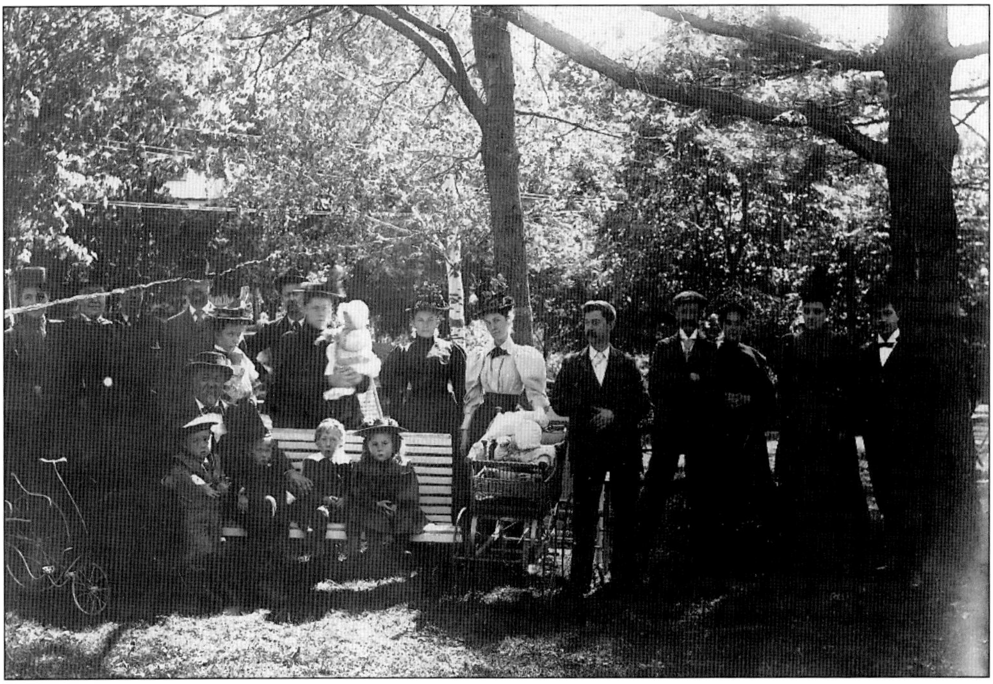

The Goddu family gathers in a grove across from the residence at 13 Madison Avenue in the 1890s. Among those pictured here are: (front row) Grandpa Louis (the inventor), Paul, Warren, Louis Jr. (trainer of many Winchester High athletic teams), Doris, and Ida with Ellen; (back row) Florence, Rose, Bill, Elwar, Della, Charlotte, Napoleon, Fred, Vienna, Irene, Isabel, and George. The inventor had a close-knit family and built homes for several of his relatives.

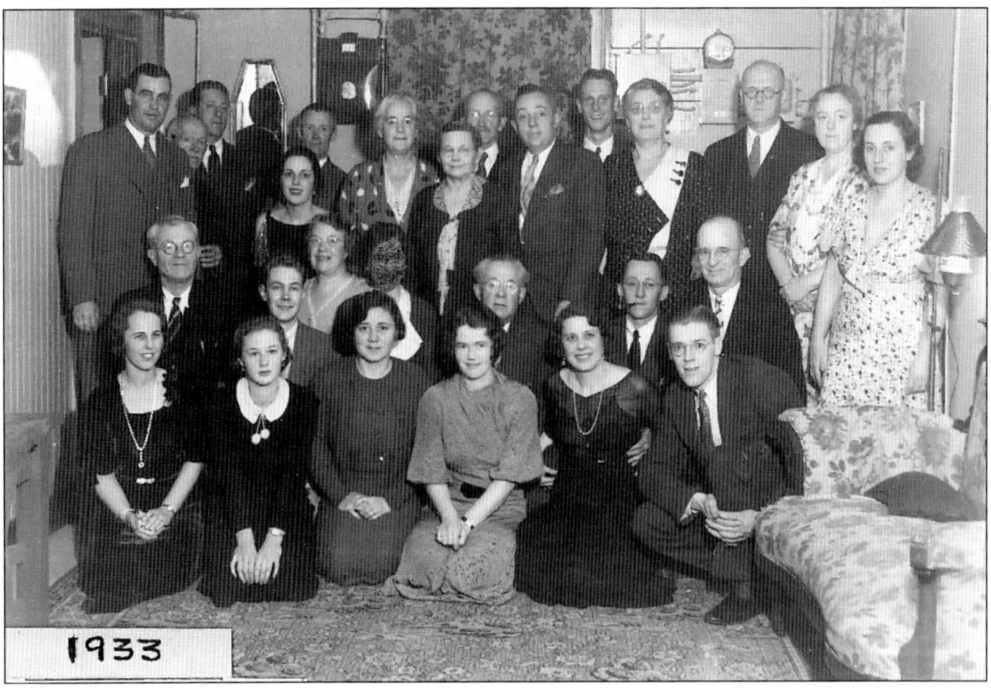

A Goddu family reunion November 11, 1933, at the residence.

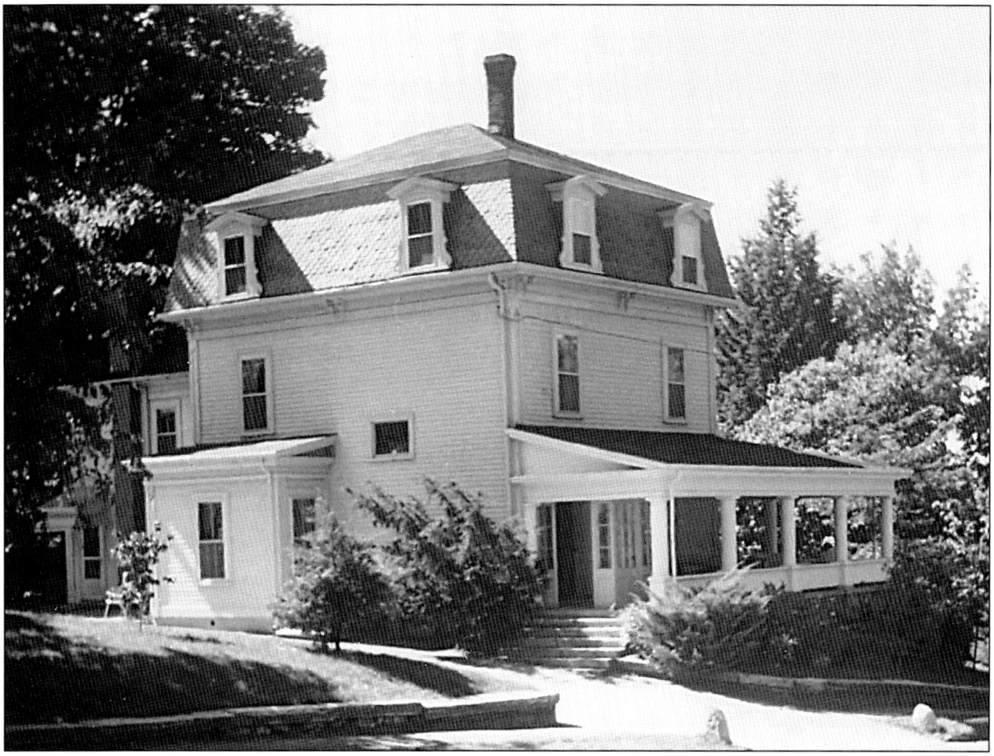

The residence at 13 Madison Avenue.

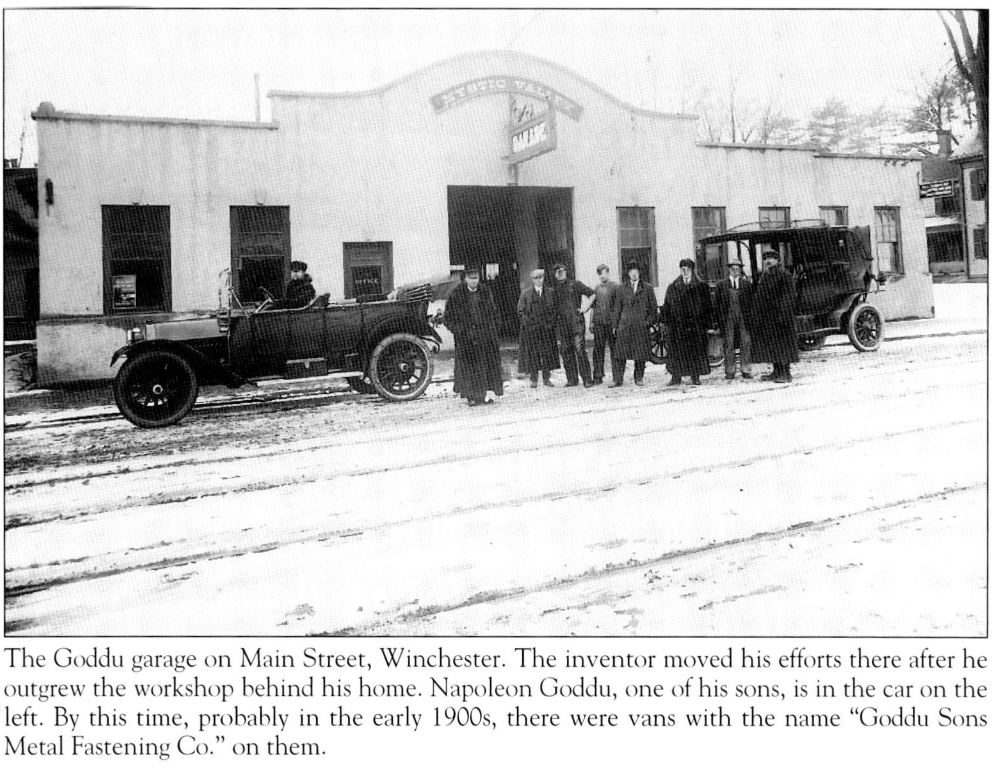

The Goddu garage on Main Street, Winchester. The inventor moved his efforts there after he outgrew the workshop behind his home. Napoleon Goddu, one of his sons, is in the car on the left. By this time, probably in the early 1900s, there were vans with the name "Goddu Sons Metal Fastening Co." on them.

Illustrated Catalogue

OF

THE GODDU SONS'

Complete

Metal Fastening System.

GODDU SONS'

METAL FASTENING COMPANY,

BOSTON, MASS.

The Goddu Sons' Metal Fastening Company had its own catalogue. Note the Boston, Massachusetts address. The company was actually located in Winchester, 7 miles from Boston.

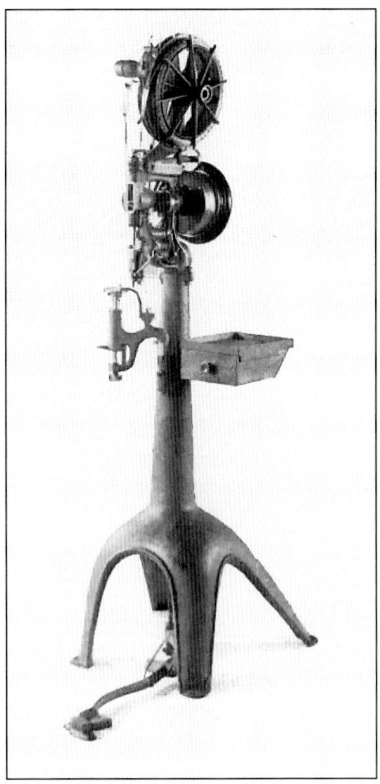

One of the more than two hundred inventions Louis Goddu provided for the shoe industry.

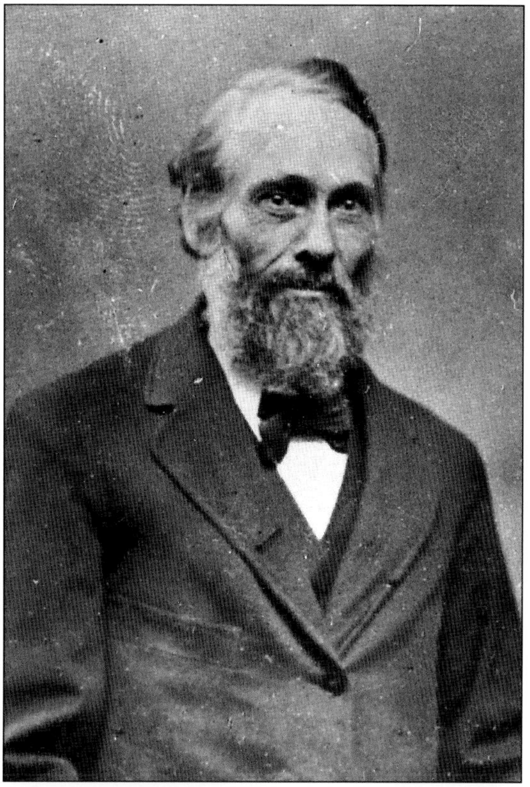

Isaac Holmes Kendall (1823–1905). This is a Winchesterite with a very interesting face.

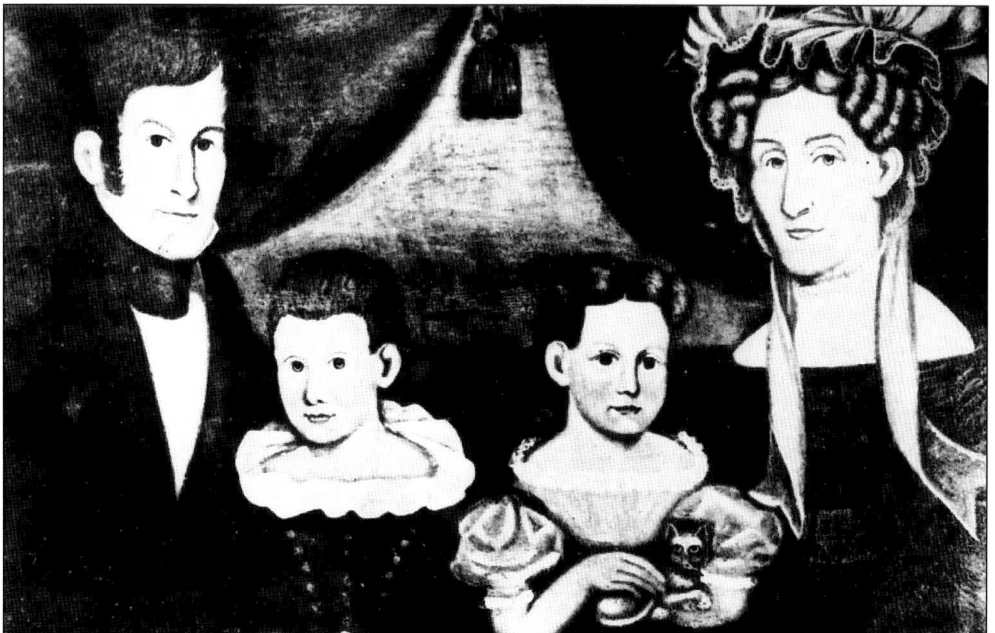

The Benjamin F. Thompson family, *c.* 1835–36. This is taken from an oil painting by a traveling painter named McLean. Deacon Thompson was active in the movement to split off from Woburn.

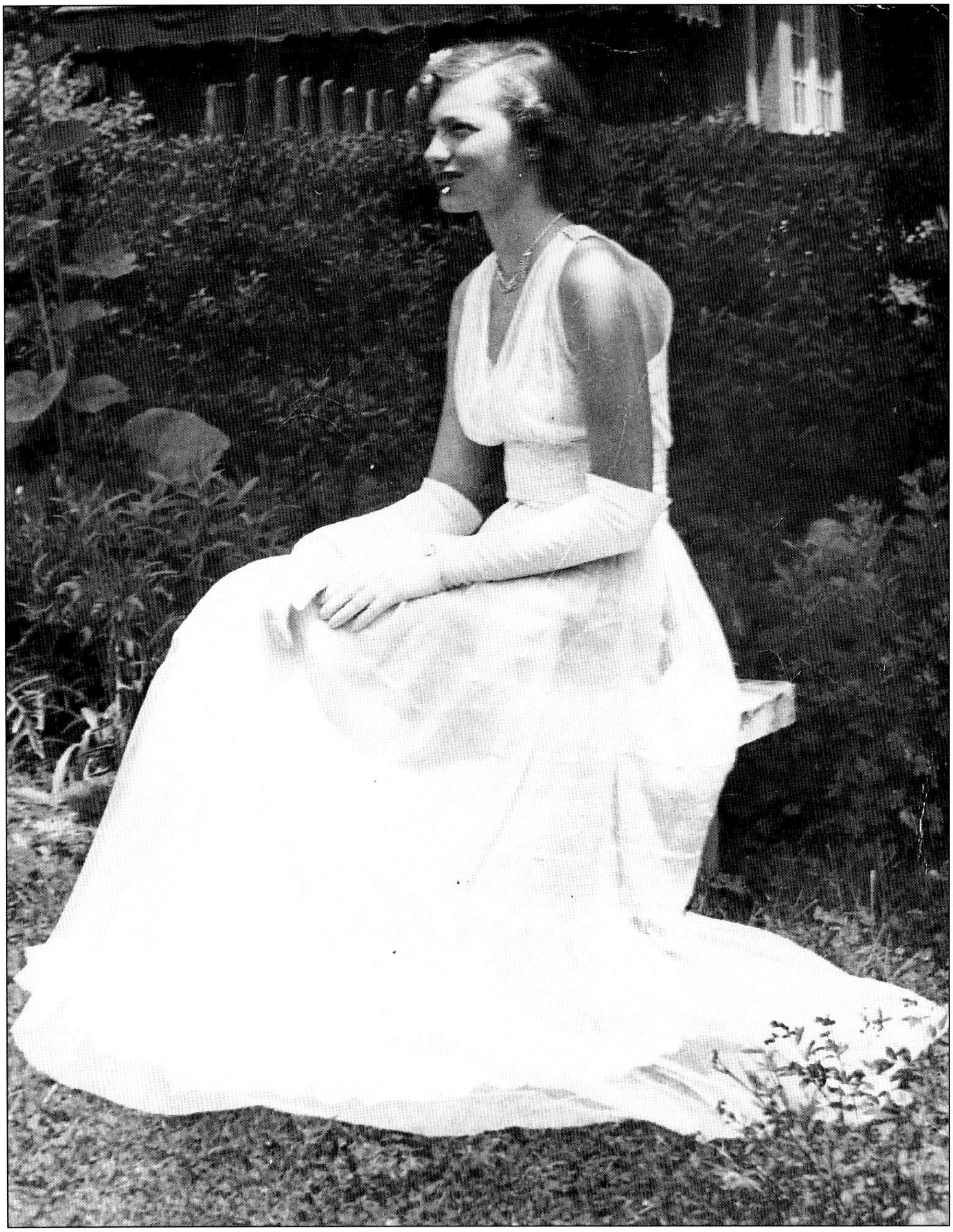

There is beauty everywhere in Winchester. Lesley Dillingham Wilcox sits in her coming-out debutante dress at the Copley Plaza Hotel, Boston, in 1949.

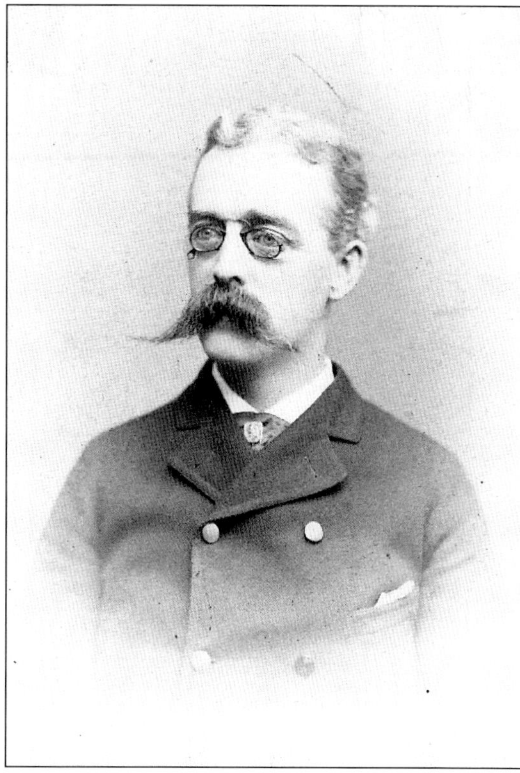

Elisha D. Bangs was president of the Boston Stock Exchange. We have already met him, in connection with the Rangeley development where he had his mansion.

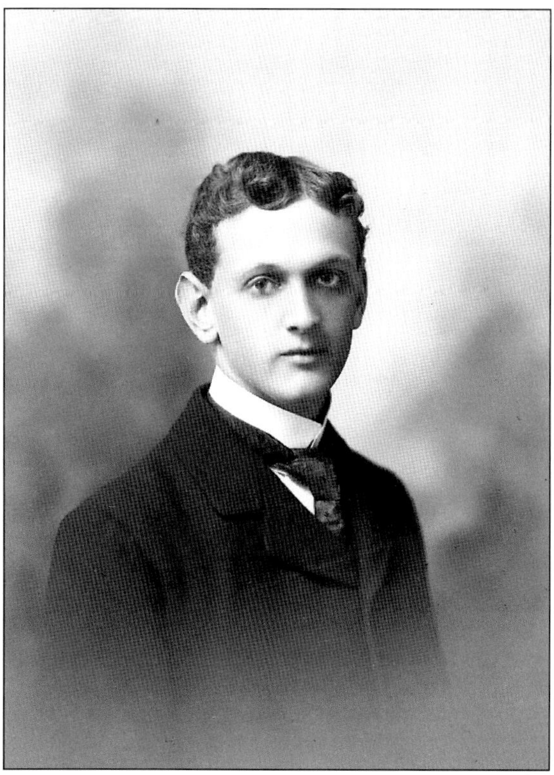

Walter J. Brown, husband of Lesley Bangs, son of Edward Jadson Brown and Mary Eliza Brown, c. 1897. He was a member of one of Winchester's most prominent families.

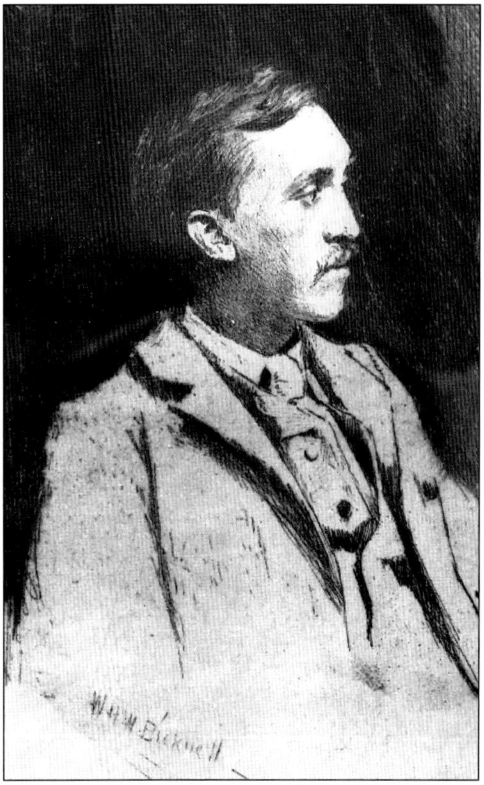

A self-portrait of William Bicknell, 1889, artist, etcher, founder of the Winchester Orchestral Society (1909–1917), and accomplished cellist.

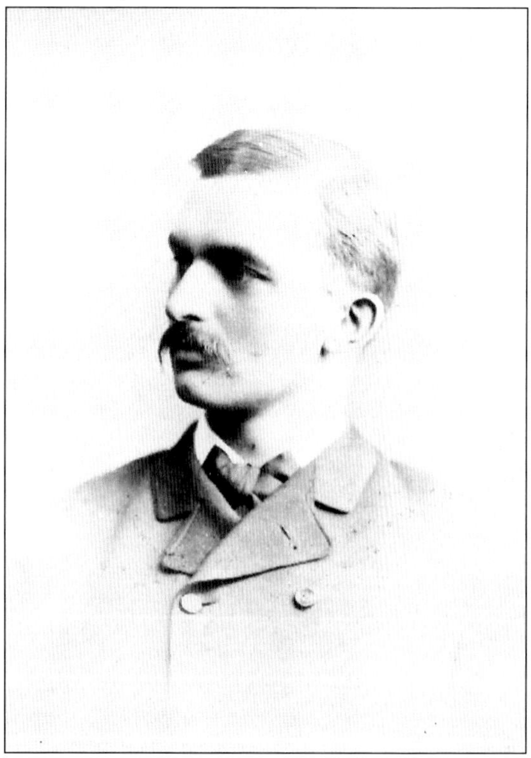

Lewis Parkhurst, who was long active in Winchester affairs and was the principal of Winchester High School several years. Among other matters, he was an eminent Unitarian, a helper in the beautification of the town center, a major owner of Ginn & Co. (the publishing firm), chairman of Winchester's 100th anniversary celebration, and served on many boards.

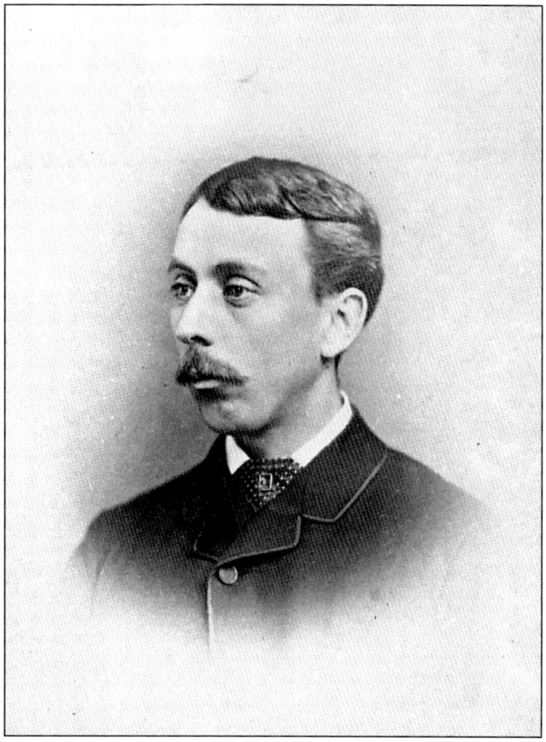

George W. Blanchard, *c*. 1900. He was a business partner of Charles E. Kendall; Kendall eventually sold that business to him.

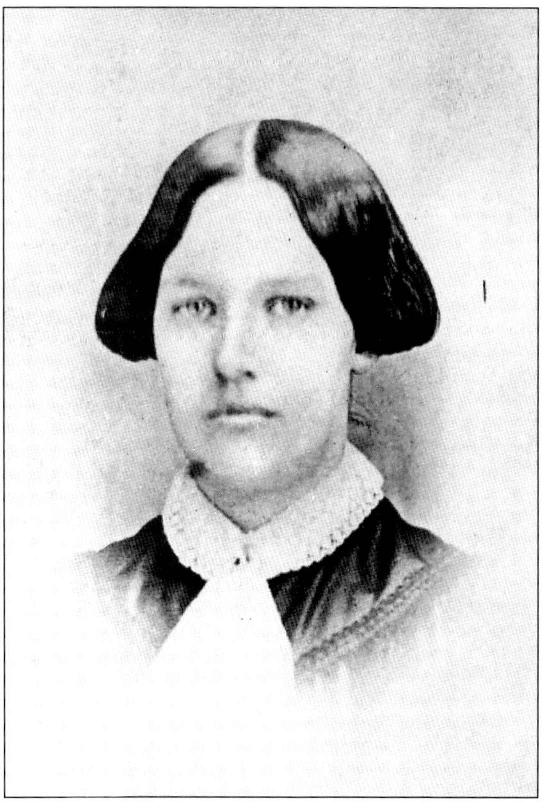

Mary Elizabeth Kendall (1830–1901). Mary was the daughter of Jason Richardson who was a firebrand at the Woburn town meetings and builder of a stone house on Forest Street. He collected the stones in his travels as a teamster.

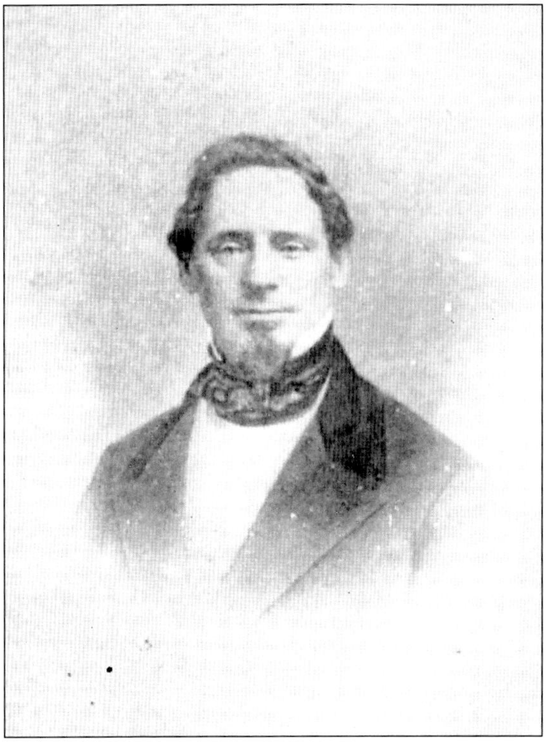

William P. Winchester, for whom the town was named.—it was not named after Winchester, England. A prominent Boston businessman who lived in Watertown, Colonel Winchester was a friend of Frederick O. Prince, Winchester's first representative to the Massachusetts legislature in 1851. Prince told the new town's leaders a gift would come from Colonel Winchester if the town was named after him. The $3,000 gift was used in the start of Wildwood Cemetery. Winchester died in August 1850, at the age of forty-nine, and never received an official welcome for his gift.

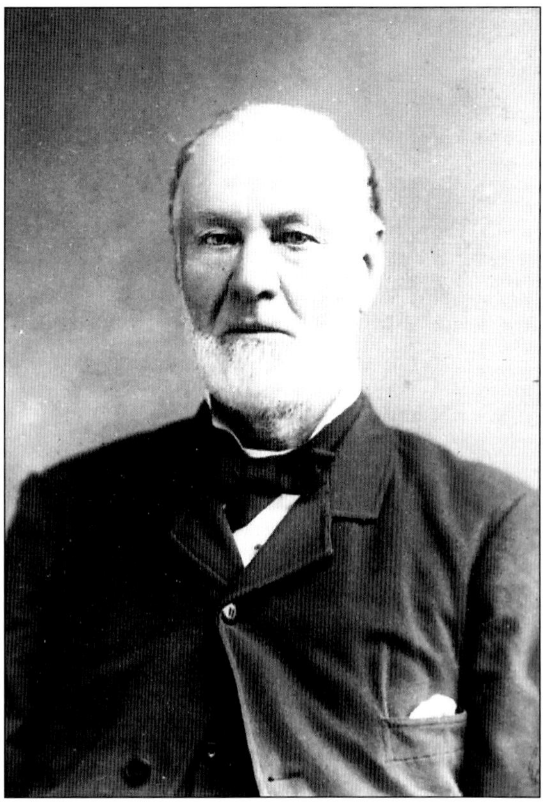

Alvin Saswel Richardson, son of Jason Richardson and brother-in-law of Isaac Kendall. Early in Winchester history what is now Washington Street was known as Richardson's Row because so many Richardson families lived there.

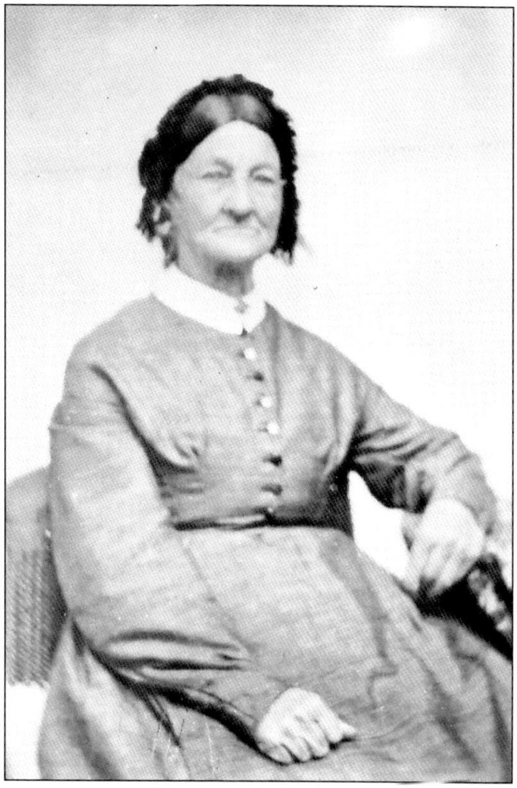

Mary Wyman Richardson (1793–1884), wife of Jason Richardson. The marriage was a combination of two of Winchester's oldest families.

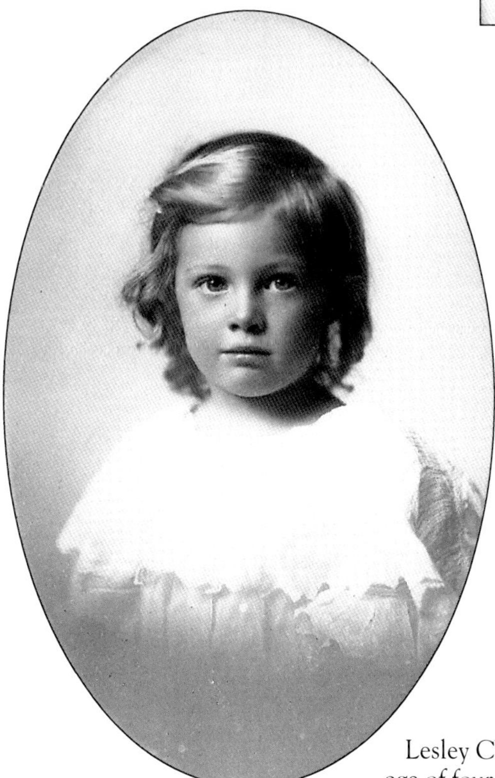

Lesley Chillingsworth Brown (Wilcox) in 1904 at the age of four.

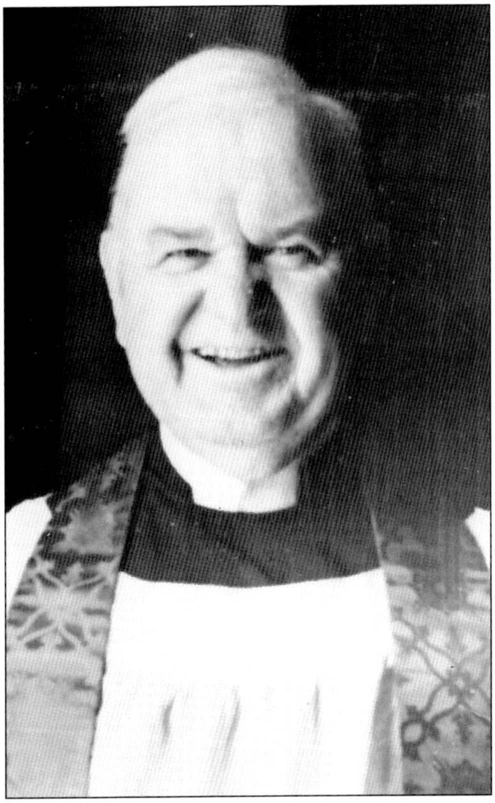

Dr. Howard J. Chidley, pastor of the First Congregational Church in Winchester from 1916 to 1953. Dr. Chidley was a leader in the fight that kept a movie theater out of Winchester until December 1937. A good-humored man, Dr. Chidley was no conservative and was a civil rights pioneer. North Carolina College, then an all-black institution, named a hall after him.

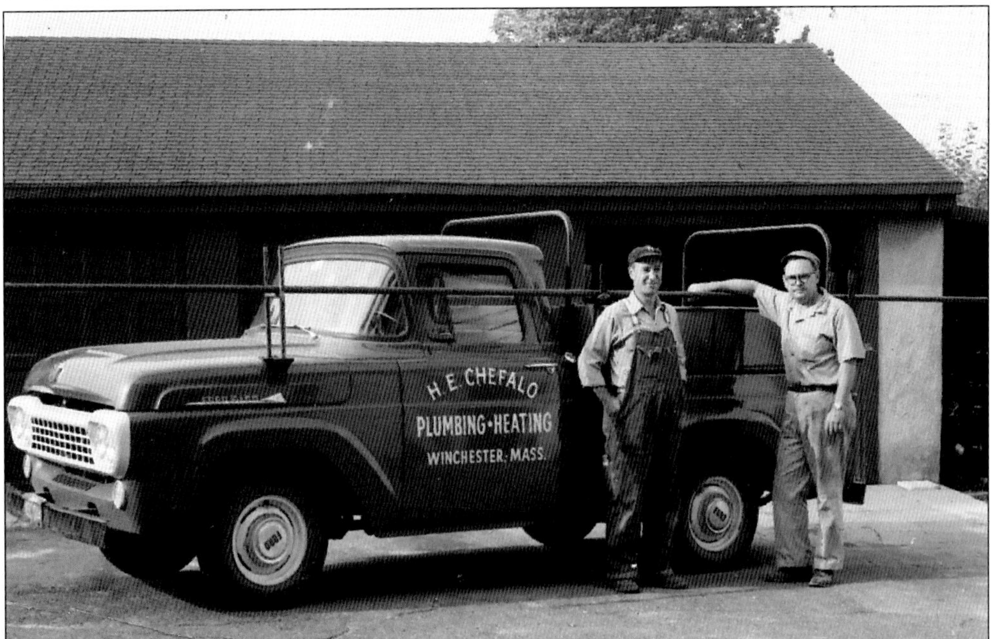

Dom Provinzano and Chick Flaherty with Harry Chefalo's plumbing truck. This photograph shows that the Italo-Americans and Irish-Americans in Winchester did often work well together.

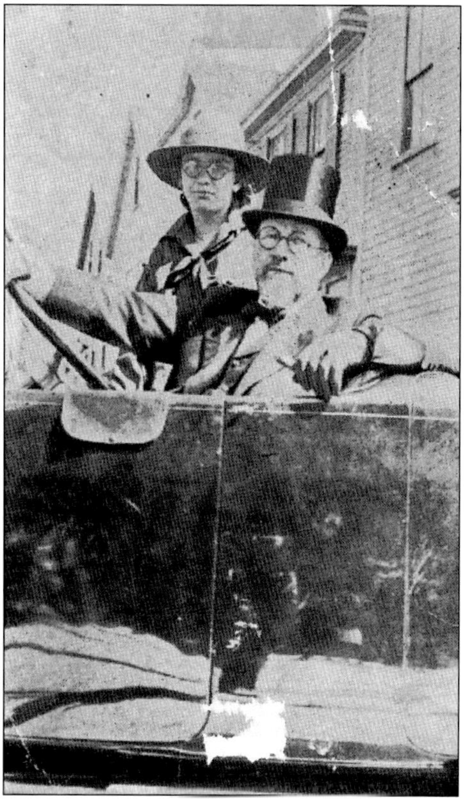

Jonas A. Laraway, known as the "Mayor of Winchester," in a car with Dorothy Laraway during a c. 1917 parade. Born in Canada, Jonas was a plumbing contractor who was very active in town meetings.

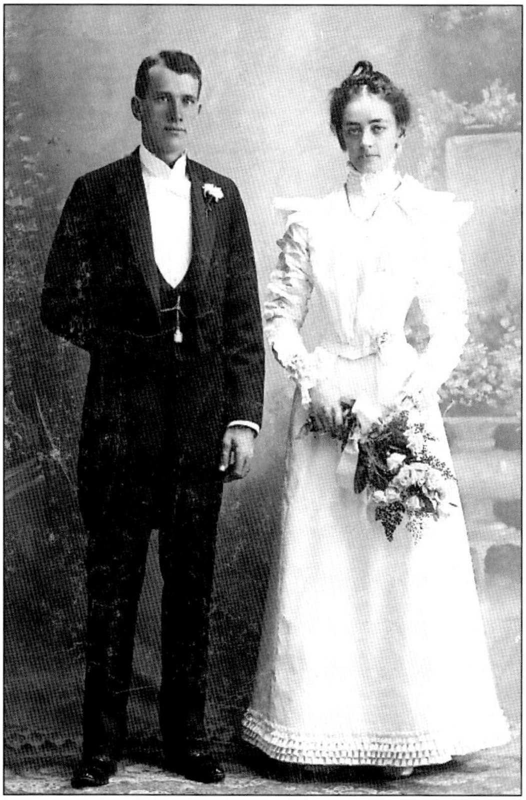

Jonas A. Laraway (born in 1871) and May Laraway (born in 1874) were married July 12, 1898.

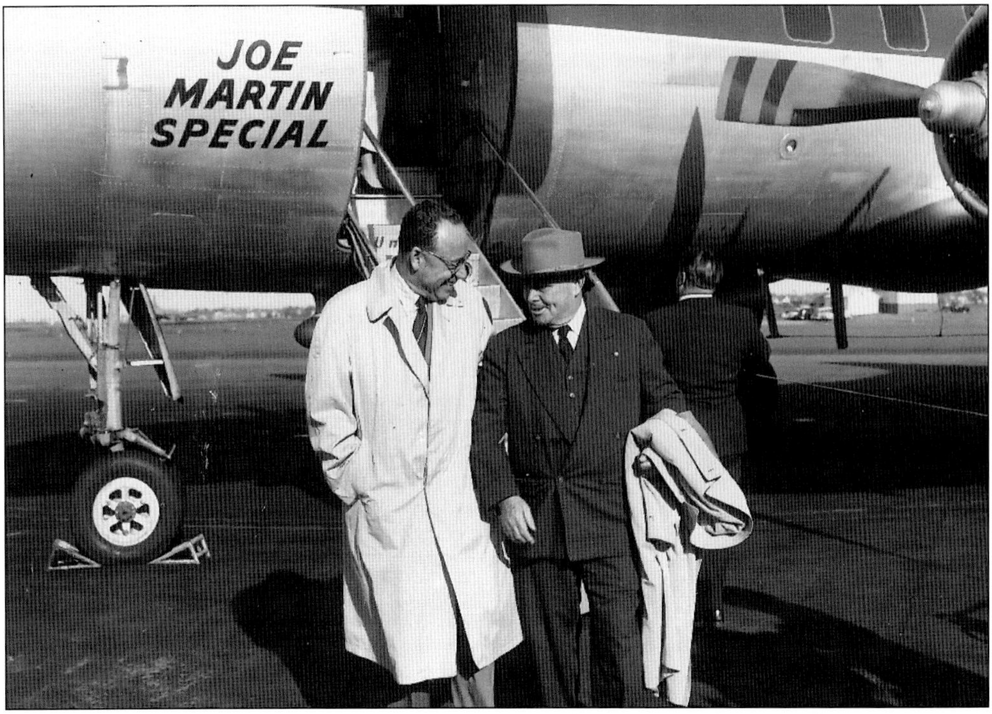

It's politics. Massachusetts Republican Committee Chairman Ralph Bonnell Sr. meets U.S. House of Representatives Speaker Joe Martin of Attleboro, Massachusetts, at Logan Airport in Boston in the 1950s.

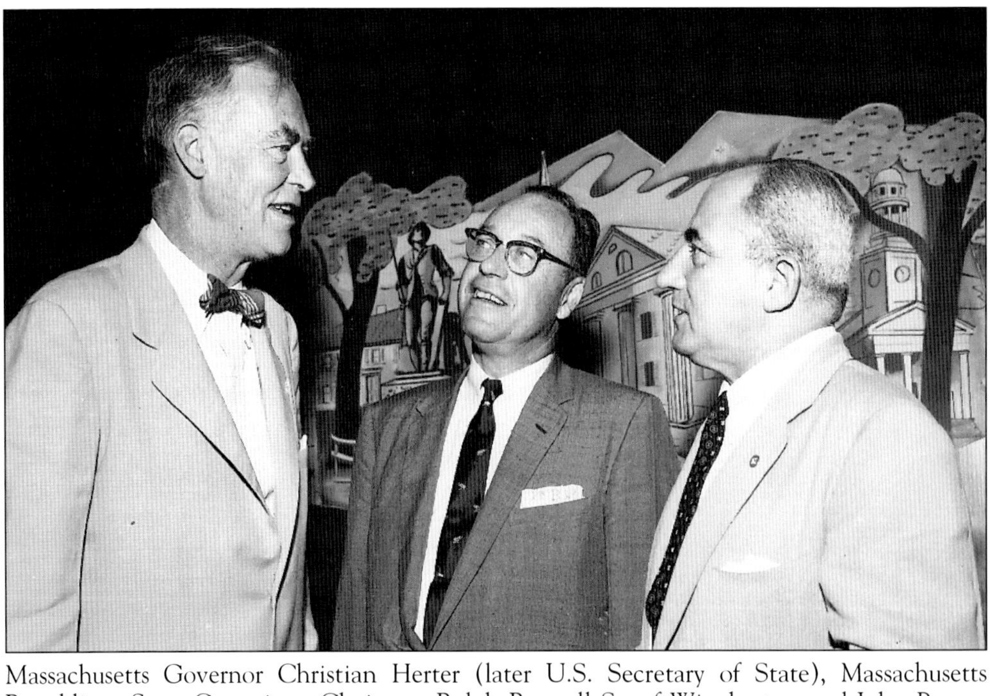

Massachusetts Governor Christian Herter (later U.S. Secretary of State), Massachusetts Republican State Committee Chairman Ralph Bonnell Sr. of Winchester, and John Pappas (the largest Greek-American contributor to the Massachusetts GOP) talk things over.

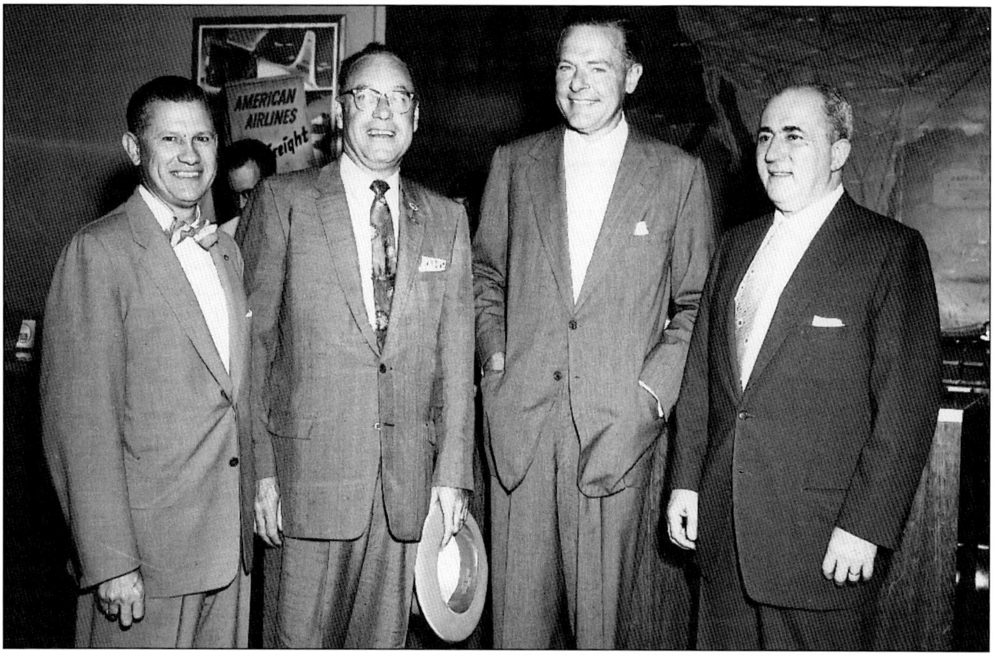

A photograph of three-term Governor of Massachusetts John Volpe of Winchester, Chairman of the Massachusetts State GOP Committee Ralph Bonnell Sr. of Winchester (whom some say was the man most instrumental in getting Volpe elected governor), U.S. Senator Henry Cabot Lodge Jr., and John Pappas.

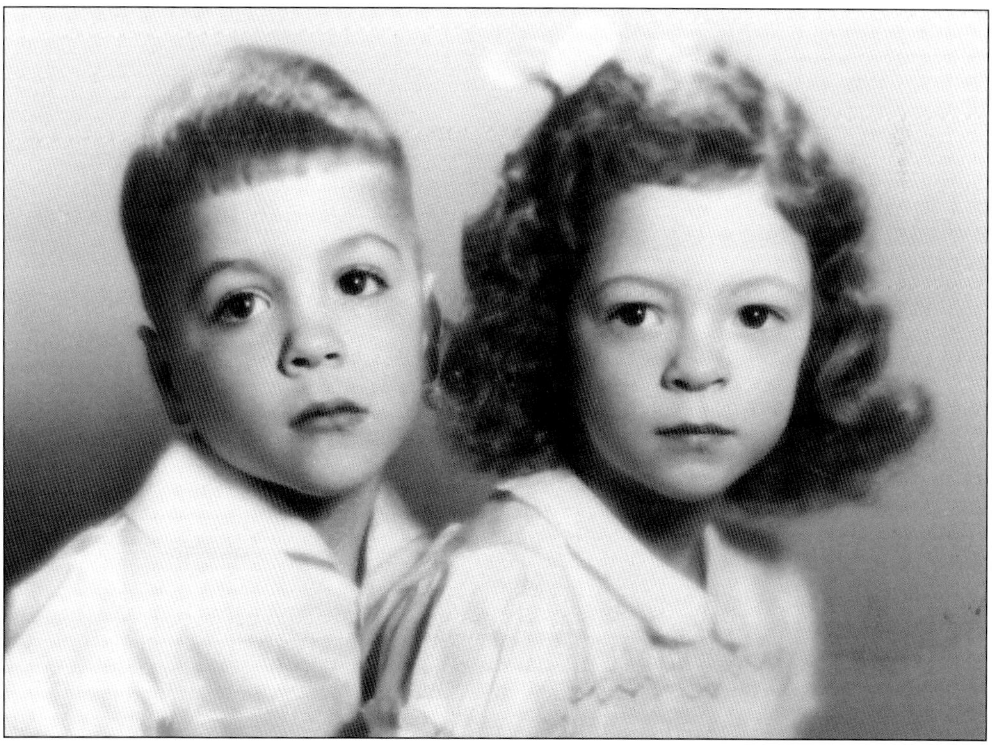

Twins Bruce and Beverly Bonnell, c. 1946, about six years old.

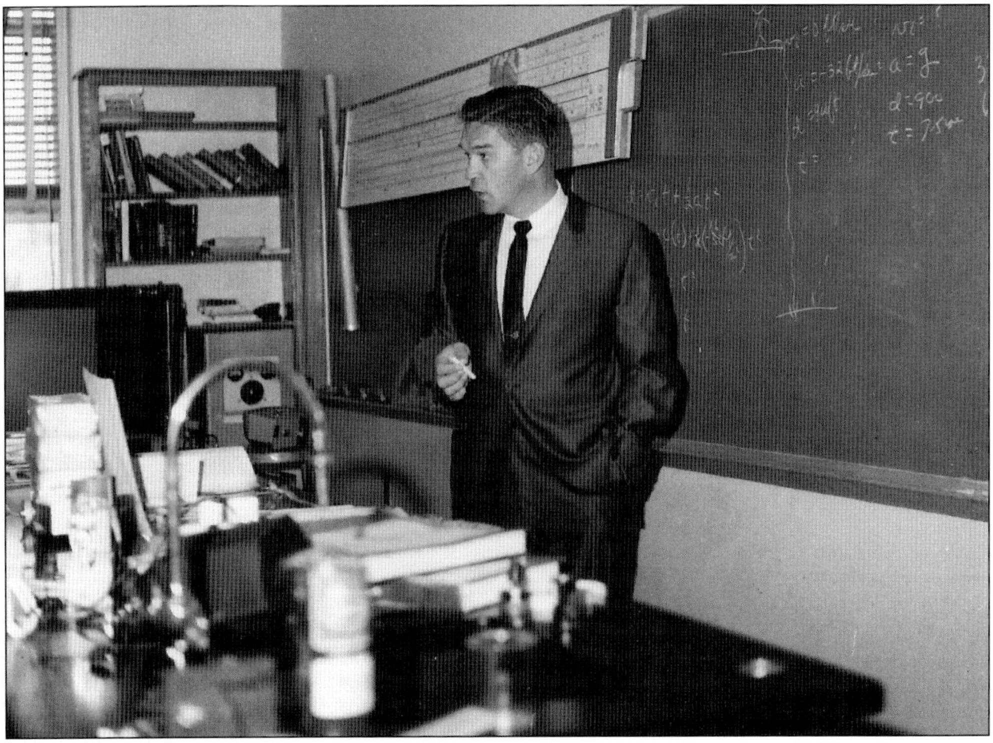

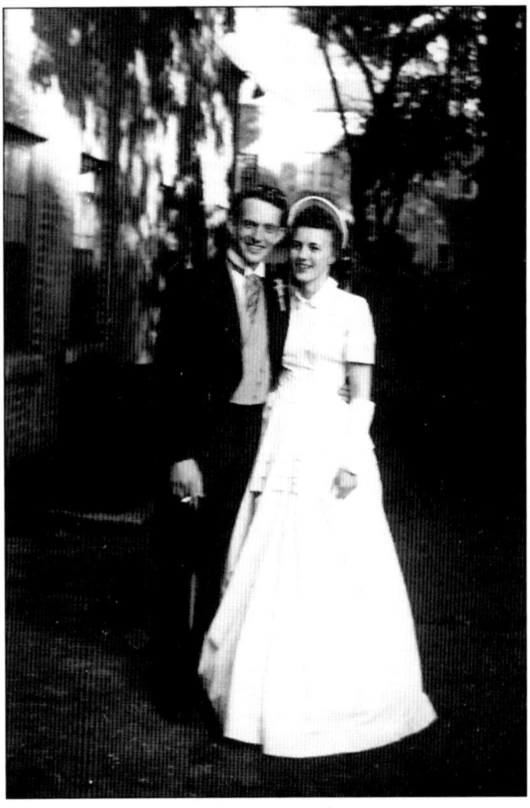

Francis X. Finigan, c. 1958, in his science classroom at the old junior high school. That's a piece of chalk in his hand. In 1995, Finigan was named the outstanding science educator of the year at the annual meeting of the Massachusetts Association of Science Supervisors. He taught physics and science at Winchester High many years and has been a member of the Northeastern University faculty for more than thirty years.

June 5, 1948, was the big day for Dick Preston and Marilyn Chefalo.

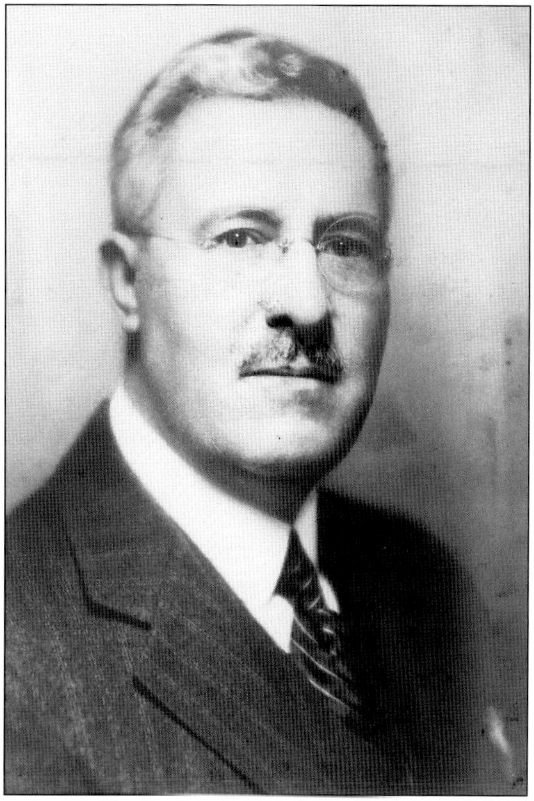

A *c.* 1930s photograph of Jere A. Downs, the son of Elizabeth Blank. Downs rose from being a runner for Hayden Stone & Company, one of the nation's largest stock brokerage firms, to being its president. He also was president of the Boston Stock Exchange and was a director of twelve companies and vice president of Eastern Steamship Co. He had a fortune of about $8 million before the 1929 stock market crash. After that crash, his fortune amounted to "only" $3 million. He died in his late fifties.

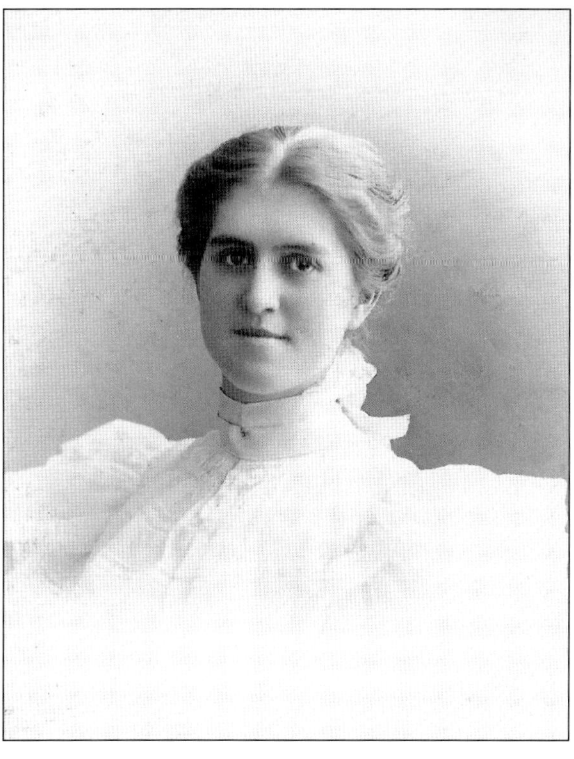

Elizabeth Stanton Downs in March 1898. She lived with her brother Jere Downs at their homes on Highland Avenue and 1 Arlington Street until he died, when she inherited his wealth. Elizabeth married Lewis Wadsworth at the age of sixty and died at age sixty-six. She and her deceased brother gave $44,000 to the Winchester Public Library. The Downs Memorial Room for works of music and fine art was dedicated November 3, 1950.

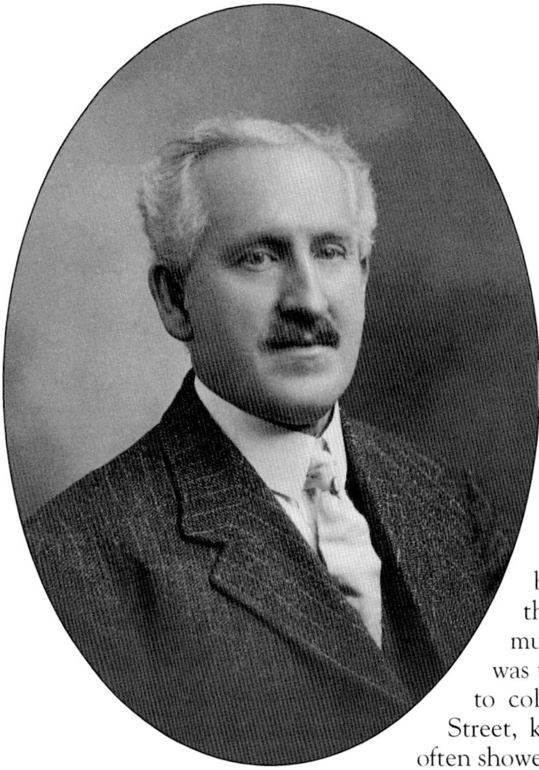

Benjamin Franklin Blank, c. 1890s. His brothers were Philip and John Blank. The three owned Blank Brothers Tannery and much real estate in Winchester. Benjamin was the best loved of the three. When he went to collect rents in the area around Middlesex Street, known to some as "The Bowery," he was often showered with gifts.

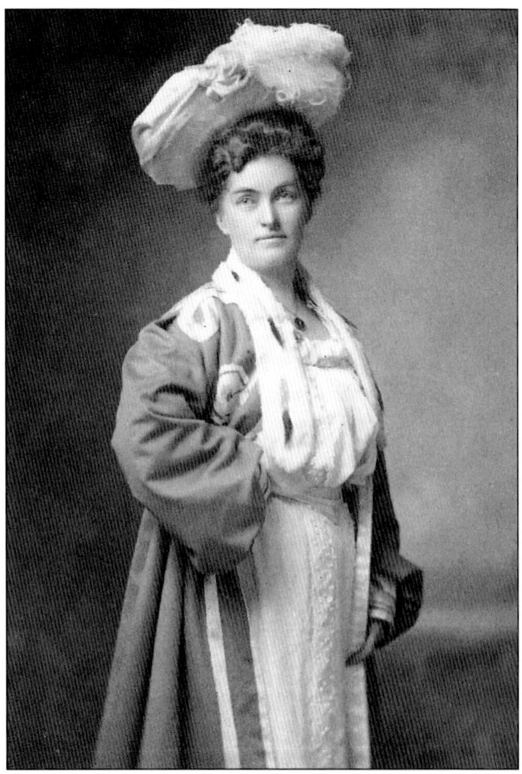

Grace Belle Manning Blank, c. 1910.

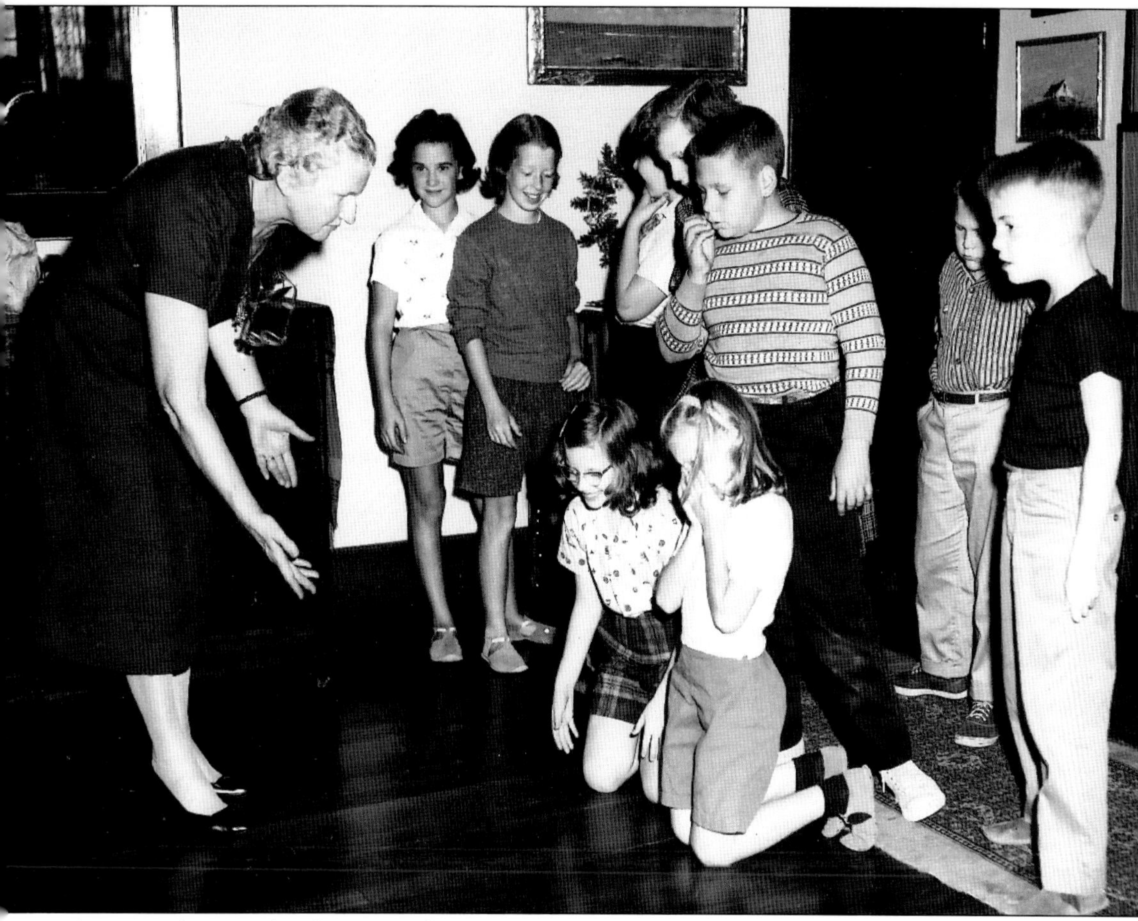

A 1960 photograph of Mrs. Carlene Murphy Samoiloff, with children at the Winchester Children's Theater, founded by her in 1955. In the 1920s, Mrs. Samoiloff was the first American student to travel with the Moscow Tsarist Art Theater in Europe. She studied four years with Maria Ouspenskaya, the famed theater and move acting instructor, who appeared in many films. She met her future husband, Alexander Samoiloff, when he was a Harvard student, at the Moscow Theater's production of *Tsar Feodor*.

Acknowledgments

I can't start this any better than with high praise for Marilyn Chefalo Preston, who motherhenned this project from the start. Without her, it just wouldn't have happened. It's not everyone that can go from high school cheerleader to history buff. Dick Preston, Marilyn's husband, also came through at some critical points.

Other members of the Winchester High Class of 1945 and their relatives who helped greatly were: Mike Boodakian; Joe Errico; Bob Quine; Al Samoiloff; Sally Sherburne (Finn), the sister of Dale Sherburne; and Harry Chefalo, at age eighty-eight the oldest licensed master plumber in Massachusetts, the font of Italo-American information, and Marilyn Preston's father.

With Marilyn as the starter on sources, the search for old photographs of Winchester rapidly spread beyond the Class of 1945. Two must be underlined at once—Lesley Wilcox, one of the most delightful, and sharp, ninety-five year olds I've ever met (on par with the late former U.S. Senator Margaret Chase Smith of Maine at the same age), and Mrs. Susan Keats, the volunteer archivist for the town of Winchester. Mrs. Wilcox had photographs that record a semi-gilded age in Winchester; Mrs. Keats gave photographs providing a broad background base for this book.

Then there was the Courtney Crandall run. Pictures from Court—but more. At his suggestion, a contact was made with Paddy Mullen at Winchester Hospital who, in turn, alerted Debbie Trask, the hospital's only public relations person. The result was the first pictorial history of the hospital in a book.

Marilyn Preston suggested Sam Rotondi, the Winchester lawyer who is the power behind the Winchester Hall of Fame Dinner. The writer attended the 5th annual event and, while there, made the contact that that resulted in photographs from Althea Hersey Shirley. Dr. William Barone was another name on the Preston source list. From the good doctor came the pictures of Joe Bellino and Jonas Laraway. Pete Provinzano provided photographs; Mrs. Frank Provinzano supplied information about her late husband. Now we come to the Winchester Public Library: Virginia Symmes White gave great beginning help and Lynda Wills had the newly discovered photographs of the library.

Ralph (known to me as Bunny) Bonnell Jr. was another Marilyn source—and a good one. I listened to Francis X. Finigan at the Hall of Fame Dinner. The former Winchester High hockey coach and science teacher was an exceptional source. Jean Randlett popped up at Dr. Barone's house and supplied critical photographs. Joe Gibson contacted Lesley Wilcox for my very enjoyable meeting with that lady. And Marjorie Bradford helped immensely with the Goddu pictures.

To anyone I've missed, I apologize mightily. Let me know and I'll put you in if there happens to be a second book on Winchester. I must not forget the two-volume *History of Winchester* by Chapman and Stone. It was a great help. Finally, I must send huge accolades to my editor, Kirsty Sutton, who has been able to bear with me and has taught me much.

Frank H. Sleeper